Urban Education: Student Unrest, Teacher Behaviors, and Black Power

Allan C. Ornstein
Chicago State College

Charles E. Merrill Publishing Company
A Bell and Howell Company
Columbus, Ohio

To
Francine and Phil
and to
Mark and Steven

Published by
Charles E. Merrill Publishing Co.
A Bell & Howell Company
Columbus, Ohio 43216

International Standard Book Number: 0-675-09106-3

Library of Congress Catalog Card Number: 77-189271

1 2 3 4 5 6 7 8 9 10—76 75 74 73 72

Printed in the United States of America

Foreword

Although it is often good to be where the action is, sometimes the thick of things is a poor place to gain perspective on what is happening.

This is particularly true with respect to urban schools, which frequently are not well understood even by educators who have spent decades working in them. It is all too easy, of course, to become immersed in an institution and to take its assumptions for granted even though the institution may be functioning poorly and its underlying rationale may make little or no sense. Particularly because urban schools almost everywhere face a series of crises ranging from inadequate financing to student dissatisfaction to bureaucratic ineptitude, it is difficult to see their problems realistically either from the perspective of the harried insider or the completely detached observer.

Urban Education: Student Unrest, Teacher Behaviors, and Black Power is a book from one who has been there and knows at firsthand that problems in urban schools are not as simple as is often suggested either by their unrepentant apologists or their supercritical attackers. Allan Ornstein has taught in inner-city schools and has worked closely with teachers and administrators in low-status parts of the inner city as well as middle-class sections of the central city and its suburbs. He has made it a point to observe developments in urban schools dispassionately while maintaining a commitment to understand and help alleviate the problems of each group (e.g., teachers, students, community organizations) directly concerned with schools in the cities. As a result, he is a sympathetic critic who combines a "feel" for the situation of an insider with the impartial perspectives of an informed outsider. From this vantage point, he is unusually well-situated to write a book addressed to readers intent upon understanding urban schools.

Perhaps the most distinguishing characteristic of Mr. Ornstein's writing in this volume is the dedication to realism which permeates the whole. Addressing himself to the most central problems in urban education, he unfailingly and unflinchingly begins each chapter with an assessment of the sad state of affairs that exists with regard to urban public education. Successively addressing attention to the status of education for the disadvantaged, the growth of alienation and unrest among secondary students everywhere, the problems of teachers in inner-city schools and the possibilities of preparing them to succeed there, and the overarching issues of integration, community control, and school district organization, Mr. Ornstein first sizes up the current situation and proceeds to outline some of the merits and demerits of proposals for reform. Most chapters conclude with a list of recommendations which in no case are offered as panaceas but instead constitute measured calls for change based on a pragmatic reading of existing weaknesses and feasible alternatives for improvement. One need not agree with all of the author's interpretations, conclusions, and recommendations to recognize that these proposals deserve careful consideration on the part of anyone concerned with the future of urban schools.

There are several respects in which *Urban Education: Student Unrest, Teacher Behaviors, and Black Power* stands in sharp contrast to many other volumes on the topic of urban education. For one thing, most books which deal with urban school problems have tended to ignore the metropolitan patterns and perspectives that help explain the genesis of these problems. Authors concerned with decentralization and community control, for example, frequently have not emphasized that the movement is a last-ditch effort to improve education for youngsters condemned by metropolitan development to attend schools in communities characterized by defeat and despair. Lacking this perspective, many advocates of the concept have tended to sell it as a panacea for the ills of inner-city education rather than a grasping attempt—however inadequate—to combat the effects of segregation and stratification. Such advocates quickly wind up promising much more than the changes they call for in fact can deliver. Mr. Ornstein does not make this mistake.

Another respect in which this book differs from many others in its field is that its author demonstrates familiarity with the substantial literature which preceded it. While it might be thought that such familiarity would be almost a prerequisite for publication on so complex a topic as urban education, this is not the case; a good number of writers have all but ignored research and evidence reported by their predecessors, especially if references to basic works in the field might call into question the one-sidedness of their own interpretations. In

Urban Education: Student Unrest, Teacher Behaviors, and Black Power, by way of contrast, the comparatively up-to-date and comprehensive listing of references Mr. Ornstein has provided should constitute a valuable resource for many readers.

For a number of years now, books dealing with urban education—particularly inner-city schools—have tended to come from romantic visionaries whose writings have stimulated public awareness of the disastrous situation which exists in the schools but who have offered precious little in the way of practical guidance for change. By romantic visionaries, I mean writers who have stressed the awful things that happen to children in the schools without giving much attention to the forces that make teachers punitive or mean-spirited toward their students. After reading these rather one-sided works, many future teachers and volunteers have been inspired to take up the banner of urban education reform but have been unprepared to confront the far-from-romantic realities of urban schools. As a result, thousands of young teachers and future teachers have entered the schools only to experience frustration and defeat upon finding that problems are much more complicated than they were prepared to cope with. What has been badly needed, in this context, is a radical critique of urban schools which is grounded simultaneously in sympathy for the difficulties teachers experience there and in understanding of the larger metropolitan setting which makes the problems of urban education so inordinately resistant to solution. In providing such a critique, Mr. Ornstein has written a book that will be helpful not just to future teachers and laymen seeking an introductory overview on urban education but also to teachers and administrators so immersed in urban education to see the total picture. It should fill much of the vacuum in analysis which has been created by other writers who have shed less light on urban education than one might have expected given the heat of their torches.

Daniel U. Levine

Preface

Writing a book is an exhausting struggle. One should never undertake such a project unless one has something impelling to write, and he is driven by a compulsion to have other people read it. Morning and evening, for many hours, writing involves words and notes—and also for me index cards where I can work out my thoughts. Writing involves solitude and aloneness, organization and creativity, ego and confidence. For myself, it also involves a morning jog, coffee and cigars, background rock-and-roll music, and lunching out so that I can unwind.

This book is geared for courses in urban education, sociology of education, and social foundations of education. It can be of value for the student, teacher, curriculum specialist, administrator, or professor who is interested in urban education and urban society. The content of the book is mainly polemical, and, therefore, I assume that the reader who finds fault with my ideas will criticize me for failing to refer to research findings and for making unjustified generalizations.

At this point, I wish to acknowledge the old friends whom I grew up with, Marcia Levinson, Stu Baden, and Bill Bass, who teach in New York City; my good friend and neighbor in Chicago Doris Samuels should also be mentioned. I would like to express my continuing gratitude to my former thesis committee members—Hulda Grobman, Virgil A. Clift, and W. Gabriel Carras—of New York University. I should mention my former colleagues and good friends at Fordham University, namely, Sheldon Marcus and Philip D. Vairo. A special word of thanks goes to W. Eugene Hedley, University of New York at Stony Brook; Harriet Talmadge, University of Illinois—Circle Campus; and Nancy L. Arnez, Northeastern State College of Illinois—all of whom permitted me to procrastinate on various projects that I am co-authoring with them so I could complete this text. Deadlines and commitments have overwhelmed me, and I am thankful for their friendship and understanding.

Next, I am appreciative to Glen Thompson who read the last part of Chapter V and Daniel U. Levine, at the University of Missouri at Kansas City, who read Chapters I and V and also took time out from a busy schedule to write the Foreword. A special word of thanks is extended to Babs Inglehart and Virginia McDavid who provided editorial counsel for some parts of the manuscript. Thanks is also extended to Cecilia Daniels who again typed the final draft of a book for me and whose warm comments were always welcomed.

Some portions (most of Chapters II and III and the first and fourth parts of Chapter VI) of the book were written in the late 1960s, and the remaining content was written in 1971. Portions of the book have been adapted from my previously published articles in professional journals, i.e., *Illinois School Journal, Journal of Secondary Education, Notre Dame Journal of Education,* and *School and Society.* I am grateful to the publishers of these journals for allowing me to reprint this material.

Allan C. Ornstein
June 1971

Contents

Introduction:
The Nature of the Setting

At the turn of the century, about 40% of the nation's population was urban, and the remaining proportion was rural. By 1970 the Census Bureau estimated that 75% of Americans lived in urban areas, and projections of this figure to the year 2,000 bring the percentage to totality. Of the more than 160 million people living in urban areas, approximately 50% live in central cities and the remaining half live in suburban settings.

Recent population trends to and from cities are generally related to the in-migration of the rural poor to the cities and the out-migration of white middle-class families to the suburbs. For example, between 1950 and 1970 nearly 2 million blacks and Puerto Ricans moved into New York City and replaced nearly 2½ million white middle-class residents fleeing to the suburbs. Whereas at one time the dominant group helped the white newcomer to the city to assimilate, this is no longer the case because of the color barrier and the widening gap between the material abundance of the "haves" and the absence of many of the basic elements of subsistence for the poor.

The cities are fast becoming the home of the rich, the poor, and the unmarried young who desire the excitement and social opportunities of the city. The rich are sending their children to private schools; the poor are sending their children to public schools. While the rich are becoming less "liberal" because of the disappearing middle-class buffer zone against the poor, the poor are becoming more alienated from the power structure—or the "haves." Thus, for example, New York City residents living in Lincoln Center or Chicago residents living on the Gold Coast no longer feel safe and insulated from the less fortunate slum dwellers.

The cities are becoming economically divided into the rich and poor, like 18th century Paris and 19th century cities of the Austrian, French, German, Italian, Russian and Turkish empires which produced revolution after revolution. Today's cities consist of the exploited poor and the wage earners whom Karl Marx wrote about, but the division between the "haves" and "have nots" is intensified today by racial barriers. Moreover, the few remaining middle-class communities will probably begin to organize themselves into militant pressure groups—against increasing taxes and diminishing public services and against the trend for special treatment for the poor and racial minorities, especially since the economy is no longer healthy and jobs are threatened by middle-class blacks.

Also, the cities are becoming more alike. Once we cross the Manhattan bridges or travel two miles outside the Chicago Loop, we might be almost anywhere, in any city. To live in the outskirts of Manhattan or the Chicago Loop is to live in a working-class or slum area, or to live in some little-known suburban community. We might be in the heart of middle America—say Kansas City, Missouri, or Topeka, Kansas, or even on the outskirts of Paris or London—and find a similar setting. In speaking of the city, especially if we are out-of-towners, we usually refer to a tiny commercial and entertainment area, actually a very menaced island whose problems have become insurmountable and a very menaced group of residents who find themselves living in the midst of a hostile asphalt-paved jungle of people with whom even the police can no longer cope.

There is little romance in living in the city, unless one is rich and can afford the luxury of dining at a restaurant which offers French service, followed by boxseats at the playhouse. The city is dying, strained by a depleting tax base; a loss of political power to the suburbs; "municipal overburden," that is, high costs of and inadequate public services (e.g., police, fire, sanitation, transportation, housing, welfare, and schools); mounting crime and social problems, even increasing symptoms of emotional disturbance among residents; problems of slums; increasing pollution; newspaper strikes, stoppage of public transportation, strikes by policemen, firemen, sanitation workers, and teachers; electric failures and blackouts; rising taxes and rents; racial tensions, even race riots; student unrest; female activism; middle-class backlash; and "confrontation politics." New York City is continuously confronted with these problems, and other cities are becoming painfully acquainted with many of them—symptomatic of the growing doubt about whether it is worth living in the large cities of America.

In analyzing the problems of the city, it is important to consider that the city consists of many local units of government, e.g., counties, districts, wards, and communities, and is surrounded by suburban towns and districts, which in turn comprise an urban or metropolitan area. It is also important to recognize that the city and urban area consist of many social systems which influence the people and which the people influence. For example, Levine and Havighurst (1968)[1] have listed some of these major urban social systems.

Chart 1

Major Social Systems of the Urban Area

1. *Local government system.* Includes a multiple number of smaller subunits.
2. *Public service system.* Includes the following departments: police, fire, sanitation, water, and sewage.
3. *Cultural system.* Includes museums, art centers, play houses, libraries, and television and radio stations.
4. *Recreation system.* Includes parks, sports and recreational facilities and associations.
5. *Social welfare system.* Includes agencies for youth, the elderly, employment, and the family.
6. *Religious system.* Includes various congregations, churches, and church-sponsored associations and clubs.
7. *Economic system.* Includes individual businesses, management associations, labor unions, and industrial and banking councils.
8. *Civil system.* Includes neighborhood charity groups, self-help and "social betterment" agencies, and the local chamber of commerce.
9. *Political system.* Includes political parties, coalitions, and clubs.
10. *Leisure system.* Includes social and country clubs, fraternal organizations, and various special activity groups.
11. *Health maintenance system.* Includes private and public facilities, agencies, and associations.
12. *Transportation system.* Includes rapid and mass transit units and agencies, parking facilities, and bus, railway, and air lines.

---

[1] Levine and Havighurst (1968) list 14 social systems. Number 15 is derived by the author.

13. *Communication system.* Includes telephone and telegraph companies, newspaper and magazine companies, advertising agencies, as well as television and radio stations.

14. *Educational system.* Includes private and public schools and special educational services from prekindergarten to the university level.

15. *Ecology system.* Includes conservation groups, research agencies, and activist groups.

This book will deal with only one of these urban social systems—the schools. The first chapter will deal with a summary of past, present, and future trends concerning the disadvantaged. Then the book will focus on three important aspects of urban education: student unrest, teacher behaviors, and black power.

I

The Disadvantaged: Overview and Trends [1]

Introduction

Since 1960 concern for the disadvantaged has grown from the sad and lonely plight of the classroom teacher who had difficulty teaching, to a nationwide movement. It has become necessary to do something to try to solve the problems of educating the disadvantaged, not because we have suddenly become humanitarian but because we fear the newcomers to the city. Blacks are no longer "invisible," hidden in rural wastelands or submerged in urban ghettoes. Since the civil rights movement and the subsequent black power movement, blacks have become "visible," vocal, and violent. Puerto Ricans, Chicanos, and Indians are now demanding equality, justice, and power, too. Poor whites, although still largely forgotten by the public, have become more "visible" since Harrington's *The Other America,* the "War on Poverty," and the recent investigations of hunger and malnutrition in the United States.

The Decade of the 1960s

Educators have reflected the nation's concern by focusing on the children of the poor and racial minorities whom they tend to lump together as the

---

[1] This chapter is written for the individual who is relatively unfamiliar with the field; it provides a brief synopsis of some of the major factors related to educating the disadvantaged.

Throughout the book the terms "teachers of the disadvantaged" and "ghetto teachers," as well as "disadvantaged" and "ghetto students," are used interchangeably.

disadvantaged. Concurrent with this recent interest in the disadvantaged, at least 15 general themes and issues have emerged within the last decade.

1. *Growing Number of the Disadvantaged.* Although there is no exact agreement among educators as to who are the disadvantaged, the term is usually a euphemism for poor and minority-group children. School authorities tend to be sensitive about being accused of stereotyping and use the term to refer to students who are reading below the nation's norm. However, there is a high correlation between being poor and being a member of a minority group and between these two classifications and low reading scores. In any event, in 1950, approximately 10% of the students attending school in the fourteen largest cities were considered disadvantaged. By 1960, the number had soared to one out of three. In 1970, it was estimated that one out of two students was disadvantaged. This increasing trend is related to the population shifts noted above.[2]

2. *Descriptions of the Disadvantaged.* Besides the primary description of the disadvantaged in terms of class and caste, there was a tendency in the 1960s to describe the socio-psychological and linguistic problems of the disadvantaged, with a mainly negative image. This led to the (1) "deprivation theory," which stresses the importance of an enriched environment, during the early years, on the cognitive and emotional development of the child and, (2) the "cumulative intellectual deficit theory," which points out that the child's deprivation increases as he is passed from grade to grade. Several educators (e.g., Kenneth B. Clark, Nancy Arnez, and Frank Reissman) have contended that the description of the disadvantaged is patronizing and reflects white middle-class biases. Also, they claim that such descriptions foster negative "self-fulfilling prophecies" about the children's academic performance.

3. *Race and Intelligence.* Several research studies were conducted during this decade which showed racial and ethnic differences in IQ and school achievement. Although the majority of social scientists agreed that environment, not heredity, causes racial and ethnic differences, the Jensen (1969) study rekindled the outdated theory of the importance of the hereditary component and the relative immutability of intelligence. The educational, social, and political implications of the study were important: they included the stereotype of black inferiority, particularly in intelligence; reduced support for school integration and

---

[2] *Supra,* Introduction.

compensatory education; and increased alienation of blacks toward white America. Until we clearly understand the findings of most social scientists regarding race and intelligence, there will continue to be a loophole by means of which the majority of the nation's populace can rationalize, even justify, the reasons for the continued second-class status of blacks.

4. *Standardized Tests.* Standardized tests such as reading, achievement, aptitude, and psychological instruments, and especially the college entrance examinations and IQ tests, were under attack on many grounds of unreliability and invalidity. There was general agreement that many of these tests tended to discriminate against the disadvantaged. Although results of these tests should have been considered only tentative and evaluated in relation to the students' backgrounds, they were misused (and still are) as the major criteria to classify students permanently, to prohibit students from entering into academic studies and college, and to "alibi" for students' educational failures.

5. *Teachers of the Disadvantaged.* Teachers of the disadvantaged were described as having negative attitudes and behaviors, limited experiences, and substandard or temporary credentials. The period of the mid and late 1960s also saw the publication of a large number of overgeneralized and highly emotional trade books about ghetto teachers and administrators. Charges of indifference, racism, physical brutality, and the general wickedness of ghetto teachers and administrators were continually voiced. These books were usually based on the selective observations of the authors about one or two schools.

6. *Teaching Strategies.* Although there was a wealth of literature concerning the socio-psychological problems of the disadvantaged, there was (and still is) a gap between this knowledge and its implementation in the classroom. Teachers were failing to reach and teach the disadvantaged. By the mid 1960s concern was expressed for developing special methods, media, and materials for teaching the disadvantaged in a way which could be basically defined as "good" teaching. Perhaps the most significant instructional innovations were made at the prekindergarten and primary-grade levels of teaching, where there was an emphasis on research and evaluation.

7. *Teacher-Training Programs.* Colleges and universities developed new courses and training programs, even advanced degrees in some cases, to meet the problem of training teachers for the disadvantaged. In addition, special programs were funded by federal money, e.g., Teacher Corps

programs and emergency preservice summer programs in urban education for people who held bachelor's degrees and sought teaching licenses, National Defense Education Act (NDEA) institutes for experienced teachers and supervisors, and Office of Economic Opportunity (OEO) programs concerned with both preservice and inservice teachers but tending to focus on paraprofessionals. Most of these courses and programs have been criticized for emphasizing theory and ignoring practice. Although the funds for these special programs have been drastically reduced, there is still emphasis by institutions of higher learning on training local residents as paraprofessionals and eventually as teachers of the disadvantaged.

8. Recruitment and Retention of Teachers. Concern was evidenced over the problem of attracting and holding competent teachers of the disadvantaged. In particular, the problem of teacher turnover seriously affected the morale of ghetto schools and the quality of instruction the students were receiving. Incentives were propounded for persuading teachers to remain in such schools, but most of these ideas proved to be ineffective. However, the 1969–70 school year saw the end of the nation's teacher shortage with the exception of a few selected areas (rural settings) and subjects (mathematics and women's physical education). New teachers now find themselves on waiting lists without immediate job prospects. This trend has helped to alleviate the problems of recruitment and retention; however, the problem of competence has not yet been solved.

9. Growth of Teacher Militancy. Before 1960 it was considered almost unthinkable and unprofessional for teachers to strike. The image of Mr. Chips and the school marm, as well as fables of "dedication" and "sacrifice," dominated the profession. An axiomatic myth was perpetuated: "Keep teachers out of politics and politics out of education." Most of these traditional beliefs were eradicated with the growth of the American Federation of Teachers (AFT) and concurrent teacher strikes; first in large Northern cities, especially in ghetto schools where morale was low and there was a large number of young teachers, and now more recently in smaller cities and Southern school systems. Because of this growing trend, the National Education Association (NEA)—once the embodiment of torpid tendencies within the teaching profession—was forced to endorse the strike as a weapon, too; and with this change in tactics, the teachers' strike suffuses the schools of America. This new militancy has helped to improve teacher benefits and wages, working conditions, and rights. To a limited extent, the teacher strike has also helped foster compensatory programs and smaller classes, as well as concern for school integration—the last of which was relatively unsuccessful in the 1960s.

10. *Curriculum Reform.* Educators expressed concern over curriculum reform for the disadvantaged: emphasizing "relevant" materials and motivational techniques; adopting methods and materials to the learning styles of the disadvantaged; developing reading, language, and cognitive skills programs but mainly stressing the early years and the need for enriched stimuli; meeting the specific health, medical, nutritional, and psychological needs of the children; upgrading the curriculum; improving the image and role of minorities in textbooks and the quality of integrated content; and involving community participants in curriculum development. Also arising out of the claims for "relevant" education and the protests of black power have been the demands of black college students for black study programs, demands which have filtered down to the high school level.

11. *Proliferation of Compensatory Programs.* Compensatory education is an effort to counteract children's deprivation, to bring them up to a level where they can be reached by existing educational practices. The idea stems from the 1957 Banneker Project in St. Louis, known as "Operation Motivation," the 1958 Ford Foundation Great Cities Improvement Project involving 13 large cities, and the 1959 New York Higher Horizons Program, initially called the "Demonstration Guidance Project."

Most of the compensatory programs have been funded by the federal government and have concentrated on both extremes of the educational continuum—prekindergarten and college. The major criterion of the programs' "success" has been academic achievement; however, most programs have been considered ineffective. They have been characterized mainly by a piecemeal approach, inappropriate shifting of federal authority over the programs, mismanagement at the federal and local levels, inadequate personnel at the local level, vague objectives and poor evaluation procedures, little change in the content or quality of the programs, only increased quantity of services, and limited utilization of community participants. Some educators (e.g., J. McV. Hunt, Carl Bereiter, and Charles Benson) have contended that the failure of compensatory education is largely linked to lack of funds, that the extra money spent per disadvantaged child ($200) is hardly enough to make a difference. There is speculation that a threshold of about $1500 extra per child may be needed before differences will be noted.

12. *Federal Role in Education.* The federal role in education greatly increased in the 1960s and basically involved two patterns: (1) funds for compensatory education and (2) the impetus for school desegregation and integration. Between 1957 and 1964, federal funds doubled; during the next fiscal year 1965–66, they doubled again as a result of the Elementary and Secondary Education Act, reaching a peak in the 1967–68 year, but since then they have slowed down and decreased. Title I of the ESEA represented the largest federal commitment, involving more than $1 billion per year or nearly 50% of the federal commitment to educating the disadvantaged. However, it should be noted that rural and small-town schools received more (and still do) federal air per child than those in urban areas. While on a nationwide basis city schools received slightly more money per child than those in the suburbs, the latter spend more than $100 extra per student than do the cities.*

During the ten years that followed the 1954 Supreme Court decision concerning desegregation, the federal role in enforcing that law was limited. The expectation was that Southern school authorities would desegregate the schools at a reasonable pace; these expectations were not met. In 1964 the Civil Rights Act set down stricter guidelines for promoting desegregation. Tokenism followed; HEW eventually demanded that the schools desegregate within prescribed time intervals or lose federal funds, even if it meant the closing down of schools or the shifting

---

* *Postscript:* In the summer of 1971, the California Supreme Court announced what may become a landmark decision as the 1954 case of *Brown* v. *Board of Education.* In the present case, *Serrano* v. *Priest,* the California court concluded that the state's method of financing school systems denies students equal educational opportunity guaranteed under the Fourteenth Amendment, because it results in substantial disparities among school districts in the amount of revenue for education. For example, based on 1968–69 figures, the Beverly Hills school district spent $1,232 per student, while the Baldwin Park school district, in the same county of Los Angeles, allocated $577 for each student. In the county of Alameda, the Emery school district allocated $2,223 to educate each of its students and the Newark school district spent $616 per student. The main reason for this inequality was the difference in local assessed property valuation per student. For example, in Beverly Hills the figure was $50,885 per student and in Baldwin Park it was $3,706 per student, a ratio of 13:1; in Emery the figure was $100,187 and in Newark it was $6,048, a ratio of 17:1.

While the Supreme Court has declared that education must be made equal in terms of race, it has affirmed that equality of education does not apply to school financing. However, the Warren Court attacked discrimination based on wealth with regard to the rights of defendents in criminal cases and the rights of voters and thus eliminated the poll tax. It is feasible that the *Serrano* case, or a similar one, will be appealed to the Supreme Court. Whether the Court reverses its position on school financing is speculative. The more conservative nature of the present Court will certainly be a factor worth considering.

of student populations. Desegregation gains were made in the South, but they were offset by growing Northern *de facto* segregation.

13. *Big Business Interests and Educational Technology.* Since the mid 1960s, large business corporations (e.g., General Electric, IBM, and Xerox) have focused on the educational market, with special concern for educating the disadvantaged since extra money was available in programs for educating these children. Education is the nation's largest peacetime industry (representing about 7% of the GNP or an average of $550 per student), and business saw education as an important source of investment, especially in the closing period of the decade when it was clear that defense and space spending would eventually be reduced.

Linked with business' interest in education was the growth of technological equipment—computer and electronic equipment, video communication systems, talking typewriters, language laboratories, and microfilm. In particular, "Sesame Street," though not a business-sponsored venture but supported by foundation grants and federal money, proved the value of television and mass communication by its success in reaching more than 8 million children on a regular basis, many of whom were disadvantaged, and improving their readiness for education. Although educators have expressed concern about the motives of business and the need to control technology, it is clear that big business is expanding its educational investments and that technology can provide both feasible and flexible instruction for *all* children and, thus, improve the productivity of the already overburdened teacher.

14. *Description of Schools.* Most schools serving the disadvantaged have been negatively portrayed. Two groups of school critics developed: (1) the popular critics and free-lance writers, among them John Holt, Herbert Kohl, and Jonathan Kozol; and (2) the social scientists and researchers, such as James S. Coleman, Irwin Katz, and Alan B. Wilson. The first group relied on commentary and described the schools' physical deterioration and depressing conditions. Teachers and administrators were viewed, at best, as incompetent and insensitive and, in many cases, as racists and tyrants. The school system was considered to be inert and unwieldy, reluctant to meet the demands of minority groups.

The second group of critics saw the schools as being unequal in the amount of economic and physical resources devoted to educating the disadvantaged; in such specific characteristics concerning their teachers as experience, education, and turnover; and in such vague intangibles as motivation, student expectations, and morale, thus leading to inequalities in the education of the disadvantaged. No matter what definition of "equal educational opportunity" is used,[3] there is ample evidence that the schools did not provide "equal educational opportunity" for poor and minority-group children, and there is little evidence that they are coming closer to its achievement.

15. *Methods for Reorganizing Schools.* New ideas were set forth to reorganize schools (e.g., linear city, educational parks, and open air schools) and to provide alternatives (e.g., storefront schools, student-centered schools, and schools sponsored by industries, labor unions, colleges and universities, foundations, and federal, state, and local agencies) for educating the disadvantaged and providing "equal educational opportunity." In the first half of the decade, a controversy developed between the relative merits of compensatory education and integration—over which of these goals should take priority. By the second half of the decade, the controversy tended to shift to integration vs. decentralization and community control.[4] As the decade came to a close, proposals were being discussed to hold teachers and schools accountable, and voucher plans were being developed to permit parents a choice of which schools they wanted to send their children to. We will return to these concepts later in this chapter.

The Decade of the 1970s

At the time of this writing, the following seem to be the directions and problems of the 1970s.[5]

1. *Research and the Social Scientist.* Attacks on the presumed validity of the research and objectivity of the social scientist were leveled in the late 1960s and will probably continue in the 1970s. The role of the social scientist, the merits of reporting research that negatively depicts

---

[3] Varying concepts of "equal educational opportunity are": (1) opportunity to get a free education; (2) opportunity to get the same education; (3) opportunity for the disadvantaged to get a better education than more advantaged children; (4) opportunity to be educated at the level of one's potential; (5) amount of community input; (6) specific teacher characteristics and variables; (7) income distribution of students; (8) racial composition of student body; (9) effect schools have on students with equal backgrounds and abilities; (10) effect schools have on students with unequal backgrounds and abilities. These items can be defined in moral, legal, or mathematical concepts. Also see Coleman (1968) and Thompson (1968).

[4] *Infra,* Chapter VI.

[5] Although there is no order of priority, wherever possible, the themes of the 1970s tend to be listed in relationship to the previous themes.

a class or ethnic group, and the right of free inquiry are bound to lead to controversy and conflict. Low-income and black communities will become increasingly suspicious of research that depicts them in a negative light. The white, middle-class social scientists will no longer be welcomed in such communities and will find it more difficult to find willing subjects there. The concept of inequality will probably merge with those of poverty and race as a major trend in research. Whereas, in the 1960s research was devoted to describing problems and changing and assimilating the poor and minorities, in the 1970s research will be devoted to finding solutions and changing society.

2. *Hunger and Malnutrition.* Lack of nutrients, besides affecting a person's health, decreases his productivity and learning capabilities and results in apathy and lack of initiative. The person needs to conserve energy. Furthermore, the underprivileged child's apparent sluggishness which was frequently attributed to laziness, indolence, and other so-called "ethnic traits" was found in some studies to be owing to malnutrition.

In 1968, affluent America began to discover, incredulously, widespread hunger amidst its plenty. Soon there arose a national demand for federal action. President Nixon's 1970–71 fiscal year budget devoted $2.8 billion to help 13 million people, more than double the amount of money spent and the number of people that Johnson's last budget had planned to help. The 1970s should see increased federal spending to put an end to hunger and malnutrition in the nation, ultimately reaching the 24–28 million people living below the federal poverty standard. By the mid or late 1970s, the children of the poor should be able to obtain free breakfast besides the free lunch many now receive.

3. *Open Enrollment at the Colleges.* Following the 1970 example of the open enrollment procedures of The City University of New York, various kinds of increased open enrollment policies probably will be tried at other city and state colleges, with special educational and financial assistance for the disadvantaged. However, if the money crisis continues, the number of institutions of higher learning involved in such policies will be reduced. In either event, many educators and middle-class parents will voice concern about academic standards and the value of the degree at these colleges. Regardless of whether these opinions are correct, the traditional view that college should bring together students of different backgrounds, and the traditional view that education should serve as a means of upward mobility for the poor will be enhanced as a result of this new procedure.

4. *Radicalization of Teachers.* Although relatively few college radicals are going into teaching, there seems to be a small but growing number of white dissident and black militant students entering the teaching profession in large cities. These new teachers have a revulsion for the old order and old system. They reject their own schooling as authoritarian and oppressive. They resent the inequities of society, especially between the poor and affluent, and no longer believe in what society has told them. They have read Jerry Rubin and Frantz Fanon as well as Paul Goodman, Herbert Kohl, and Edgar Friedenberg, and they identify with their revolutionary ideas. A number of these new teachers should serve as catalysts of the new educational "revolution" and "reform" movements. These teachers will probably band together with each other and with radical students and militant community groups against conservative teachers and administrators. The target will probably be the large school system which tends to be inbred and *status quo* oriented, and the battlefield will probably be the schools. Some of these radical teachers will be dismissed, in part because they will be easy to discharge in view of the increased supply of teachers and the growing school budget crisis.

5. *Teacher-Training Programs.* Teacher-training institutions will begin exploring the uses of (1) modular instruction, substituting mini-courses for regular semester courses and stressing mastery rather than time in determining how long an individual works on a module; (2) behavioral objectives, stating precisely what is intended and how behaviors are to be accomplished; and (3) competency-based criteria, that is, defining objectives and holding participants accountable for meeting them.

Due to the black-white polarization as well as federal pressure on schools to integrate their students and faculty, summer teacher institutes on racism should emerge, or at least inservice training which will include increased use of sensitivity training and other methods of changing attitudes.

6. *Differential Staffing.* Differential staffing should become a popular trend by the late 1970s, whereby the profession will offer a variety of career positions and entry points and salaries appropriate to the various teaching levels, experience, responsibilities, and recognized competencies. The idea already coincides with the growing number of paraprofessionals and the teacher-training institutions which are providing inservice education for paraprofessionals and teachers, as well as the trend for employing clinical professors and cooperating teachers to work with student teachers. The idea also agrees with the new trends of competency

based criteria, teacher accountability, and the influx of educational technology.

Differential staffing models are already in operation in small school systems, among them Beaverton, Oregon; Montgomery County, Maryland; and Temple City, California. National teacher organizations and educational associations will probably soon develop such models, and large city school systems should subsequently modify and adopt them. Moreover, if the city school systems are decentralized and controlled in part by the community, as the trends seem to indicate,[6] the local school boards most likely will approve of the idea since it coincides with their demands for requiring changes in teaching behavior and rewarding merit as well as with their general demands for hiring, promoting, and evaluating school personnel.

7. *Teacher Militancy.* Teacher militancy may decline for the following reasons. The decentralization of city schools will mean that teaching conditions, problems, and morale will vary in different school districts. The increase of black teachers in the profession should eventually splinter the AFT, for black teachers will voice different concerns than white teachers and form their own associations. There is now an oversupply of teachers and this trend will increase. Consequently, nontenured striking teachers, or for that matter even tenured striking teachers, may be intimidated by local school boards with lists of new teachers looking for jobs. In an emergency, paraprofessionals, with the aid of nonstriking teachers and with the utilization of educational technology, could teach the students—making the striking teacher's position less secure. Finally, the schools will find it difficult to finance education and simply cannot meet as many of the teachers' demands as they were able to in the 1960s.

To offset the potential decline of teacher power, there are signs that the AFT and NEA may merge in the 1970s. By the same token, there is indication that the United Federation of Teachers (UFT), the largest local of the AFT with more than 70,000 members, may merge with the New York State Teacher Association (NYSTA), a state affiliate of the NEA, whose strength is in the suburbs and rural areas of the state and with a membership of more than 105,000. This city-state teacher organizational merger may set in motion the AFT-NEA national merger— toward a single, giant teacher organization.

8. *Hiring and Promoting Practices.* There will be increased demands for and possibly eliminating formal examinations for teaching licenses

---

[6] *Infra,* Chapter VI.

and especially supervisory promotions. Various civil rights organizations will refer the case to the courts, claiming the examination procedures discriminate against minorities. (The elimination of objective tests raises the problem of patronage, nepotism, and pork barrel.) Due to federal pressure to integrate teaching staffs, central boards of education will assign an increased number of black teachers to predominantly white schools (and vice versa with white teachers and black schools). However, this trend will be partially offset and superseded by the growing demands of black power and black community control of the schools in which there will be increased preferential hiring and promoting of minority school personnel. Coinciding with the demands for teacher accountability and differential staffing, the claim for merit pay will increase and different teaching indices may be adopted by the close of the decade.

9. *Teacher Accountability.* In the past, it was the students who were primarily held accountable for success or lack of success in school. Now the finger is pointing at the teacher and school. In 1969, the contract between the United Federation of Teachers and Board of Education of the City of New York recognized that the school system was failing "to educate all students . . . especially minorities." The Union and Board agreed "to seek solutions to this major problem and to develop objective criteria of professional accountability." In 1971, the Educational Testing Service was retained to devise an accountability model.

Many educators and community groups have voiced interest in the idea of teacher accountability, and it has already spread beyond New York City. But unless implementation and procedures for teacher accountability are carefully regulated by the profession, the notion could have negative effects—threatening the rights and job security of teachers and causing reduced morale and increased tension among teachers, administrators, and community groups.

10. *School Accountability.* Contract performance programs are gaining in popularity across the nation and provide a means for holding schools accountable. The idea is that a business firm guarantees to raise the students' academic performance in terms of grade level units in a prescribed amount of time. Instruction is usually in reading and mathematics, involving low achievers, mostly from minority groups.

The first contract performance program was carried out during the 1969–70 school year between the Texarkana, Arkansas, school system and the Dorsett Educational Systems; by the end of the year the company was criticized for unethical practices. (Dorsett taught the test questions to the students and administered many exit tests but counted only the highest scores for purposes of payment.) [7] Nevertheless, the federal government and many school systems have provided funds to business companies for performance contracts and the trend is increasing. Restrictions and guidelines, modes of proof and retention, auditing procedures, and the mutual responsibilities of the schools and contractors will have to be developed in order to protect children against intense pressures to perform, to safeguard against educational quackery and unethical practices generated by the profit motive, and to identify viable contract programs.[8], *

11. *School Reorganization.* Southern schools will probably continue growing more integrated than Northern city schools, at least statistically [9] —a result of federal pressure to eliminate state-imposed racial segregation and the increased migration of Southern blacks to Northern cities and white out-migration from the cities to the suburbs. Northern school systems will increasingly decentralize their schools and local communities will obtain more control of the schools, thus helping to perpetuate Northern segregated schools. Bussing in the North will become a major political issue.

In the early 1970s, the OEO is scheduled to implement a number of experimental voucher plans, probably in California, Illinois, and/or Washington, mainly in school systems with approximately 12,000–15,000 students. Parents of elementary school children in a specific area will be issued vouchers. The parents will take these vouchers to an accredited school in which they want to enroll their children, and the school will convert the voucher to cash. The idea is to force mediocre schools to improve. If the plan is adopted on a mass scale, several experimental schools will probably open and, unless carefully regulated, these schools will be of dubious quality, predominantly white or black,

---

[7] See Andrew and Roberts (1970) for the final evaluation of the Texarkana-Dorsett program.

[8] See Ornstein (1972) for a discussion of the problems inherent in contract programs as well as recommendations for improving such programs. Also, see December 1970 issues of the *Journal of Secondary Education* and the *Phi Delta Kappan,* as well as the January 1971 issue of *Educational Technology.*

* *Postscript:* The May 1972 issue of the *Nation's Schools* is tentatively scheduled to have a feature issue on professional accountability. As guest editor of the issue, the author listed several problems and unresolved questions regarding teacher accountability and school accountability. It was concluded that accountability was a bandwagon movement, and like other bandwagon movements in education it would probably cease.

[9] According to 1971 governmental statistics, 38% of black students in the South are attending integrated schools, compared with 27% in the North and West. Also see Chapter V.

thus increasing segregation. In this connection, ghetto children will have to be provided with a voucher of higher monetary value than white children in order to make the former more attractive to schools outside the inner city, as well as to avoid increasing the middle-class flight to the suburbs.

12. *School Finances.* School districts will continue to face deficits with no relief in sight. While schools will compete for state and federal funds, money probably will be diverted to assist parochial schools, thus increasing the trend toward segregated schools in the cities. The cities will be forced to find new sources of revenue, for, in many cities, residents are already taxed beyond practical limits. There will probably be a call for cost benefit studies, in turn increasing the trend toward competitive schools which is implied by vouchers, as well as contract performance programs and performance criteria. Legislatures of the states will be reapportioned; thus we can expect some extra state aid in the cities in a variety of areas—including education. Still, it will eventually be necessary for the federal government to come to the rescue of the schools. This increased federal spending on education may possibly reduce the amount of increases specifically earmarked for compensatory education.*

13. *Compensatory Education.* Funds for compensatory education, which have recently declined, will continue to decline for a few more years because of the failure of recent compensatory programs; the present administration's attitude toward reduced educational spending; the unhealthy economy; and the current public backlash against increased

---

* *Postscript:* As 1971 drew to an end, millions of students in both large and small cities as well as suburban areas faced the prospects of extended winter and spring vacations, and especially an early summer recess. Large cities such as Chicago, Cleveland, New York, and Philadelphia, smaller cities such as Dayton, Gary, and Newark, and suburban schools in Clovis, California; Malverne, New York; and Mansfield, Ohio are each in the red for exceedingly large sums—ranging from several million dollars in each of the large cities to several hundred thousand dollars in the suburbs.

School districts across the country are caught in a squeeze between operating costs and teacher demands for increased salaries vs. citizen revolts against further tax increases and inflationary spending. In cities that have a mayor who is in political opposition to the governor of the state, the situation is aggravated by the unlikely prospect of increased state contribution to the city schools. In order to stay open, some schools are borrowing against next year's school budget, freezing teacher salaries, reducing teacher health benefits, reducing the teaching staffs between 5% to 10%, limiting school repairs, reducing compensatory programs, increasing class sizes, and reducing the work week of janitors and other ancillary personnel.

taxes, high school and college unrest, teacher militancy, and the growing demands of minorities for special treatment. Although most of the trends that are producing this current public backlash are not expected to subside in the near future, the economy should eventually regain most of its health, and there are signs that military, defense, and space expenditures will be reduced. In the event that a more liberal administration gains control of the executive and legislative branches of government, increased government funding toward education and compensatory programs should reappear by the mid or late 1970s. Increased compensatory spending will coincide with a growing desire among the public for optimizing the educational achievement of the disadvantaged; moreover, this spending will be used as one of the main ways for camouflaging the reluctance of white America to integrate the schools. Thus, again, these programs will probably become one of the nation's educational priorities.

14. *Drugs.*[10] The problem of drugs recently became apparent, especially when it was found that white middle-class youth were also using and becoming addicted to them; it was no longer a black vice. The problem of drugs has reached epidemic proportions at almost all levels of society, and many city schools already find the problem beyond their control. Trends indicate that community drug education programs and centers will continue to spring up in urban areas. The state and federal governments will increase funding to schools and other educational and social agencies that are burdened with the problem and trying to cope with it. The topics of drugs and drug abuse will become required in one or more of the following curriculum areas: science, health education, English, and social studies, at both the elementary and secondary school level.

15. *Suburban Students and Schools.* Educators should soon take increased notice of the problems of suburban students and schools: the widespread socio-psychological discontent of students in the suburbs and the overrating of their teachers and schools. In many respects, suburban youth are also disadvantaged, and their schools are also unable to help them fulfill their human potential.

Whether the white suburbanites like it or not, the suburban setting will become altered by increasing numbers of blacks. The white influx to suburbia has been so great that the percentage of blacks in suburbia has

---

[10] A related topic is student unrest, which also became apparent at about the same time that drugs in the schools became a problem. Like the problem of drugs, student unrest involves not only city youth but suburban youth, not only the disadvantaged but also the advantaged. The topic of student unrest will be discussed in Chapter II.

risen only slightly within the last ten years, less than .05%, and still totals less than 5%. Although opposition in the suburbs has been pronounced and bitter against low- and moderate-income housing, and although the Supreme Court in 1971 ruled that the residents of a community may block housing projects by voting them down,[11] the federal government may eventually implement an expansive building policy, perhaps with a more liberal President. Such a policy would eventually affect the racial imbalance of the city and suburban schools sometime in the 1980s.

Conclusion

Reflecting upon the last decade, educators came to the realization that they lacked answers. Little was definite and consistent, excepting the obvious—i.e., poor students achieve less in school than their middle-class counterparts. Our lack of knowledge seemed to be partially due to the fact that variables and subsequent results varied because they were functional to many varied situations. As the complexities of the problem became evident, the old truism became applicable to the field— we are only at the first stage of wisdom: humble confession of how little we know. Rather than formulate ideas and programs that are based on hunches, we now have come to the realization that we first have to find what can work, with whom, to what extent, and under what conditions.

Perhaps the most distressing problem which haunted American society and spilled over to the schools during the last decade was the growing polarization of blacks and whites. Increased black and white racism in society will probably remain the most distressing problem in the future ahead and will affect many of the aforementioned trends.

---

[11] *Infra,* Chapter V.

II

Emerging Youth Deprivation

Introduction

By 1970 the emergence of high school student unrest had intensified and spread across the country and was filtering down to the junior high schools. Disruption and fear stalked the corridors and yards of many of the nation's schools. Fights between black and white students erupted. Teachers were assaulted; principals were harassed; picketing, demonstrating and the use of Molotov cocktails and chemical sprays had become common student tactics; underground student newspapers and political clubs called students to action in some schools. Guards and policemen were stationed in the halls with handcuffs, clubs, and sprays. Barricades encircled several schools, and many of these schools were closed.

According to a recent two-year study by Havighurst, Smith, and Wilder (1970), comprising 700 high schools (with a total of 1.6 million students) in 45 large cities, 53% of the principals who were surveyed reported some kind of student protest in their schools; as many as 56% of the junior high schools reported student disruptions. The Center for the Study of Violence a Brandeis University affirmed that the nation's public schools have become the number-one battlefield in America.

Though the recent yippie, hippie vogue and the New Left and black power movements seem to serve as sources which triggered the new student consciousness, the manifestations which made its emergence possible had been maturing in the schools for decades before their convergence in this consciousness.

The "wisdom" of teachers', administrators', and school board officials' policies has rarely been questioned in the past by students. Having perpetuated the *status quo* and having deluded themselves into thinking that the students were content because there were no signs of overt dissidence, the caretakers of many schools were (and in many cases still are) besieged by student disruptions; and the students had blasted holes into their phantasms.

For example, in their study of 7,000 high school students in the New York and Philadelphia metropolitan areas, Westin, De Cecco, and Richards (1970) pointed out that the great majority of students were angry and frustrated by school. Students saw school as impinging on their individual rights, and they felt victimized by authoritarian teachers and principals. They believed that complaining did little good and that there were few chances for improvement.

Bryant (1970) randomly selected 1,100 students from 74 high schools in Ohio. As many as 90% of the students believed that they should be involved in decision making involving curriculum, dress codes, and disciplinary procedures. These students contended that lack of communication between students and school authorities was a major cause for student activism. More than 50% believed student activism was an effective tactic in bringing about change.

On a nationwide basis, a recent poll of 100 schools conducted by Louis Harris and Associates for *Life* Magazine (1969) revealed that more than 50% of the students were unhappy with their limited part in school decisions. More than 60% wanted greater decision-making powers. However, conflict arose when it was pointed out that only 20% of the parents and 35% of the teachers believed that students should participate in decision making.

A survey of 512 high school and college students in thirty states, conducted by Parker (1970), revealed that more than 90% believed that the schools were "unsatisfactory." Overwhelmingly, these students maintained that courses were irrelevant, teachers were incompetent, learning was replaced by stress on grades, and school was boring.

In this atmosphere of chaos and conflict, we will now examine two groups of students—(1) middle- and upper-middle-class white students, and (2) black students of all classes—who, according to the previously mentioned surveys, seemed the most dissonant and active among all the student subgroups. Then we will proceed to a discussion of (3) the conflict between the students' and schools' norms and values, (4) the conflict between the students' and teachers' organizational behavioral roles, and then end with (5) some recommendations for curtailing student unrest and humanizing schools.

Besides focusing on the problems of middle- and upper-middle-class white students and black students in general, we will learn that almost *all* students and youth are generally denied their basic constitutional rights in school and society by virtue of the existing cultural patterns. They are deprived in the sense that they are culturally deviant from the larger society and within the school which reflects the dominant culture, and, subsequently, they are treated as second-class citizens in both settings. For the greater part, we will find an authoritarian, dissentient school machine, designed to cause distaste for learning and to exacerbate disconnection and discord between students and teachers—all of which can be viewed as part of the seeds for the recent student disruption. Although the majority of students are still nonactivists, they tend to dislike school and find it inane, boring, mismanaged, and oppressive. Those who try to maintain the *status quo,* or ignore the students, or rationalize that they are immature or going through a witless phase of development, underestimate the reality of the growing ill-feeling and potential for unrest among the students. Students can no longer be expected to be quelled by the myths and promises of school and society.

Granted, some of the overt dissonance among college youth seems to have subsided for the present. The reasons are probably due to the affirmation of the eighteen-year-old vote, the seeming de-escalation of the war in Southeast Asia, and the present inflationary economy and tight job market. Indeed, college students are more concerned about their job future than reforming future society. However, the high school student is still angry and alienated by the adult-controlled schools and society.

Middle- and Upper-Middle-Class White Students: The Anomic

The news from mainstream U.S.A. frightens the caretakers of the system. Many children and youth of managerial executives, doctors, and lawyers are still mocking the system and rioting in the schools. Although they grew up within the system, many no longer believe in its institutions. Worse than being disillusioned, they find they are culturally deviant and marginal to the system—helpless and powerless, too.

Their favorite criticism against caretakers is their hypocrisy and contradictions between what they say and what they practice. We believe in justice and equality, but not for blacks. We believe in ecology but continue to allow private industry to pollute the water and air. We believe in peace, but thousands of Americans and Vietnamese continue to die in what is now considered by most of us to be a senseless war. Many of these students often condemn their caretakers as dollar-grab-

bing, conspicuously consuming, chain-smoking, pill-gorging, gin-guz-
zling, bed-hopping frauds who have the audacity to pin dirty names and
labels on anyone who doesn't fit their bag. They disdain being judged
by others, especially by adults. With vivid and angry language, they
confront their critics:

> Look at you, blowing up whole countries for the sake of some
> crazy ideologies that you don't live up to anyway. Look at you,
> mindfucking a whole generation of kids into getting a revolving
> charge account and buying your junk. (Who's a junkie?) Look at
> you, making it with your neighbor's wife on the sly just to try
> and prove that you're really alive. Look at you, hooked on your
> cafeteria of pills, and making up dirty names for anybody who
> isn't in your bag, and screwing up the land and the water and the
> air for profit. . . . And you're gonna tell us how to live? C'mon,
> man, you've got to be kidding! (Simmons & Wineograd, 1966,
> p. 28)

Adults offer middle-class high school youth a world that is no longer
relevant. For many of these youths, the values we cherish are viewed as
defunct, American whoop-de-do, pilfered from the graveyards of the
past to serve as a source of needless guilt rather than a barometer for
present living. These young people's values are in flux; they are anomic;
for the greater part, their lives are meaningless, empty, purposeless. They
question the future, or if there will be one because of the bomb. Thus,
they are *now* people; they refuse to postpone gratification as their parents
did or as the schooling process demands.

Many middle-class youth are bored and cynical and feel unneeded or
useless. There are no frontiers to conquer. There is no real work for
them. According to Bettelheim (1969), these youth have become "obsolete." They can do very little except fight the nation's wars, but they
question these priorities. They can get good grades, but school doesn't
interest these youth—and not because they reject knowledge and learning. If anything, these youth have soaked up knowledge and are quite
intelligent. Many reject school because they view it as impersonal and
irrelevant, false and oppressive.

In effect, youth's activism helps reduce their useless feelings and empty
waiting; it helps reduce their boredom and enhances their desire for
immediate gratification; it provides a source of hope for changing their
derogatory image of school—falsely proving they are masters of their own
destiny. Many of these high school students now seek new elements of
pride and identification, a sense of purpose, power and worth, and, in
pursuit of this personal integrity, a goodly number have become rad-

icalized. Their faith in their group, their distinctive dress and idiom, their unified action and almost pathetic need to confront the system, as well as to forge their own life style, serve as substitutes for their personal void, powerlessness, and lost faith in the system and its values. Youth's zealous drive to improve the world, to consume themselves in peace and civil rights marches, their devotion to justice, equality and freedom give them a new meaning, and they find this exhilarating. Having lost faith in the system, they are willing to crusade recklessly against it. They are driven in part by their sense of powerlessness, for those that have power think the system is good and are against change; those who are powerless favor change. They realize that power must often be taken away through violence or the threat of violence since few people relinquish power on their own will. Some are ripe, in fact, to serve as the pawns in a *sturm und drang,* left-or-right cause. If they appear nihilistic, it is because they are often naive. Yet it is their naïveté that serves as a source of strength in the sense that they are unaware of the dangers and curvatures in the road ahead. In the exuberance of their age, they remain potent in spirit and resilient in the throes of force and danger; they often tease, provoke, and manipulate rather than surrender to their enemies— whether they be local vigilantes, law-enforcement agents, or public officials from city, suburban, or rural areas, Southern or Northern U.S.A.

In particular, their mockery serves as a unifying spirit, as a means for confronting others and coping with what they feel is their victimized and absurd relationship with society. According to Lifton (1969), there are times when such "incongruity can be dealt with only by the combinations of humor, taunt, mimicry, derision, and ridicule contained within the style of mockery [pp. 51–52]." Their mockery, combined with their potential for innovation and spontaneity, often confuses and misleads their opponents. Many adults (including teachers) become repulsed and jarred by their behavior; in turn, such adults often become angry and, if they also possess power, repressive. A few adults are able to sympathize with these youth and feel that something should be done to correct the abuses which are being exposed.

Although radical students usually claim nonviolence as a virtue, they do not turn their cheeks the other way; they often turn to violence themselves or elicit it from their opponents. (However, a distinction should be made between the high school and college radical. By virtue of high school students' ages, the police rarely react with violence to their behavior as they often do with college radicals.) The failure of high school radicals is the work of the system, and their success is a triumph over the system. They heed the messages of the new folk-rock and protest songs; they mouth the rhetoric of and sometimes join with the hippies, college radicals, and black militants. However, often their suspicion of adults is so great that even college radicals have difficulty being accepted by them. In fact, high school radicals themselves are often divided by competing ideologies. They tend to be suspicious of opposing groups and test each other to see whether they are true radicals.

Many of these high school students see schools and teachers as agents and apologists of the system. They see the discrepancies between the ideal and real, between preaching and teaching. We have taught students to think for themselves, or at least we have tried to do so, and we are witnessing the fruits of our labor. They sense they are being homogenized and used to "beat the Communists," as well as to swell their school's reputation and parents' pride. Some of these students see themselves mobilizing against the forces of stagnation: the old, unresponsive, impersonal institutions of society—the school is considered as one of these institutions—and spurning dehumanized caretakers who run these institutions. Thus, their need for intense personal relations and their growing number of communal groups should be viewed in part as a rejection of such bureaucratic structures and behaviors.

The students' ferment also stems from the need to change school and society and gain some mastery in a situation in which they have been rendered impotent. Their actions are a means of expressing their individuality and culture, as well as nursing their grievances and showing their disdain toward the system and its agents—the teachers and schools. They are sustained by the faith that what they are doing is right as well as by their growing numbers. They are revolting not only against the evils of the school but also against its weaknesses. Conditions must be right for rebellion, and the schools have been weakened by recent internal strife among teachers, centering around racism and union policies, as well as by outside political forces such as community groups and local, state, and national governmental agencies.

Although the main point of the radical students is that the schools and system must be humanized, they are not sure how to bring about such change. There is no formula or doctrine of what is to be done to accomplish these changes or what will be done once the schools are "revolutionized." Foggy, prodigious ideas are more important than concrete, feasible goals, for then there might be some reconciliation and their holy crusade, revivalist spirit, and individual fulfillment might cease. Since they are "true believers," they do not need to know exactly what they are doing or where they are going. However, although their goals are undefined, they are able to concentrate on specific wrongs that need changing; these wrongs will be examined later in this chapter.

Black Students: The Alienated

We now change our discussion from the anomic to the alienated. First we should note that the high schools, especially in rural, suburban, and small communities, wherever provincialism is pervasive, have been destructive and discriminatory toward lower-class youth, both white and black. The devious and covert methods through which the schools "civilize" and teach them their place in the social order have not changed since the classic studies of *Middletown, Elmstown,* and *River City.* The school performs a sorting job, and, as the lower-class students' first encounter with the system, it is there they learn that the poor members (of school and society) are virtually helpless and powerless. Over-whelmed by middle-class teachers who often dislike and disparage them, these students either fall in line and learn to exist and avoid conflict or become too harried and drop out. They learn that if they do not suc-ceed it is their fault, not the fault of the school or society.

At this point a distinction should be made between the white and black students. White lower-class students are often destitute and de-moralized, and the destitute and demoralized dream no dreams and see themselves incapable of changing the system or school, or of shaping their own future. For the greater part, they have no hope, no sense of awakening power, and no spirit to unite collectively. They are too shattered and awed by their surroundings to think of confronting them. They feel unable to control the circumstances of their existence in school or society.

Although blacks (no matter what their class) are the lowest on the student totem pole of status and power, they are no longer as destitute or demoralized as white lower-class students. The reason is that they possess a new faith in their undertakings and possess an irresistible drive in context with the black power movement. The schools are viewed as part of the white power structure, which has always been the enemy of black people. It is natural for black students to strike out against the school, the aspect of the white power structure they come into contact with most often.

As part of the concept of white paternalism, blacks are told to go to school and uplift themselves. Those who cannot make the grade are blamed for having poor home environments and low IQs. Most fail and score low on tests and eventually drop out of school—either in fact or by virtue of tuning out. Those who make the grade often are still perceived as "niggers" in the white society. They cannot escape the eye of persecution, even if they become "super Toms." Judge Marshall is still considered a "nigger" by many Southern Congressmen, Senator Brooke still incites American racist feelings when he is accompanied by his white wife, and Dr. Martin Luther King was killed for challenging white society—the American populace that wanted to think he loved them. Many young blacks today refuse to be "niggers" in school and society and also refuse to accept the myths and promises of school and society.

Black student unrest in school is linked with a throbbing belief in better things to come. Each new advance in the black power movement makes blacks fully appreciate what further progress can mean, and part of this progress is linked with education. As conditions improve, their discontent increases and they are more prone to rebel in school. Student ferment is a means for eradicating the Negro stereotype and self-image of submission, withdrawal, and escapism. Black students are involved in a battle to recognize their selfhood and identity. In effect, it is mentally healthy for the black student to lose himself in the intensity of the struggle against the Northern white power structure, including his teachers and school. He has almost a desperate urgency to be angry and protest, to make it clear to many white teachers to move out of his way, to gain a sense of hope and power, to prove he can shape his own destiny.

Indeed, the black student is not seeking new values, as with white middle-class students, but demanding that old democratic values be realized. Like his white counterpart, however, the black student sees the school as the first of several institutions of society, which he terms the white power structure, that seeks to destroy his individuality and culture. However, unlike the white high school radical whose ideologies cover a broad range and who is often suspicious of different and older radicals, the black high school militant concentrates on racial issues and is less suspicious of older black militants. Although the white radical and black militant sometime join forces, in most cases, they work independently of each other and often oppose each other in low socio-economic and low middle-class integrated schools. In the final analysis, the black high school militant should be counted as part of the larger black power movement. And in an era when "confrontation politics" has become both a creed and a psychological weapon, the black student has projected himself into the broad sweep of this advance in order to negotiate with the schools for identity and self-respect, as well as to tear down the restrictions that it imposes upon him. This indeed is better than resigning in apathy and submitting.

By themselves, white radical or black militant students are not a political or educational danger; nonetheless, they tend to cause adult backlash and increase repression in school and society. In turn, both extremes tend to feed on each other, and, followed to its logical end, both dissonant students and repressive authorities can threaten the school's foundation and society's stability. Ironically, almost all students (including most white radicals and black militants) would like to improve the schools, not dismantle them. Their desire to improve school coincides with the desire of most educators, only that their life style, philosophy, and tactics differ and threaten school authorities. As adults, it behooves educators to understand youth. Similarly, it is important for those in power to recognize the needs and aspirations of those who are powerless. The need is for educators to reach out and make the first peace gesture, to compromise, to form an alliance—to step forward with the students and rectify the schools.

Conflict between Students' and Schools' Norms and Values

Although the students come to school to learn, no matter what their class or color, they get grades instead. Grades become equated with learning. Our grading system is designed to separate the "sheep from the goats," the "intelligent" from the "ignorant." One of the major functions of the school is to provide the credentials for those who will work to perpetuate the system, the very system many students reject now. The school helps determine who will drop out of society, who will become second-class citizens, who will hold a union card, and who will enter the professions. The schools also help perpetuate the theory of the "survival of the fittest" which in wartime until very recently with the introduction of the draft lottery was perverted into a theory of eugenics where the unsuccessful dropout was drafted and faced death.

Since grades are the key to school success, the students become hypnotized by right answers and pigeonholed by their tests. Many students spend numerous hours doing homework and preparing for tests, and their teachers spend numerous hours devising and marking the tests. The students learn it is unsafe to question, interrupt, or evaluate; it is wiser to copy the material, and parrot the teachers.

Besides being overworked, the students are underpaid. They are forced to live on a poverty level, receive money from their parents and be grateful. Today many high school students are beginning to "opt out." No longer impressed by or afraid of teachers and schools, they seek other means to make the system take notice of them. Maybe what the students need is a union to improve their working (school) conditions and to provide salaries (scholarships). Perhaps the recent student ferment will improve their status.

The students are being "had" and most of them realize it. What the student studies is saturated with irrelevant, mechanical, nonessential hokum. We are in danger of trying to teach so many facts to keep up with the explosion of knowledge that we seem unable to go beyond the realm of knowledge, beyond what is now considered by many educators to be the lowest level of intellectual development and inquiry. Students are often required to memorize trivia, the same trivia their teachers have difficulty recalling without referring to the text or lesson plan. Who is the twelfth President of the United States? What is the capital of Alaska? How many legs does a spider have? What is the pH of sulfuric acid? What is the formula for the sine of an angle? How many teachers reading this chapter can answer these questions? Most students today work harder than ever before because there is more knowledge to know. The problem is not a lack of effort but a waste of effort; the problem is not that students are uninterested in learning but that what they are supposed to learn is uninteresting and usually taught in an uninteresting way.

Seldom has the *Record* of Teachers College, Columbia University, published an article by a thirteen-year-old student; however, when it did, what she had to say characterizes the trivia and boredom that students must face daily. Wrote Patty Wirth (1970), "Sometimes when we are reading page 307 in class I feel like jumping up and saying, 'Who is really interested in this? Who thinks that this is fascinating [p. 57]?' " She goes on to say, "I learn morpheme strings, not necessarily because they'll help later in life, but because how else could I pass to eighth grade. In the eighth grade I'll learn equally useless stuff so I'll pass to ninth grade, tenth grade, eleventh grade . . . [p. 57]."

Fraternity pledges and army privates are required to learn trivia, too. It serves to remind them of their lowly and menial position, and it gives their superiors an opportunity to harass and chastise them for being unable to recite useless information. While the pledges and privates are permitted to improve their status, students are indentured to their teachers as long as they remain in school. They cannot escape the teacher's watchful eye, sensitive ear, and red pencil. Some teachers are brutal—continuously testing their students with written quizzes and oral questions related to homework and previous lessons. Their assumption is the student must be coerced to learn, and this is true if he has to learn trivia.

When students claim their courses are irrelevant, they mean that they are unable to apply what they learn in school to problems outside of school. Similarly, they are unwilling to accept the teacher's future orientation; namely, that it is important to study a subject so that in the future they will be better citizens or be able to get better jobs. To be sure, the curriculum should be alive, real, and relevant. Contemporary issues dealing with sex, drugs, war, racism, poverty, etc., should be examined in depth, not just mentioned as a supplementary thought or on special days. For example, there is no reason not to relate student personal experiences with sex and drugs to work in literature and findings in science. We delude ourselves into thinking that only a small minority of American students engage in such "immoral" activities. It is ludicrous that hundreds of school systems are losing bond issues over courses in sex education while an increasing number of students are losing their virginity before attending their high school proms. It is even more ludicrous when we count the large number of balding teachers who speak, when among themselves, about their covert desires for certain pistil-bearing students; or when we include some young, side-burned high school teachers, especially in the large cities, who are deflowering them.

The teacher who seduces his student is usually not sick but selfish. It is the school that is sick—for losing one-third of its clientele when they have no other place to go except for "deadendsville," for graduating another one-third as functional illiterates, and for being for the remaining one-third not a place to learn but a boring place to go in order to get a good job. Indeed, it is a sick school that makes students sick of learning.

Holt (1964) points out that the student, when he begins school, is eager to learn; he is curious, open, receptive, not afraid of mistakes, and persistent in responding to and evaluating this new learning experience. Learning is fun, exciting, interesting, and natural. The young child is willing to explore the unknown and put together—or at least try—the pieces that puzzle him. As the student passes from grade to grade, his creativity, spontaneity, and zest for learning eventually become stifled, sometimes squashed. Learning becomes boring and irrelevant. His intellectual curiosity usually is diverted into areas unrelated to learning such as sports, extracurricular activities, and clubs, as well as drugs and sex. In class, the student often squirms in his seat and writes graffiti on his desk, daydreams, whispers, doodles, and figures out ways to fool the teacher and do the least amount of work and still get by. At home his main task is to get his schoolwork out of the way as quickly as possible so he can do his "thing."

A bored student is more conscious of his voidness; he has more time for being an activist. The student ferment is in part motivated by an attempt to alleviate boredom. A student who feels the subject matter is irrelevant has little difficulty in formulating demands for improving the curriculum, to give meaning to going to school and to give meaning to his life. Similarly, he is more prone to use drugs to escape from boredom or to challenge the system that bores him.

As for most teachers, they offer a picture of the world that for students is false and hypocritical and in conflict with the students' sense of reality, behaviors, and emotions—all of which have been sharply sensitized by the new trends in the media of mass communications and music. Music and dancing are a means of expression and communication, and the difference between adult and youthful music and dancing reflects differences in their life styles. Witness adults waltzing across the floor to the hallowed deadening music of Guy Lombardo or Lawrence Welk. Then visit a throbbing, stomping loft party or teenage discotheque. Ultraviolet lights make light-colored clothing fluoresce. Psychedelic posters and bright clothes are everywhere. Teenagers gyrate wildly under flickering strobe lights to the beat of incredibly loud and intense music. The senses are awakened and eroticized. You get the feeling of being stoned just by watching and listening, and sometimes just by sniffing.

Today's youth do not repress their feelings or emotions, nor do they become embarrassed by interpersonal relations—many teachers do. Youth tend to be impulsive and impetuous; they tend to be more humane, sensitive, and sincere than their teachers. They often seek honest communication and trusting relationships, and they usually do not have the defenses that adults do, nor do they have the need to always feel in control as adults often do. They tend to reject the dishonest and nonpersonal type of communication that often evolves from their relations with their teachers. Some manage to find honest and personal relationships with their peers, especially through communal living and through the intimacy of sex. Sex is to be enjoyed and helps fulfill their need for intimacy and capacity for enjoying life.

The students flaunt their authenticity and honesty, and in doing so, make many teachers aware of their own falseness and dishonesty. The students, in their quest to change the schools, are often teaching their teachers to doubt, to criticize, and to act upon their convictions. While most teachers—as adults usually do—learn to go along with the system, students tend to be more outspoken and fearless for they are not the stooges of the system; they do not have to worry about nonexistent $15,000 jobs and nonexistent families to support. Many high school students are willing to act *now,* even in small numbers, rather than wait for two or three years until a contract expires and confront the system with the safety of large numbers.

If the students make any display of warmth of feelings in school, for example holding hands in the hallway, they are usually reprimanded by the teachers. Their teachers are generally anti-erotic and anti-sensual; they are unable to teach students to enjoy life because they are often restricted by a Puritan morality; moreover, many are often envious of their students' youth, freedom, and hedonism. Many, in fact, believe it is unwise to smile in class for the first two or three months; they believe the students will construe their smile as a sign of weakness. The idea is not to be friendly or kind but aloof and firm so the students will not take advantage, so that the teacher will maintain control.

Many teachers are emotionally repressed and are unable to teach in the affective domain—involving attitudes, feelings, and emotions. Factually oriented by their teacher training and the demands of the curriculum, secondary school teachers usually view feelings and attitudes as subjective and rationalize that there is insufficient time to discuss what is subjective. Even worse, many teachers are afraid to express their own attitudes and feelings in front of the class. What they often do is ask students to share their feelings without revealing themselves. They ask students to be honest without being honest themselves. Under the guise of objectivity, some teachers refuse to take a position on a controversial issue and reveal their real attitudes. In short, most teachers are unable to treat their students as real people—to relinquish their facade and be their honest selves.

Often teachers are disturbed by students addressing them by their first names; it is construed as a sign of disrespect and a potential threat to their authority. Teachers demand privacy from their students; they usually have their separate bathrooms with locks on them and their separate lounges and cafeterias which are "off limits" to the students. This is where the teachers are themselves, and they are afraid to have their students see them. Most teachers do not want their students to get to know them as persons, for they feel such familiarity will lead to a loss of respect and authority and, in turn, threaten their egos. In fact, teachers tend to feel threatened if they live in the same community with their students, and those who do often try to avoid their students for they feel embarrassed and uncomfortable when their students greet them outside of school.

Furthermore, most teachers are reluctant to admit that they lack rapport and communication with their students as people. For the greater part, many are too old to relate to students, too ignorant of the mood and style of youth, and, after a few years, too engulfed in an organization that pays their salaries and has dehumanized them. Many teachers have become frauds without even knowing or admitting it, and the older they become and longer they remain in the system, the worse they usually become.

The teaching-learning process is supposed to be a mutually satisfactory relationship between students and teachers, but what usually transpires today is mutual mistrust, resentment, even hostility and alienation. It has degenerated to a situation where students often see teachers as patronizing caretakers, frequently authoritarian and oppressive, and where teachers often see students as ungrateful and untamed, too immature and lacking in intelligence to know what is best for them.

In all fairness, teachers are probably no worse than other professionals in their relations with their clientele. Some start with zeal and energy and have good intentions of helping their students and imparting knowledge. But a combination of factors—years spent in a dehumanizing and bureaucratic system, the general disdain many adults have toward youth, and boredom with the same work over a long period—makes most teachers grow to dislike their students and work. In other fields, however, the professional-clientele relations last for a brief time so any professional dislike or impatience with the clientele is not as visible or aggravated as it is with teachers. For example, a doctor can treat his patient in ten minutes and prescribe medicine. Win or lose in court, or once the contract is signed, a lawyer need not further associate with his client. Unfortunately, young clients are more vulnerable than adult clients, and over a period of years, they may be gravely affected by their relations with teachers.

Sociologically speaking, students need to feel that they belong, but many do not feel a part of the school or that the school belongs to them. If they thought it was theirs, they wouldn't be breaking windows and wrecking classrooms; they wouldn't have to be bribed and coerced to keep the school clean and perform services for it. The students' rights tend to be ignored by the school; moreover, disciplinary procedures are usually based on the premise that students are guilty until proven innocent. Students are often suspended by the whim of a principal and are subjected to hearings without counsel. The school often permits the police to search and interrogate students for hours without notifying their parents; it often applies arbitrary dress codes and harasses students' political activities; it outlaws many social functions and many of the students' freedoms of expression and emotion. (In this connection, some of the students' basic rights are summarized later in this chapter.)

Conflict between Students' and Schools'
Organizational Behavioral Roles

One need not be a cliché-monger to affirm that the schools reflect the values of society, and though there is wide opinion of what values should be taught, democracy is a sacred value that the schools preach and try to teach. But while the school attempts to teach the value of democracy, it operates as an authoritarian organization. In a democracy, the mass have a check upon the abuse of their leaders at the next election. In the schools, the students have relatively no check on their teachers and principal. As with the masses in a dictatorship, the most effective way for the students to initiate change is to rise up and revolt. Widespread enthusiasm and zeal are needed for the realization of such change, an upsurge of fervor, an awakening or exhilaration of power— student power.

In a democracy, decisions are made through accommodation and compromise. Policy is subject to debate and bargaining; it has the approval of the majority group, and each of the majority groups will have achieved some aspect of what it wanted. Although the students are the majority group in school, they have very little, if any, influence in decision making. Decision making in the schools is vested with the top echelons, and it is the teacher's role to maintain and enforce these decisions, and the student's role to listen, obey, and be grateful. Even student elections are a sham; the school authorities usually decide who has the right to vote and hold office. Restrictions are imposed upon nonconformists, those who have the life and energy to assert their individuality. What the students want is usually irrelevant; it is con- sidered that they do not have the ability to govern themselves. They are told to think and be responsible, but if they dare stand by their convictions or criticize the school's operation, they are often chastised and branded as "troublemakers."

One of the best ways to study the democratic process and learn to value it is to participate in it. Democracy in the schools means the majority are heard, have power, and can influence their own destiny. We fail to recognize that no democratic society, or for that matter no democratic organization, needs to fear different opinions and life styles. Only a society that seeks order, conformity, and regimentation needs to fear differences. The school is supposed to be a democratic institution which claims it tolerates, even encourages, diversity. However, in reality the school is coercive and authoritarian because the students are com- pelled to attend it. Thus, by its very nature and function, the school is undemocratic and does not tolerate or permit real differences. In the meantime, students are losing faith in the democratic process because they do not experience it in school or society. Indeed, we cherish and defend democracy, but we fear it too, especially if students and youth are treated democratically. Students are rebelling for the same reason adults do: a desire for their basic rights, the need for equality and justice—the so-called virtues of democracy.

Most teachers feel safe and satisfied as long as they control and coerce their students. The thought of not being in complete control in a classroom disturbs and frightens teachers. Teachers often claim, "I've tried democracy, but it doesn't work in the classroom." They overlook that students who have been stifled and repressed by a system for years, suddenly experiencing democracy, will have trouble adjusting. They conclude, then, that students' modern impulses and free expression must be checked and choked. Indeed, efforts to change teacher behavior and school operation do not reflect the sophistication that we have with regard to changing and manipulating student behavior.

The bureaucratic school organization legitimatizes the teacher's power; he is responsible for controlling and regulating the behavior of the students, who serve in the organization as subordinates—powerless and penurious. Of course, those who have power think it is a good organization and are against change. The powerless recognize their abject position and favor a different system.

Control is essential for the organization. The school's procedure is that of regulating student behavior, of reducing their behavior to the predictable patterns necessary for organizational functioning. Every formal organization, including the school, attempts to reduce the variability and spontaneity of individual human acts. The teachers must obtain from the students reliable performance—which can be defined in terms of conformity. Rather than encourage uniqueness and diversity, the teacher requires obedience and docility.

The student is no longer treated as a human being, but as a cog in the organization—one of the nuts and bolts in the school machine that must be wrenched, pressed, and oppressed. The student is forced to surrender his individuality; he is told what to do and when to do it. The process of going to school, in effect, becomes a process in which the student surrenders his rights as an individual; it is a process of submission. It is his first encounter with the system, transmitting to him his position in the order of the hierarchy, putting the student in his place —last place, conveying to him a powerless and impotent self-image.

The students who break a regulation must be warned, scolded, or punished—shaped into routine. The students who accept the teacher's authority without reservation by obeying and reacting positively to a whole set of stimuli that strips them of their identity are prized by their teachers for being cooperative—cooperative victims. Their cues become the teacher's instructions, commands, and whistles and the school's bells, chimes, and gongs. Somewhat reminiscent of Pavlov's manipulative operation, the school conditions the students to sit, stand, line up, and file out. Most students learn the rules of the game; others refuse to or cannot play the game, assert their identity, and in turn threaten the teacher's identity. These are the "flibbertigibbets," the potential student activists whom teachers resent and scorn. Since the minimal function of the teacher is to be sure the incumbents obey the organization's rules, corrective action must be taken against these students. If the teacher fails, a higher authority is often called upon to enforce the school's routine.

The teacher's authority is vested in his position; his authority is taken for granted, at least by the organization's rule book. Although the student comes to school to gain intellectual experiences, his first requirement, not listed in the official aims or educational goals of the school, is to respond to and listen to the teacher. Indeed, there is no more important law of any organization than that the performers of certain roles shall heed the requests from superior role-performers.

The lowest subordinates in other organizations have coffee breaks. However, students are rarely given time or a place where they can unwind—smoke a cigarette, sip a coke, listen or dance to a record—and escape from their teachers. Even prisoners have many of these privileges. One might expect that the school—the system's shrine of enlightenment, its generator of knowledge—would treat the younger generation as respected human beings, at least as prisoners. As role-superiors, the teachers are provided free time and a lounge to have their cigarettes and coffee.

Instead, the student lavatory serves as their sanctuary, a place to meet friends, smoke a cigarette or perhaps a joint, relax, and escape role-superiors. Their ten- or fifteen-minute escape here can be considered the institutionalized coffee break of the modern machine or bureaucratic organizations. For a teacher to venture into the students' bathroom, especially in a "difficult" school, is to invite abuse and unnecessary conflict. Only a bold or inexperienced teacher intrudes into their "crib of euphoria." Consequently, many students' bathrooms today are locked and opened only at prescribed time intervals.

The school curriculum may stress "citizenship" as one of its major goals, but it is unlikely to specify "obeying the teacher," which for the sake of the school's functioning is equated with "citizenship." Often the citizenship grade merely reflects the degree to which the student listens to the teacher and conforms to the rules of the school.

Excellence in "citizenship" often means the student has done what the teacher has told him to do, and not annoyed the teacher, thought for himself, or questioned the teacher's authority or "wisdom." He has taken his sedative pills; he has been submissive and docile; he has, in fact, adopted the qualities that least fit a citizen to meet the problems of the twentieth century.

The best way to become a good citizen is to practice citizenship. In order to practice citizenship, whether it be in school or society, the individual must have confidence in himself as a person who can influence what goes on. Many students today are stating they want to feel they can alter what goes on. They want to control, at least influence, their own destiny in school, not be exploited and manipulated by the school and its caretakers. They are seeking their constitutional rights so they can become a citizen of school and society. If resorting to rebellion is their only means of achieving their citizenship, then, they claim, so be it; so did our founding fathers claim their right to rebel. Many students no longer seem willing to behave "properly" unless they see themselves as responsible members of the school, not suppressed by it. To change their status from victims to shapers, from powerless to influential, is basic for preparing students for citizenship in schools and society.

While the teacher's authority and power is taken for granted by the organization and made a matter of policy, an increasing number of students no longer feel they should obey their teachers just because of their position. In most organizations, new members join with full understanding that they are subordinates and will have to abide by the regulations. Furthermore, these people often have options to work somewhere else if they dislike the organization. The child who begins school is not cognizant of the school's rules; he has to be taught them. As the child grows older and advances through high school his role is still formalized and prescribed without his having a voice in the matter. The rules define his expected behavior, and he has little opportunity to transform his role according to his personality. For the sake of the organization, his behavioral procedures are outlined and supervision is administered with penalties for deviant behavior. Whether he enjoys carrying out his appointed role and related tasks is beside the point. With the exception of dropping out of school or attending a private school or one of the few free schools, the student has few other options open to him.

Nobody enjoys a situation where his identity, needs, and problems are diminished for the purposes of someone else such as a teacher or for some organization like the school where he feels exploited. If a student feels his identity is conceived in terms which conflict with his personal integrity and self-actualization, he has three choices: repress his needs, withdraw from the organization, or confront the organization directly. In the past, most students decided it was easier to accept than to rebel and allowed the school to define them until they either dropped out or graduated. While their mental health suffered, the school's functioning was secured and the teachers were satisfied. The overt rebellious students were either tamed or expelled. Unique and unorganized, the school was allowed to label them as "problem" students. Blinded by tradition, the school is still unable to conceive that its own functioning may need adjusting, not that the students need adjusting. Today, in some parts of the country, many high school students seek the third alternative. Since it is ridiculous to label the majority in these schools as "problem" students, the schools rationalize the students' unified action as the "problem." The authorities fail to recognize that the schools' process is the original problem, not the students' unrest. However, as the students become more active, their behavior is perceived by most educators as the problem.

No organization, including the school, can function without substantial recognition and acceptance of authority. Consequently, student unrest and disruption are considered as the breakdown of such recognition and acceptance. To avoid this—at least to minimize the number of crises today—the organization devises several ways to make the student conform and make his behavior reliable and predictable, ranging from man's primitive reverence for fear to more subtle techniques of brainwashing. Part of the brainwashing technique is to siphon off the bright members of the group, to get them interested in the myths of the organization and the value of succeeding within the organization, to provide them with extra awards and recognition: awards for attendance, achievement, conduct, and service to the school—educational hokum. In each case, the rewards are for those who fulfill or go beyond the role expectations and requirements. For example, among the many useless and boring functions of the school assembly is that it is the time and place where rewards are usually given and received. Weakened rules are also reaffirmed, warnings are frequent, and inspirational messages and pep talks along with certificates and awards for "merit" are given. During the proceedings, many students become bored and lapse into a torpid coma.

In the bureaucratic organization, personal relations among members of the hierarchy are frowned upon in order to enhance the predictability of behavior. In the schools the teachers are warned by their colleagues about becoming too friendly with students; likewise, students who become the "teacher's pet" are usually ostracized by their peers. These unwritten rules of the school merely reinforce the already strained teacher-student roles.

An *esprit de corps* develops among the shared members of both groups, creating an "us-them" distinction. Members of both groups tend to support and defend members of their group against the other group. It is not uncommon to hear teachers in their lounge or cafeteria describing their students derogatorily; and in the bathrooms, hallways, and their own cafeteria, students denounce their teachers. Confined to the same classroom, selected members of both groups sometimes ridicule, shame, harass, and manipulate each other. Since the teachers are supported by the authority of the organization, the cards are stacked against the student. This is a "civilized violence"—subtle but inherent in the teacher-student role—which over a period of time is perhaps more destructive to the student's selfhood than is the "uncivilized student violence" to the school's operation.

One of the main goals of the teaching-learning process is for the teacher to make himself unnecessary, to replace fear and doubt with trust and knowledge, to instill in the students the ability to learn without the teacher's help. Most teachers fail to accomplish this goal, in part because they are incompetent and in part because they want their students to depend on them for ego reasons. Although the teacher's aim should be to make each generation of students better than the previous one, better than the teachers themselves, this is difficult, if not impossible, when the role conflict between them is too visible and repugnant. In this connection, the student rebellion should be viewed to some extent as a student backlash against their impotent and ineffective status and against their teacher's covert hostility and suppression. Much of the thrust of the student ferment is an acting out of repressed and rejected feelings. It is a self-defining process—a method of retaliating against the school's operation, a desire to gain a droplet of power. It is an attempt to shatter the assembly-line, coercive rules and regulations of the school, to force the school to be less exploitive and more humane.

Recommendations

Students and educators now contend that the schools must change, but most youth and adults do not know just how or what to do. The following recommendations, if observed, should help reduce student unrest and make schools more humane. Of course, there are risks involved, but this is true with almost all innovations. To sit back and maintain the *status quo,* however, is to invite greater risk.

1. Teachers and administrators must recognize that good intentions and a clear understanding of contemporary youth alone do not suffice, although they are important prerequisites for working with youth. Common sense and experience are also important. School authorities should understand that change is relative to a given situation and recommendations should be viewed in relation to one's own situation. Indeed, each school is different, consisting of different students and teachers, faced with different problems and pressures.

2. A teacher who is sensitive to the needs and interests of the students and who has good rapport with students, teachers, and administrators should serve as an ombudsman. The idea of the ombudsman assumes that student problems will be heard. The students should have a voice in determining the ombudsman, and ideally they should be allowed to vote for the person since he will have the responsibility for understanding their problems and representing them in decisions involving school policies.

3. There is need for a semiannual, perhaps even monthly, school-wide dialogue, one that honestly examines what changes need to be made to improve the school. The dialogue should take place during school hours, say for the entire afternoon, and it should be open to students, parents, teachers, and administrators.

4. School authorities, when talking for the need of student unity and cooperation, should avoid ideological rhetoric and emotionalism as well as threats and patronizing "wisdom." Reason, respect, and veracity should prevail in such dialogues. It should be explained to students that they represent only one power group or subgroup in relation to other groups such as parents, teachers, administrators, and community organizations.

5. "Conventional wisdom" tells us that people who are involved in decision-making aspects of the organization are more committed to it. There is need to find ways in which students can meaningfully be involved with the responsibility of decisions concerning school life, since it affects them. A student-faculty advisory committee could be elected which would represent the different student clubs, classes, grade levels, school tracks, and other student subgroups, as well as the different teaching departments and grade levels. This committee would work with the administration to decide policy concerning curriculum, classroom methods, discipline, school dress, assemblies, and recruitment and evaluation of teachers and administrators.

6. If teachers and administrators are going to relinquish some of their decision-making powers and limit their organizational roles, and if

students are going to fill the vacuum, the three groups may need to attend training programs and workshops to work out their new roles and behaviors. The schools should consider hiring intergroup trainers to organize effective encounter groups among the three groups and subgroups. Indeed, there is need to confront attitudes and problems through open discussion. Different groups and subgroups will articulate different needs and interests; there will be need to work together and learn to respect opposing views.

7. Guidelines may have to be developed for students to negotiate and articulate changes in school policy. Grievance procedures may have to be developed to protect students against dictatorial teachers and administrators (the grievance procedures should be based on the procedures employed by teacher unions in large cities). Students, teachers, and administrators may have to learn to reach compromises, similar to the way unions and management reconcile their differences.

8. A student court should be organized to enforce the basic school rules, especially those concerned with dress codes and disciplinary procedures. If rules are to be acceptable to students, they should help in enforcing them as well as in devising them.

9. School authorities should stress the concept of the student as an integral and necessary aspect of the success of the school and community. They should point out how the student can contribute to the school and community and how he can become actively involved in constructive reform. Students should have the opportunity to share leadership roles, to originate plans, to work with adults in the school and community on an equal basis. Students should be encouraged to peacefully organize, picket, and demonstrate for purposes of being influential and gaining respect and power. Students must be allowed to make mistakes, to learn from adults, and to see that they are often more competent in running and organizing things.

10. Student government fails not when students make mistakes but when the school denies students their constitutional rights. Today, more than ever, the students' rights need to be defined. Some of these rights are summarized below and (with the exception of the first item) are primarily based on a handbook published by the New York chapter of the American Civil Liberties Union (1969).[1]

---

[1] It is presumed that the students' rights will not endanger the health and safety of the student population or disrupt the educational process. If any of the students' rights lead to such problems, the school officials should intervene and curtail those specific rights which are causing the problem(s).

It is also presumed that it would be more practical to introduce students gradually to their rights at an early age instead of suddenly confronting them with freedom they might not be able to handle.

1. *Equal educational opportunity.* No student should be denied the right to attend a school, unless specifically geared for a special academic or talented group. The student's course of study should be appropriate to his abilities. Transportation services, whenever necessary, should be provided by the school.
2. *Freedom of expression and communication.* The school should not interfere with the students' expression and communication concerning controversial issues. "The students have the right to express publicly or to hear any opinion on any subject which they believe is worthy of consideration [p. 11]." They have the right to plan forums, select topics, and invite guest speakers. Student publications should be permitted, and the context of the material should be based on the decision of the student editorial board. The students should be assured that they will be "free from coercion or improper disclosure which may have ill effects on [their] careers [p. 12]." Although the school may provide information about the students' character and academic performance to outside business or governmental agencies, it should not answer questions about the students' values and political opinions. Answers to such questions are an invasion of the students' privacy and academic freedom. Also, the students have the right to observe "their own religion or no religion [p. 13]." The recitation of a prayer, a Bible reading, or the use of public school facilities for religious instruction has been declared unconstitutional.
3. *Freedom of assembly and the right to petition.* Students have the right to organize associations or clubs within the school for athletic, social, or political reasons, provided the organization does not deny membership to other students because of race or religion, or for any other reasons unless they are related to the purposes of the organization. The forming of political organizations should be permitted, and the school administration should not discriminate against the organization. The student and/or student organizations should be permitted the right to assemble within the school or on school grounds. Peaceful demonstrations and picketing or the collection of signatures for petitions concerning nonschool or school issues (even for the dismissal of the principal) should be permitted and "subject only to reasonable restrictions of time and place [p. 16]."
4. *Student government.* The organization and processes of the student government should be clearly specified by the school. All students should be allowed to vote. Similarly, they should have the right to run for and hold office, subject to the qualifica-

tions of the school's constitution. Candidates seeking office should be allowed to express their opinions and should have opportunity to campaign, subject to equally enforced rules. Vote counting should be scrutinized by representatives of the different candidates, and the winners of the election should be declared elected without a faculty veto.

5. *Student discipline.* Students' lockers should not be opened without their consent, unless a warrant is presented. Corporal punishment should *never* be instituted. Punishments should not affect students' grades, credits, or graduation, except when the infraction is related to academic dishonesty. Serious penalties (i.e., possible suspension or expulsion from school) should be reached as a result of a formal hearing—where the student is presented in writing with the charges prior to the hearing, and where the student's parents may be present and where he may be advised by anyone of his choosing. Involvement of the police should not lead to harassment. If a student is questioned by the police, he should be advised of his rights, and the principal (or his representative) and his parents should be present.

6. *Personal appearance.* Uniformity should not be equated with responsible citizenry. The students' appearance—their dress, length of hair, personal adornments, badges, or insignias—should not be restricted (so long as it does not disrupt the school); these personal belongings are a form of the students' freedom of expression and communication.

7. *Pregnant and/or married students.* The students' education should not be abrogated because of pregnancy or marriage. If temporary separation from the school is warranted, "the education provided elsewhere" should be as equal as possible to "the regular school [p. 20]."

A vast number of recent court cases have confirmed the basic tenor of the above list of students' constitutional rights.[2],[*] In addition, Highland (1971) maintains that (1) the courts have made it clear that schools have "no absolute authority over [students] and never had";

---

[2] Knowles (1971) lists and briefly describes nineteen recent court cases which confirm these rights. The February 1971 issue of the *Bulletin of the National Association of Secondary School Principals* discusses students' rights and the change in school law.

[*] *Postscript:* The American Civil Liberties Union revised its booklet during the summer of 1971 to include an appendix which lists the recent court decisions on students' rights.

(2) "schools may not be enclaves of totalitarianism which confine students only to those sentiments officially approved"; (3) the Bill of Rights applies to students as well as adults, and "students do not shed these rights upon entering a schoolhouse"; and (4) "to uphold arbitrary school rules which" contradict the students' legitimate rights "for the sake of some nebulous concept of school discipline is contrary to the principle that we are a government of laws pursuant to the United States Constitution [p. 115]."

Conclusion

If the reader is looking for a broad psychological explanation of why some students seem willing to crusade against schools and society, then the Keniston (1970) model of "youth" as a new stage in development seems worth considering. Keniston describes youth as a new stage, in between adolescence and adulthood, for some members of society. He points out that adolescence was recently invented to describe behavior for older children and teenagers. However, the descriptions of adolescence do not seem operational today for many students, and this may be one reason why we are unable to understand them or are confused by their dissenting and militant behavior. Education has prolonged adolescence and has rendered students relatively useless and impotent.

Keniston maintains that, while attending college seems to intensify the stage of "youth," going to college is not a necessary factor in prolonging this useless and impotent position. For some youth, the beginning of the stage might start in high school, or for others it may extend beyond their thirtieth birthday. In this connection, student unrest, as well as the demand for new values and life styles and freedom from adult authority, could be viewed as part of the acting out behaviors of youth against the facets and institutions of society which render them useless and impotent. According to Keniston, this unrest occurs "when the potentials for zealotry and fanaticism, for reckless action in the name of the highest principles, for self-absorption, and for special arrogance are all at a peak [p. 637]." Youth is the time when many members of society work out their conflicts between rejection of self and society and personal integrity and achievement of self within society.

Whether the reader is willing to accept this model as a partial explanation for student unrest reflects in part his own values and life style. Nevertheless, there is a danger in an education which renders its clientele powerless—restricting their freedom and individual expression. The danger is these forces mutually reinforce each other and may lead us down a path contrary to the American ideal of a common man who is free, responsible, and significant. The operation of the schools, if un-critically accepted and continued in an era of specialization, technology, automation, and bureaucracy, could lead to the powerless man in a powerful society. Given the assumption that the students have the greatest stake in the schools—and future society—do we give them the right to judge and change the schools—or do we continue to organize the schools so that future adults are unable to shape them?

III

Why Ghetto Teachers Fail

Introduction

Despite our concern and huge outlay of money, despite our talk about providing "quality education" and "equal educational opportunity," we are not making significant gains in educating the disadvantaged. More than ever, we seem faced with an increasing crisis: generally, low-income and ghetto students are not really learning; their teachers are not really teaching; the schools are driving their students away, if not literally, then psychologically; students are at war with their teachers (as indicated in the previous chapter) and teachers are at war with each other; communities are waging war against principals, and principals find that the grievance machinery of the teacher union is ready to confront them; racial conflict and drug problems are seriously enervating the schools; educators, social critics, and lay people are demanding change without offering viable and tested alternatives; the rigid, bureaucratic nature of the school system is preventing honest and worthwhile reform; schools and society seem bankrupt; and "confrontation politics" now threatens many of our cherished values and institutions.

We seem to have reached the point where we no longer know what to do in order to solve the educational ills of the children and youth referred to as the disadvantaged. There is a loss of genuine objectives, purposes, and reason. Spasms of rhetoric, name calling, emotionalism, scapegoating, "jabberwockery," and "fads and frills" seem to be increasing and contaminating what it logical and valid. Many of us have become impatient, cynical, and taut over the issues of class and race and power and politics. A host of moral-ridden terms, half-truths, simplistic solutions, threats, and counterthreats are waxing in the literature, college education courses, and schools. Under the guise of educational reform and with the license that academic freedom permits, many of us seem to be madly vaulting off in several directions—verbally assaulting one another, pounding our fists, and smashing our heads against the wrong walls.

My purpose here is to come to grips with the problem and suggest why we are failing. I am governed by a major assumption as to the reason for the problem and the stage that it has now reached. None of the public's concern, money, and talk has created a substitute for good teaching; no amount of compensatory education, integration, or community control is adequate if teachers are doing an inadequate job. New schools, smaller classes, and integrated textbooks are meaningless if teachers are indifferent. In short, it profits us little to voice our interest, spend billions of dollars on compensatory education, or reorganize school districts and then place the students under ineffective teachers.

The fact that teachers are failing to reach and teach the disadvantaged is not new, but I suggest that we explore some of the reasons. The teachers are the victims of improper teacher training as well as victims of their students, supervisors, the school system, and professors of education. These forces cause them to become frustrated, angry, and, finally, indifferent; so that almost everything we attempt, at that point, is a waste of time, money, and effort. Furthermore, instead of being helped, teachers are often subjected to constant and unjust attacks by many professional and nonprofessional educators who are often remote, not a part of or not strongly attached to the actual school situation. With this in mind, it is worthwhile to outline the major aspects of this chapter, or, the ways in which teachers are victimized by: (1) improper training, (2) their students, (3) their supervisors, (4) the school system, and (5) professors of education.

Teacher Training

Most teacher-training institutions do an appalling job of preparing teachers. Even the distinguished, "big-bellied" colleges and universities fail miserably in their attempt. It is possible for a teacher to possess an advanced degree in education and instruction and still be ineffective in the classroom. Teachers who are assigned to "good" schools usually manage to get by, since their students have the ability and intrinsic motivation to behave well and learn on their own. However, whenever teachers are assigned to work with the disadvantaged, poor teacher training becomes obvious because these students depend on good teaching. That a limited number of ghetto school teachers do succeed may be attributed to their unusual ability, which despite their poor training allows them to gain experience and effectively teach the disadvantaged. Here, however, we are confronted with a style—characteristics that seem to work well with disadvantaged youth but were never developed by our teacher-training institutions. This occurrence implies, to some extent, that teachers are born, not made (certainly not by our present teacher-training methods) and that those who are in the business of specifically training teachers should go out of business or improve their training methods.

Almost any normal person can teach students. A college degree per se is not a key factor, though it is important at the high school level; education is basically a criterion used to maintain a facade of professional standards for teachers. Certainly, it is possible for a mother with no college degree, who likes children, to be a more effective teacher at the primary-grade level than a young lady with a Ph.D. who can intellectualize the theories of Jersild, Piaget, or Bereiter and Engelmann, but cannot put them into effect. Similarly, it is possible to take some adults, former high school dropouts, who are capable of comprehending the *Reader's Digest,* off the street and turn them into relatively good junior high school teachers in a couple of months. Even lacking the background and knowledge of the field they are teaching, they can read the student's text and prepare his lessons the previous night, just as many teachers, who know very little about what they are supposed to be teaching or who are teaching out of license, do now. Of course, very few readers are expected to agree with these descriptions since they are ego threatening to teachers and have serious job implications for them and their professors of education.

We fail to recognize that it is nearly impossible to teach teachers how to develop common sense and a feel for teaching, how to use hunches and sentiments—all very intangible, yet important for successful teaching. Teachers can only learn limited techniques about teaching, which, with the present methods employed by most training institutions, can be supplied in advance in six to eight weeks. The rest must be learned on the job. To be sure, only limited aspects of methodology can be supplied in advance of teaching, but virtually all the skills and knowledge basic to teaching are learned while teaching. Teachers develop competence and become aware of their role as teachers during the first two or three years of teaching, and not while they are in undergraduate school. Courses and textbooks require consolidation after teaching has begun, but, as soon as prospective teachers graduate, their colleges usually abandon them. Thus, the most crucial period of training becomes the time when training is ended or there is a break in continuity.[1]

Courses consist merely of descriptions, recommendations, anecdotes, and success stories, much of which is nothing more than opinion, but often taken as gospel. Readings usually consist of glowing reports and advice but fail to explain how or why the advice works. Even our best advice is a dead-end approach, a "gimmick" at best. What works for one teacher will not necessarily work for another, even with the same student. The best advice, in fact, can sometimes do the most harm. We often fail to recognize that each teacher and student is unique, as are their interactions. These interactions consist of hundreds of variables that make every classroom situation different.

While the research in teacher education may be impressive in quantity, very few worthwhile changes and innovations have resulted or are forthcoming. We are basically using in the classroom the same methods which we were using fifty years ago and, even worse, when our landscape was dotted with one-room schoolhouses. On the other hand, the innovations and improvements in science, technology, and medicine within the last five years have been impressive and have affected almost all of our lives in some way. Had Rip Van Winkle been a teacher and slept for fifty years, he could return to the classroom and perform relatively well; the chalk, eraser, blackboard, textbook, and pen and paper are still, today, the main tools for most teachers, as they were a half a century ago—or longer. If Mr. Van Winkle's occupation had been related to one of the other three fields, and had he dozed off for five years, he would be unable to function effectively, for his knowledge and skills would be drastically dated.

Teachers and Students

Eager but unprepared, the ghetto school teacher is usually doomed to failure. The disadvantaged are astute appraisers and knowing manipulators of their environment; they easily see through "gimmicks"; they often learn the educational clichés about themselves and answer or behave as they are expected to. They know what will upset the teachers,

---

[1] The reader might argue that the author is contradicting himself, first contending that almost anyone—with little training—can teach, then maintaining that teachers are poorly trained. This is not a contradiction. Most teacher training is so inadequate it is as if the teacher were not trained, that he just wasted his time in most educational courses. In addition, with or without training, most teaching techniques are learned on the job.

often better than the teachers know; they know just when to stop before it becomes unsafe or the teacher gets angry. They realize that threats are ineffectual and that the teacher's authority is limited. They usually assess the teacher as a person before they become interested in him as a teacher. A negative assessment—which is common because of the different values and life styles of the teacher and students—can provoke a dramatic incident, or it can be drawn out into a series of minor clashes. In either case, the students usually proceed to capitalize on the teacher's weaknesses, then ridicule and abuse him as a person, for example, derogating his personality and physical appearance. Having demolished the teacher's self-respect and authority, they readily express indignation and contempt, and their general hostility and resentment often are directed at him.

The outcome is the teacher soon tends to see his students as adversaries. The major task of teaching is replaced by discipline, and the teacher judges himself by his disciplinary prowess. Each day leaves him emotionally and physically exhausted. Anxiety overwhelms him, too, as he soon becomes aware that almost anything can happen. He is confronted by a bored and hostile class, thirty or thirty-five students he can no longer control. He sees little tangible results of hard work and feels little sense of accomplishment. For his own mental health, then, the teacher often is forced to learn not to care. His apathy protects him; it is his defense. It is his way of coping with the meaninglessness and possible danger of his situation. Weekends and holidays become more important; he needs to rest, recuperate, and regain his strength and rational outlook. Sometimes he cannot wait and becomes "ill" a day or two before the weekend. Sometimes he does not finish the term, or does not return for the next term.

The problem of "illness" and teacher turnover—the latter of which often leads to unfilled positions—results in excessive class coverages and loss of preparation periods and detrimentally affects teaching morale and performance. The inability of ghetto schools to find willing *per diem* substitute teachers, even with recent increased salaries, adds to the dilemma. The fact that teachers are required to cover additional classes —in most cases strange ones, which means the teacher is merely performing custodial work—creates uneasiness and emotional stress for many. This, in turn, further undermines teaching morale and performance and causes more teachers to become "ill" and eventually quit. More classes have to be covered; the students are not learning because they have many different teachers; the school's discipline problem increases; and substitute teachers become even more difficult to recruit. Teaching morale and performance continue to deteriorate, resulting in still more absenteeism and departures and the curtailment of the teaching-learning process. The cycle finally ends on the last day of the school year, but usually begins again in September.

Even when a teacher is sincere, the children often greet him with what to him is unwarranted cynicism. Constant questions and advice from social workers, police, and even other teachers have helped to create a feeling of suspicion in the child. The disadvantaged child is surrounded by authorities who seem to castigate and further reject him for failing to appreciate what they have done for him. Authority becomes suspect. The child long since learned that the police are enemies. The teacher is now a new kind of "cop" who only keeps him in a different kind of jail, but a jail nevertheless. Some students are willing to learn the new rules but many cannot, or will not.

Unfortunately, castigation and rejection are an almost intrinsic part of teaching. The developmental lesson is the type that most teachers use most of the time with most students. The teacher questions and the students answer, and when more than one student wishes to answer at the same time, it is the teacher who decides who will speak—or, from some children's point of view, who will be rejected. One is called on, and the others who were raising their hands cannot answer. The disadvantaged child is present oriented and is unable to cope with this type of frustration, and, since it occurs so often, it leads the child often to withdraw or shout out answers—to reject the teacher and the learning process.

Delays are common in all lessons, too. For example, in the lower grades the teacher may work with one group of students while another group works at something else. Some students are bound to finish before the teacher is ready for them, and often he asks them to find something else to do until he finishes, possibly chastising them if they do not. With the exception of the radicals previously mentioned, most middle-class students tend to obey the teacher or at least will manage to appear busy, but the disadvantaged child has difficulty coping with delay and lacks self-control and the ability to be "good" without a structured environment.

This kind of delay can also be observed in the secondary schools. The teacher gives the students an exercise to do; some students finish before others and are unable to cope with the prospect of sitting and doing nothing. The teacher senses the problem and often asks, "How many need more time?" The teacher may be concerned with slower students and give them more time, making no provisions for faster ones or merely advising that they do "busy work" and frustrating them further. On the other hand, if the teacher discusses the exercise before everyone is finished, he is castigating the slow-performing students and confirming their stupidity.

Then there are the minor delays—waiting to use the pencil sharpener, waiting to use the lavatory pass, waiting to line up for lunch or dismissal. It is precisely these delays that the disadvantaged child cannot cope with and which lead to disciplinary problems. Similarly, minor interruptions are common—students going to the teacher for advice, borrowing a pen or pencil, asking a question about obtaining a lunch pass or permission to turn in today's homework tomorrow. Middle-class students can ignore these distractions or at least quickly resume their lesson; however, the disadvantaged have difficulty resuming work once they are distracted. These minor interruptions may result in a major delay or in the teacher's losing control of the class.

The most common method of evaluating students is with tests. The child's success or failure in school depends on his ability to take tests, and the "cumulative, intellectual deficit"[2] of the disadvantaged child almost guarantees failure as he is passed on from grade to grade. In effect, the test becomes just one more area of frustration and castigation, one more blow to the child's already weakened self-ego.

The child cannot escape being evaluated. Daily, the teacher judges his work or lack of work and communicates these judgments to him, not necessarily with grades, but with facial expressions or comments such as "Who can help James?" The child realizes when he is confused and cannot cope with the learning situation but rarely voices his plight in the classroom because the teacher seems to be castigating him for being stupid. It is little wonder that the child retreats from learning; the longer he remains in school, the more evident is his retreat. Similarly, if one is looking for additional reasons why students are becoming activists, these classroom interactions should be considered.

Teachers and Supervisors

Isolation is usual for teachers in American schools. Formal observations and discussions of their teaching behavior are limited to one or two a year. Even the freshman teacher goes generally unobserved and unassisted, and the shock of the initial year of teaching becomes his own private struggle. Inevitably, he makes many mistakes. Teachers who are assigned to "good" schools usually learn from their mistakes and piece together solutions to problems. However, those who are assigned

---

[2] *Supra,* Chapter I.

to ghetto schools are usually unable to stand up alone under the cultural shock and process of getting adjusted to teaching the disadvantaged.

The teacher turns to his supervisors for help but usually learns that he must solve his own problems—or wait until he has been assaulted, threatened, or a knife has been flashed. His supervisors rarely can provide assistance on more than an emergency basis; even then, many teachers do not receive any assistance until weeks or months after the term has begun.

Often ghetto school supervisors are suffering from many of the same problems as the teacher, for example, lack of training and experience. Many are unwillingly appointed to the school; and like teachers, are "marking time" until they can transfer to a "better" school or are promoted for not figuring in "the wrong headlines." The only difference is that they can shut their office doors, which some do, thereby divorcing themselves from the teacher's problems. They can divert their energies to writing impressive reports and devising programs that appear good on paper or look good to a visitor but rarely, if ever, work. Completing reports and turning them in on schedule is often considered more important for advancement than helping teachers; moreover, the longer these supervisors are out of the classroom, the further their experience takes them from the classroom and their being able to help teachers.

Of course, some supervisors are concerned and eager to provide assistance. Nonetheless, it is hard for them to avoid becoming inspectors and treating the teachers as subordinates. They start with the unfortunately true assumption that most teachers are not teaching enough and conclude that these teachers must be coerced and controlled, checked and counterchecked, somewhat similar to the way teachers feel they must coerce, control, and check their clientele. However, the unanticipated consequence of this teacher-supervisory relationship is the fostering of minimally acceptable teaching performances. These minimum standards tend to become common for most ghetto school teachers and thus become maximum standards as well. The teacher who deviates is often frowned upon and considered unrealistic. Minimum performance convinces the supervisors that their assumptions are correct. It puts added pressure on the supervisors to check more closely on the teachers and to further treat them as subordinates, which leads to increased tension and further decline of teaching morale. The teachers soon realize that they must battle both students and supervisors. Thus, the supervisor's derogatory beliefs about ghetto school teachers become "self-fulfilling prophecies."

Every ghetto school has a few effective teachers, but they are rarely, if ever, adequately rewarded or recognized by their profession. The teaching profession is probably the only one which does not reward superior performance, even superior performance under difficult circumstances. In effect, it rewards mediocrity. The absence of merit pay rewards the incapable and ineffective under the guise of professional equality. Furthermore, many incompetent teachers are promoted to supervisory echelons because they have played it by the rules and either they have the paper prerequisites or have passed some kind of formal test. The very fact that the teacher, especially the male teacher, remains in the classroom often implies that he is a failure. At the present, the usual compensation for effective teachers—as long as they are favored by their supervisors—is that they are usually given "good" classes and fewer classes to teach or are given the opportunity to leave the classroom entirely on a nonteaching assignment. Although this type of patronage system exists in almost all schools, it is more pervasive in ghetto schools, primarily so that these teachers will not leave the school.

The result is that the new teachers, weak teachers, and those who are out of favor with their supervisors often teach the most "difficult" classes, teach a maximum load, and are assigned to police the hallways and lunchroom. In most cases, it is precisely these teachers who cannot cope with the "difficult" classes and who need extra time to prepare themselves for their classes. Similarly, it is disheartening for a teacher who has to battle his students and supervisors to find out that some of his colleagues not only teach most of the "good" classes but are able to spend long periods in the teachers' lounge or cafeteria. Not only does this practice pit teacher against teacher, but it lessens professional integrity. Teachers in the nonprivileged position often react by refusing to give assistance to the administration or to their colleagues, by spending less time on lesson preparation, or by losing interest in teaching. The situation fosters an attitude whereby teachers worry more about what they can get away with than about what they can do. When teachers no longer care or are willing to help the growth of the school, morale often deteriorates. Instead of teachers supporting each other, they may purposely work against each other. The situation may become so bleak that the nonfavored group, perhaps half the staff, may be "marking time." In many large cities, the teachers' union attempted to remedy this situation by writing into their recent contracts a rotation system for nonteaching administrative positions. The result has been that many supervisors have rotated the nonteaching assignments within the same favored group of teachers.

Then, there are the intangible, vague problems and petty chores that, when added and accumulated over a long period, have a grave and detrimental effect on almost all teachers, especially those who work in ghetto schools: the inability to find chalk or an eraser so that a well-prepared lesson turns into confusion; the receiving of supplies a year late and having to work with an incomplete set of texts; the falling plaster, dimly lit hallways, stale urinal odors or the cracked window pane that goes unfixed for the whole winter; the unbearable June heat; the bells, gongs, whistles, loudspeakers, meetings, memos, and forms; the rushing between classes; the tasteless food in the teacher's cafeteria, and the shabby, ill-furnished teacher's lounge; the stolen purse or wallet; the chalk-stained clothing; the constant student harassment, abusive language, students fighting among themselves and with teachers; and finally, the student who flashes a knife or accuses the teacher of racism or sexual advances. Thus, teaching becomes at best a drudgery and at worst, a horror.

For the greater part, the serious problems have racial and violent overtones. Many white teachers now find their black students, especially the secondary school students, overtly antagonistic toward them. Years of white prejudice have collided with current black militancy within the larger society, and the schools reflect an intensification of this racial antagonism because of the nature of the superior role of the teacher and the tendency of youth to have a low frustration tolerance and to resort to physical aggression and violence as a means to alleviate frustration.

The teachers have increasingly become the victims of student assaults, which many supervisors and administrators are reluctant to report, since it may be construed as a blot on their records and career aspirations. Furthermore, many colleagues and supervisors do not support the victimized teacher, even during the immediate crisis, since the staff members are sometimes divided along racial and political lines as well as demoralized and desiring to avoid additional problems themselves.

Teachers are reluctant to press charges because the students now have attorneys and civil rights organizations which are willing to provide free legal services, and the teachers are not always provided with these free services. The common legal strategy is to shift the blame and accuse the teacher of provoking the attack. In addition, the courts are often powerless because adequate schools or facilities for housing "dangerous" or maladjusted students, even those who are considered homicidal or suicidal, are crowded and even nonexistent in some places. If the principal wishes to take action himself, he is often powerless to suspend the student for more than a few days, the exact number varying among the different school systems. If the principal takes sterner action, he often risks conflict with student and community groups. Thus, the students are learning that their actions are going unpunished, even encouraged by militant student and community groups.*

Teachers and the System

If the teacher is a provisional, his colleagues sometimes advise him against returning for the next term before he gains permanent certification and is regularly appointed; he learns to "mark time" until he is allowed to transfer to a "better" school. If the teacher is regularly appointed, unless he is not trapped by approaching retirement or by deferment from the army, he may be so depressed that he leaves the system or even the profession entirely. Nevertheless, most teachers reluctantly remain in the system because they cannot find a better job. The teacher often grows to dislike teaching and the students he teaches; moreover, he resents the idea that he is a teacher with little avenue for escape. If, however, the teacher is asked whether he enjoys teaching or his present school, he often paints a favorable picture in order to maintain his self-worth and ego, as well as to hide his guilt feelings.

Thus, many, if not most, permanent, certified ghetto school teachers feel trapped by the school system. In order to reduce the turnover of teachers, many urban school systems require several years of service before a teacher can even be eligible for a transfer. What happens during the interim? The longer the teacher has to wait to be transferred from a school where he is "marking time," the more meaningless teaching becomes and the more cynical he becomes. Involvement, commitment, dedication, the joy of teaching, and the rest of the splendid educational clichés disappear from his thinking, although he often continues to regurgitate these types of clichés for the aforementioned reasons.

Who suffers more, the teacher or students, is questionable. Both are victims of the system and both victimize each other; both often have dropped out in fact, if not in name, from the teaching-learning process. As for the teacher, his students seem disinterested and pay little tribute to his work; often they are hostile and alienated. Yet, a teacher's success and professional gratification mainly depend on his teaching his students, knowing they are learning. Teaching is contagious, but contagion can be

---

* *Postscript:* In recent conversations with the author, teachers from Chicago, Detroit, and New York City confirm that even the police stationed in the schools are unable to control the violence in many of the schools; moreover, it is not uncommon for a teacher or student to be raped, knifed, or shot in the lavatory, hallway, or right outside the school after 3 PM.

good or bad. Both students and teachers are aware of their own feelings and communicate these feelings to each other. If teachers don't care, then students learn not to care. The reverse is also true. When students are apathetic, teachers become apathetic. Hostility and alienation breed more hostility and alienation. If students come to school angry, teachers become angry. If students fail, in effect, teachers fail.

One hundred eighty days a year many ghetto school teachers feel trapped—engulfed with a feeling of helplessness and hopelessness—perhaps one of the bleakest existences any person can experience. Instead of teaching, they often find that they must face a long-drawn-out humiliation, a state of loneliness and despair, in which the worst still may be to come, and the only certainty is that there is no solution to their predicament in sight. The school year becomes a kind of jail sentence; the class becomes a kind of a cage; and "torture" is not too strong a word to describe some of the things that teachers have experienced in the classroom. Like prisoners who have given up hope, they often adopt an air of indifference and willing incompetence; moreover, they act much more indifferent and incompetent than they normally are. Is this not a partial explanation of the indifference and incompetence that teachers often display in ghetto schools? Is this not one reason why ghetto school teachers adopt failure strategies? They are like prisoners without hope!

Actually, the school system is frequently characterized by deceit, incompetency, triviality, and rigidity. In it, the teacher is reduced to a file number and treated as an insignificant person which, in turn, reinforces his indifference for teaching. The system operates by siphoning teachers' energies and enthusiasms; it proceeds to coerce teachers into and then prevent their escape from a nearly impossible teaching situation and meaningless existence.

While the teachers are being assaulted, the system often produces glowing reports. Pilot programs usually seem to work, especially if evaluated by their directors. Instead of consulting the teachers, the system calls upon "experts" from local universities, governmental agencies, and foundations to reexamine and reorientate. They usually voice their one or two "pet" ideas which sound good on paper—and which some have voiced for the last five years or more—but fail to consider the many human variables and are, therefore, unrealistic.

The belief is that teachers are rank-and-file workers with no legitimate right to define policy—an outmoded theory based on business administration practices and adopted by education administrators for lack of a better system of ideas. Directions and decisions are passed on to teachers with no concern for them and no avenue of communication open to them, except by disrupting the system and striking. Almost the entire system is organized to keep teachers at the bottom of the educational totem pole, or at best in a second-class position, with no ego involvement in curriculum development, no real participation in policy, and no sense of sharing credit given to the schools, although the literature recommends otherwise. There are no teacher heroes, no public recognition of fine work or outstanding achievement, no mention of classroom success stories. Now there is interest in teacher accountability, a euphemism for clubbing teachers over the heads. It appears that a teacher can gain recognition only by writing a book about his teaching experience—then he had better leave the school.

The system creates an artificial division between teachers and supervisors; in fact, supervisors are organized to enforce the system and run roughshod over teachers because supposedly that is "the way things get done in the system." Teaching is the most important and difficult part of education; however, the salary difference and rewards between teachers and supervisors are wide, and recent teacher contracts indicate a widening trend—fostered by a pay scale index. Although the activities of supervisors should be considered secondary and as assisting the major activity carried on by teachers, supervisors and administrators decide almost everything and often take whatever praise may come—which increases the gap between them and teachers—but unfailingly impute poor achievement to the inadequacy of the teachers.

The system does more than uphold the ideals of hypocrisy; it fosters the myth that teaching is a profession. Teachers often are entangled with large classes and cannot individualize their work. Professionals tend to individualize their work with their clientele. Teachers often fail to understand or appreciate research, while defending the *status quo* and rejecting innovations. Professionals, on the other hand, generally engage in research, at least appreciate it. Consequently, while notable changes have been made in the last five years in the fields of science, technology, and medicine, as previously mentioned, teaching methods have remained essentially unchanged for the last fifty years. Teachers are subject to the power hierarchy of their administrators. Professionals, however, command authority; their administration is in charge of secondary activities which facilitate the major activities performed by the professionals. Teachers are restricted by rigid bureaucratic rules of punctuality, attendance, dress, and clerical assignments while professionals operate in a relatively free and informal setting. As previously mentioned, teachers often grow to dislike their jobs and clientele, and those who remain teachers are considered failures. Success implies moving into administrative positions. Professionals, on the other hand, usually are content in their work and consider administration undesirable and time consuming. Teachers may be challenged by almost any parent or tax-payer; the community sometimes may dictate what they will teach and how, even in opposition to the teachers' "professional" judgment. Teachers have little political power, and whatever power they have is still at the infancy stage—a result of their recent unionism. Professionals have strong lobbies and are better insulated from the public. Teachers lack control even over standards of admittance to the field. Professionals often determine their own criteria for meeting standards of admittance, and they often have a voice in whom they hire. If teachers were a professional group, there would be little need to assert their collective power through a union; the AFT would not challenge NEA leadership, or lack of leadership.

To compensate for his semiprofessional status, it is important for a teacher at least to *feel* like a teacher for purposes of his own ego gratification. Feeling like a teacher means the teacher and his students are in pursuit of learning together. It implies a relationship between students and teacher, rapport, pleasure of knowing one another. Few ghetto school teachers have this feeling. Rather, they often are disheartened and feel they are wasting their lives in the classroom; they feel more like supply clerks, timekeepers, and policemen.

Teachers are also treated as children. Their lesson plans often must be checked, just as students' notebooks and homework are inspected; they often must punch a clock or sign a time book, like students who must come to school on time or be chastised; sometimes they must submit medical notes when they are absent, like the students who must bring a note from their parents; they receive warning and complimentary notes from their supervisors in the same condescending way that they often praise or voice their discontent with their students by writing on test papers or writing letters to parents. Teachers often are required to arrive at their hall patrol posts within a prescribed time, like students who are allotted a limited time to get to their classes in between the change of periods. Patronizing notes and voices over the loudspeaker often remind teachers of rules and duties just as teachers remind students of their tasks.

When teachers no longer feel like teachers, inevitably they must either quit their job or challenge and change the system to improve their status by bettering their working conditions and salary. The AFT's strength is concentrated in the inner cities where it is fast becoming a luxury to feel like a teacher. The AFT does not seek to run the schools; it concentrates on the problems that arise as teachers attempt to teach and most heavily on the problems stemming from teaching in ghetto schools. Under the guise of "quality education," the AFT seeks "special services," smaller classes, lighter teaching loads, methods for dealing with the disciplinary problems, grievance machinery against supervisors, the guarantee of teachers' rights, and, finally, more money. It is questionable whether the members' thoughts are with their students, as they claim, for most of them have already surrendered their faith and are too alienated. A dedicated teacher takes an interest in his students daily, not just when his contract expires. Sadly, with rare exceptions, most ghetto school teachers cannot remain dedicated for long but must learn the opposite if they are to survive the everyday classroom situations. Indeed, no system of mass, meaningless education can expect to recruit more than a sprinkling of exceptional teachers.

Teachers and Professors

Having to fend against the students, supervisors, and system, the teachers often turn to the university for assistance, but even this fails. The professors of education often formulate strategies for teaching the disadvantaged, but these tend to be unrealistic and too general because the professors have little or no classroom experience with the disadvantaged and are far too removed from the actual school situation—yet many are often considered the "experts" in educating the disadvantaged. Instead of helping the teachers with their problems, many professors first patronize them, then criticize them for negative attitudes, and finally, berate them for failing to understand and appreciate what has been done for them.

Professors commonly state that most ghetto school teachers are uninterested in, if not antagonistic toward, their students and lack the background and understanding so necessary to work with disadvantaged students. Surely most of the professors, who are middle class themselves and removed from the ghetto schools and communities, also lack familiarity in this area; and, therefore, they are unable to provide real knowledge by which teachers may broaden their insights into the problems of the disadvantaged.

Teachers are also condemned for believing in the so-called "deprivation theory," [3] which is unwittingly fostered by those professors who write about the socio-psychological problems of the disadvantaged. Recent research confirms the importance of family environment and early child deprivation. The "cumulative intellectual deficit" of the disadvantaged is a major cause for failure in school. When professors voice this

---

[3] *Ibid.*

theory and the related research, they are considered gallant and dedicated scholars, who deserve promotions. When classroom teachers mention the child's background and environmental deprivation, they are often accused of having low expectations for these children. When the teachers use the professors' jargon—auditory, visual, cognitive, and language deprivation—they are attacked by many professors for stereotyping and generalizing. The professors' "deprivation theory" is, in part, based upon measuring and comparing IQ and achievement scores between lower-class and middle-class students. However, when teachers accept IQ and achievement scores as somewhat valid measures of the disadvantaged child's potential and present ability and of what still needs to be accomplished, they often are condemned for being prejudiced and for confirming the child's low esteem and self-expectation.

Not only are the professors' criticisms of ghetto teachers unfair, but they are wholesale and generalized, often based on preconceived opinions and distorted "conventional wisdom" rather than on real teaching experience. Moreover, the criticisms usually overlook the reasons for poor teaching, and, therefore, are unjust. The attacks subject the teacher to the same stereotyping that they blame teachers for using on their students. The harsh tone and constant criticism add to the problem of recruiting ghetto teachers, discourage the few competent and concerned teachers from remaining, and harden the already widespread feelings of indifference and futility, as well as reinforce poor teaching morale and performance. In fact, the results of these attacks may be the cause of a reverse "self-fulfilling prophecy." The common "self-fulfilling prophecy" suggests that if the teacher treats students as if they were slow or uneducable they eventually fulfill his expectations. In reverse, if it is continuously asserted that ghetto teachers have poor attitudes and behaviors, or if they continuously read this "wisdom" in the literature, the teachers may eventually adopt or rigidify such characteristics, and they may unwittingly use this "wisdom" to rationalize their classroom failure.

Professors often fail to recognize that many ghetto teachers were once idealistic and worked harder than others in other schools but, because of lack of adequate support and impossible bureaucratic conditions, were forced, perhaps, to retreat from teaching. They fail to comprehend that most ghetto teachers would rather teach and feel like teachers and fulfill their commitments. Many professors fail to appreciate that these teachers are overwhelmed by despair and need assistance, not criticism. They fail to realize that even they often have abandoned and further alienated the teachers. It is time for professors to stop attacking teachers. The fact that teachers are criticized and need to be reminded that they are failing indicates that the professors themselves have failed with their own teaching. By criticizing their clientele, the professors are indirectly criticizing themselves and their own inadequate job of teacher training.

Consequently, the remarks of the professors are beginning to have an apologetic ring. Some professors now admit they do not have the answers, while others claim they need the cooperation and even the assistance of the teachers; some talk about using ghetto teachers as clinical professors, while others advocate having teachers formulate their own strategies and inform the universities about what seems to work. Similarly, many professors claim they are coming "down from the hill," but how far down is speculative. Most of them are still standing safely on the sidelines and professing useless theories and tired clichés. Yet, the only place where learning and practice can be consolidated is in the public schools, not the universities.

Most professors merely give lip service to what they say and will continue to do so until they go into the classroom and teach the disadvantaged, test their theories, and experience what the teachers have experienced. Professors can read the literature in quiet offices and gain theoretical insights, but those involved in teacher training need the actual experience and should have the opportunity to teach. Likewise, those involved in training teachers of the disadvantaged should have the opportunity to teach the disadvantaged—at least for an "exchange year"—as a requirement for their rank promotions. Most of these professors would do well to accept the challenge they talk about and apply for teaching licenses and positions before they vent their criticisms. There are still vacancies in ghetto schools, and there is great need for dedicated and effective teachers. If the professors had the fortitude to work in ghetto schools, they might not paint such one-sided, dismal pictures of teachers. The truth is, however, most professors look down at and resent being called teachers and are swift to indicate that they teach on the college or university level. Similarly, many would probably feel uncomfortable about going back into the elementary or high school classroom —even fear and resent teaching disadvantaged youth—and would have to be coerced.

It would certainly be interesting, perhaps amusing, to see if the professors really know what they are talking about, if they are really "experts," or if they could do any better than the teachers they condemn. Not only do I dare them, but I question if some of them could be trusted alone in the classroom, especially if they are there long enough for the students to "size them up."

The teachers realize such professors' hypocrisy, resent it, and no longer trust or respect them. The result is a widening gap between professors and teachers; moreover, as teachers become more educated and militant, the gap becomes more difficult to reconcile. The gap also widens over the discrepancy between teachers' and professors' views of reality. It is common practice among teachers to voice in their graduate courses, "That's all good theory, but it doesn't work." Of course, some professors advocate more realistic procedures for teaching the disadvantaged. They urge the use of audio-visual materials but rarely, if ever, demonstrate their use in their lectures. They remind teachers to teach concepts, but usually do not teach teachers how to teach concepts because, most likely, they do not know how themselves. They recommend the formulation of behavioral objectives but have difficulty being precise themselves. They recommend that teachers change their lockstep method, but they often use the same method in their own courses. They urge teachers to use role playing but do not show how and when to use it.

Dull, repetitious, meaningless, and false, if these courses were not required for teacher certification or promotion, most classrooms of education would be empty, and the professors would be lecturing to the walls. Education courses, for the greater part, do not help improve pedagogy, especially pedagogy with the disadvantaged. What these courses do is to help create and safeguard jobs—jobs for teachers, school administrators, state education officials, and, of course, professors.

Since the professors of education have safeguarded their jobs and are assured that their courses will continue to be required, the best plan might be for the professors to duplicate their lecture notes—which are sometimes yellowing—hand them out during the first class session, send their clientele home, and have them return only for the final examination. There is no good reason to require anyone to leave his home in order to listen to what often winds up being humdrum hokum, useless clichés, and tiny bits of information. Furthermore, since it is becoming unpopular even to give examinations, especially in classes taught by "progressive" professors, perhaps the students should be told just to remain at home.

The most amusing nonsense is the glowing reports about successful programs for the disadvantaged and for teachers of the disadvantaged, as if the professors were reminding the teachers, "If you would change your attitudes, or if you knew what you were doing, you could succeed, too." Of course, if only half of these reports were true, there would no longer be a problem concerning the education of the disadvantaged, and the "experts," whom we pay for "expertise," would no longer be saying, "We do not have the answers."

The harsh fact is that reports can easily be filled with false data, procedures, strengths, and results. Very few directors of a program will jeopardize their chances for additional funds and admit their present program is a failure. Similarly, outside evaluators are often reluctant to state the truth, because of fear of being blackballed by these directors. Funds are still available from governmental agencies and foundations for those who are in a position to write up and submit a proposal for the education of the disadvantaged. That so many "experts" have suddenly become interested in this field indicates how profitable it has become. They are cashing in on an opportunity and getting the pie while the poor remain poor and the disadvantaged remain disadvantaged—and get the crumbs.

Apparently, little time or energy is spent on validating the various assumptions or on anticipating the numerous variables that will affect a program. Guidelines and data are usually hurriedly put together to get the money while it is still available. The result is that the optimistic and portentous interpretations of these programs have ended chiefly in ambiguous or dismal outcomes. Nevertheless, because the private colleges and universities are increasingly dependent on this type of supported program, their folly is often overlooked and, in fact, many institutions of higher learning, both public and private, have established offices and executives to work full time on program planning and have hired new faculty members with friends in the U.S. Office of Education. Thus, many professors are pressured to divert their energies from scholarship into developing such programs. The entire procedure illustrates one more hypocrisy which confronts the ghetto teacher. Oh, yes, the programs are developed with the so-called best interests of the student and teacher in mind. From beginning to end, from lofty objectives to fictitious conclusions, most of these programs are a tragic, but comical sortie.

Most professors of education have been sitting idle—even though many of them know what they are doing is inadequate. They sit there, safeguarding their jobs, afraid (like teachers) that any major change will affect their security. The fact is, if they sit there long enough and fail to reexamine, much less reorient, what they are trying to accomplish in light of what they are veritably accomplishing, there will be no need to make decisions about how they can improve teacher training; it will be taken away from them—by the growing militant teacher unions or communities, for example.

Conclusion

I submit that I have probably alienated my friends and former colleagues in school, whom I have in the past defended and praised, as well as my present partisans in college. However, I feel very strongly about what I have voiced.

As a writer and educator, it is safe to conclude on a positive or hopeful key. I refuse to conform to this "game," though many of my colleagues do it, some intentionally, some unintentionally. There are no sure or permanent solutions, no straight or sagacious roads to follow. The "sacred cows" of education and the glowing reports and prophecies of success can no longer mask the dim future. Most ghetto teachers will continue to fail. Words will not prove me wrong, only time, and the old cliché is still good: time is running out.

Although it is considered inappropriate to criticize without offering solutions, this chapter will risk that appearance, too. I am not trying to satisfy my readers or suggest what is currently fashionable—and unrealistic. We are fighting a losing battle. The problem of educating the disadvantaged is so deep and intense it is probably beyond our capacity to solve, although few educators are willing to admit this fact. The problem is not a matter of diverting money to guns or butter, to defense or social and educational agencies, but spirit—spirit to teach, spirit to learn, a contagious, intangible element that is dying in the ghetto schools. The problem will worsen until the forces that are lined up against the teacher are abolished. But such a change is unlikely because many of the educators upon whom we must rely are themselves a major cause of the problem. The harsh fact is that the control of educational policies and procedures rests with those who often are working against teachers, and especially against students, but do not even realize it or are unwilling to admit to their subversive role. To be sure, power corrupts, and, as one moves up the ladder of power, the individual becomes more distant from the people he is supposed to be serving.

IV

Teacher Training for Ghetto Schools

Introduction

It was only about ten years ago when colleges and universities were actively placing their teachers in suburban schools. But the new and changing demands of society have forced educators to devote their attention to urban schools, especially those located in ghetto areas or housing a student population referred to as the disadvantaged. America has become an urban-oriented society, and the real problems of American education have become synonymous with urban education.

Since the recent "discovery" of the disadvantaged, there has been a proliferation of conferences, books, and courses on the subject. Almost all institutions of higher learning now offer preservice and inservice training for teaching the disadvantaged, and some even offer advanced degrees in closely related fields.

It is now almost impossible to discuss teacher education in an urban institution of higher learning without devoting attention to training teachers for the disadvantaged. In fact, an urban college or university that does not have an urban-oriented teacher-training program may someday lose its accreditation.

The literature and training concerning the disadvantaged generally emphasize the child's socio-psychological problems. When the teacher is the target of a discussion, he is usually attacked and ridiculed for exhibiting negative attitudes and behaviors, as well as for being inexperienced and of marginal quality, holding substandard and emergency or substitute licenses. On the other hand, it is claimed that more experienced and competent teachers usually work in "good" schools, because seniority counts when teaching assignments are made. Thus, it is not only difficult to recruit good teachers for ghetto schools, but it is also a herculean task to keep them. Ghetto schools are generally considered the "jungles" of the local school system, places to flee from rather than places to be sought out for the challenges they offer. Thus, the students who most urgently need the best teachers are usually deprived of them.

Now that a buyer's marketplace for teachers exists—the supply of teachers has exceeded the demand—some teachers are not going to get jobs. Schools will soon be concerned with quality, not with just a "warm body," and they may eventually take careful notice of the different teacher-training programs and the kinds of teachers being graduated at the various institutions of higher learning. Colleges and universities in a metropolitan area may soon be competing against one another to place their teachers in schools, for these institutions will have to furnish graduates who can compete on the competitive market. Such competition should improve teacher training, or at least force these institutions to attempt to improve their respective teacher-training programs.

With this brief overview in mind, we will now examine a modest plan for improving teacher training, specifically for teachers of the disadvantaged. Most of the ideas and suggestions are traditional in nature; that is, proper teacher training should be the cooperative responsibility of teachers and professors, as well as schools and teacher-training institutions. It should consider the realities of the teaching profession, and it should be continuous from the point of entry into the education program for as long as the teacher remains in the profession. What emerges is a partnership between teachers and professors and between schools and teacher-training institutions; in addition, admittance standards into the profession are tightened, and a career plan for training teachers is outlined, starting with the prospective teacher's second year of college. The essential stages of the career plan are itemized here but discussed later in greater detail.

Chart 2

Career Plan for Training Teachers

Time Sequence	*Professional Term*
Sophomore Year	Observer
Junior Year	Assistant Teacher
Senior Year—First Half	Associate Teacher
Senior Year—Second Half	Practicing Teacher

Time Sequence	*Professional Term*
Beginning Two-Year Period	Intern Teacher
Continuing Inservice Education	Experienced Teacher (With opportunities for becoming a Cooperating Teacher or Clinical Professor)

The discussion then continues with four methods for implementing theory into practice, which deal with procedures for organizing and evaluating objectives for teacher training—(1) objectives, (2) activities, (3) measurements, and (4) evaluation—and then ends with a commentary on the limitations of these four procedures.

The Teacher-Professor Partnership

In general, most professors of education are the scapegoats of the rest of the academic faculty. Many of these education professors tend to react by ignoring or viewing practical aspects of teaching as being mechanical or nonscholarly. They focus on theory and research, and even their discussions of teaching and teacher behavior tend to be immersed in principles of theory and research, often unrelated to the actual classroom. Furthermore, most professors feel it is an imposition to work with student teachers or to work in the public schools and prefer—if they have to work with students—to work with graduate students and doctoral students. Junior members of the faculty often work with student teachers, but as professors gain in experience and rank they tend to become removed from preservice teacher training, and often from almost all facets of teacher training.

These trends are more pervasive in the large urban universities where the professors are often too busy doing their research and writing to become involved with prospective teachers. While many of these professors have seemingly good ideas and do influence the thinking of teacher education by writing about their findings and concepts, they rarely envision their ideas being acted upon or are willing to promote their ideas into practice. They are more concerned with theory and research than with practice and implementation, since the latter detracts from the former which they consider to be their real work and interest. At best, many of these professors manage to devote a few hours monthly to a limited number of graduate students. Sometimes these students do the preliminary research or writing for the professor's forthcoming book.

It should be noted, however, that at many former teachers colleges it is still considered appropriate for senior-ranked professors to work with prospective teachers. Many professors in these colleges are former school marms and rigid, retired, civil-servant administrators, whose life style and values often conflict not only with the disadvantaged student but also with the young prospective teacher. Rather than encouraging innovation and permitting constructive change, these professors often try to preserve their mode of life and impose their outdated thinking on the preservice teachers they work with. These professors are often unable to understand present social realities and the sweep of change which is taking place in school and society; they usually resent and are threatened by the new social order and are unable to develop an honest dialogue with prospective teachers. In addition, under the guise of "expertise" they often wind up relating to prospective teachers in a patronizing and authoritarian manner and thus "turn off" these young teachers.

Considering these factors, master or outstanding teachers should be paid to help train prospective teachers. The rationale is that experienced and competent ghetto teachers, who combine ability and interest with experience and classroom reality, should do a better job of training teachers than professors whose "qualifications" usually coincide in many ways with those of one of the two portraits delineated above and who usually lack experience in teaching the disadvantaged, having only abstract knowledge. Granted, such knowledge is helpful, but there is no substitute for actual experience. As for the few professors who once taught the disadvantaged or students who are now characterized as the disadvantaged, their experience has become remote.

The master teacher should be recognized and promoted in terms of responsibility and a differential beyond the basic salary for helping to supervise and train prospective and beginning teachers as well as for teaching two or three of the most "difficult" classes ten or fifteen periods a week. The outcome would be that classes in need of a strong, effective teacher would get such a person rather than a beginning teacher, which is customary. Moreover, beginning teachers in need of assistance would have immediate help and guidance, and prospective teachers would be trained by the most qualified school personnel. In this way, the master teacher would be promoted in terms of status and salary but would remain in the classroom and school where he is needed the most.

In addition to the customary tuition waiver for an educational course, the colleges and universities should make these master teachers adjunct or clinical professors (which some institutions are already doing) and pay for their services—perhaps $500 per semester. In turn, these teachers would be expected to work actively with the prospective teachers in the school and work with the college or university on a steady basis in developing and improving the teacher-training program. The master teachers should be required to read about the latest trends and innovations in their respective fields and in education in general to improve their relationships with and the quality of their assistance to the prospective teachers and professors. These teachers also might help the professors lecture in their methods courses at the college or in educational courses which take place at the school. The professors, in exchange, should have the opportunity to take over the classes of these teachers in order to refreshen their skills and give demonstration lessons about what they are advocating. (The assumption is that at least some professors are competent teachers and would not do a disservice to the students.) In fact, both the cooperating teachers and professors involved in the teacher-training program should give demonstration lessons to prospective teachers with post session analysis. As a result of this increased teacher participation, professors would be able to devote more of their time to research and graduate work—where they can do the most good. With this new partnership, the professors might be able to develop and apply teacher-behavior theories in relation to classroom practice.

In order to develop this teacher-professor partnership, however, we need to stop blaming one another. Right now teachers are not doing a good job of teaching the disadvantaged and professors are not doing a good job of preparing teachers to work with them. Both are at fault, and it would be best to accept a collective inadequacy in this area and start doing something to correct it. To be sure, it is time that professors and teachers stop throwing stones at each other. Improved communication and teamwork are needed, and if they are not forthcoming, various groups (e.g., business, political, or community organizations, governmental or foundation-sponsored organizations, or various know-nothing cliques) will soon begin to challenge the function and status of both teachers and professors of education.

The School-Teacher-Training Institution Partnership

Perhaps one of the best ways to improve the relationship between teachers and professors is for teacher-training institutions to organize the teacher educational center, an offshoot of the old idea of the lab school which some large universities still support basically for research and experimental purposes. Ideally, the teacher educational center constitutes a cluster of schools ranging in grade levels and geographical settings.

Whereas the lab school is often turned into a private school with a homogeneous and stabilized student population whose teachers are hired by the university, the teacher educational center is based upon a partnership between the teacher-training institution and two or more public schools in one or, preferably, in several school districts and school systems within the urban area. Because several schools are supposedly involved in the teacher educational center, the student population varies and is more representative of the urban student population, thus more realistic for the prospective teacher who wishes to gain insight into a setting which corresponds with the school he will probably be assigned to when he begins teaching. However, since there is a greater student turnover in the public schools, and especially in those in ghetto areas, the possibilities of longitudinal research are hindered.

The parents who send their children to these teacher educational center schools must be made aware that their children will sometimes be serving as subjects both for experimentation and teacher training. However, the teacher-training institution program will disseminate the latest innovations and will supply the schools with an abundance of prospective teachers who will also serve as teacher aides and tutors, as well as additional experienced teachers involved in inservice training; so if the overall policy is well organized, it should provide the students with educational dividends.

The teacher educational center provides the atmosphere and resources which are conducive for the practitioner and researcher and which, in turn, contribute to the needs and interests of the students, prospective teachers, cooperating teachers, inservice teachers, graduate students, and professors. In particular, it provides the opportunity to identify theory which can be translated into practice, while refining practice into theory. Teachers and professors are encouraged to go beyond the "dos" and "don'ts," "good-bad" categorization of techniques, as well as to identify teacher behaviors which can be used to develop teacher accountability models or refine behavioral objectives and concurrent test items.

The educational center reduces the amount of restrictions and bureaucratic red tape usually imposed by other schools on university experimentation and research. Similarly, visiting preservice and inservice teachers are more readily accepted than at other schools. Various aspects of the teacher-training program, from preservice to inservice education, can be tested and research can be conducted which indicates the different effects on teacher success.

Most important, too often teacher-training institutions have little choice in selecting cooperating teachers, most of whom are selected and sometimes coerced by their supervisors because it is their turn to have a student teacher. In still other cases, teachers look forward to a student teacher since it provides them with the chance to register for a free three-credit educational course at the college or university, to vacate the class, or to have someone else teach for them and do their clerical work. Besides not being committed to helping the prospective teachers, many cooperating teachers are incompetent and, therefore, provide poor teaching models to emulate. With the increased cooperation between the school and teacher-training institution, master teachers who want to work as cooperating teachers are easily identified, and, since they may also be working with inservice teachers and cooperating teachers from other schools as well as with graduate students, professors, and researchers, their professional growth would be encouraged and easily enhanced. Cooperating teachers who might otherwise be unaware of new innovations in the field would manage to keep up with the field, thereby helping prospective teachers implement such innovations in the classroom without being threatened by their lack of knowledge.

Professional Standards and Admittance Requirements

While the problem of training ghetto teachers is complex, a major reason for its continuation stems from the teaching profession itself. In general, the teaching profession has been content to limp along, admitting almost anyone to its ranks—students who are unable to make the grade in their preferred area of speciality; students who register for a number of educational courses as a kind of insurance; people who do not like children and youth or, for that matter, teaching; people who are rejects from business or industry or feel they cannot succeed in other professions or have retired to teaching; men and women who seek security (especially minorities who feel relatively less discriminated against in civil service jobs) or find the hours and vacation attractive; women who feel teaching is a reasonably good job until they get married or their husbands finish graduate school; men who are avoiding the draft or remain in the profession until they complete law school or their Ph.D. Indeed, it seems that most teachers enter the profession for negative reasons, not because they enjoy children or teaching.

Even worse, as previously indicated, adults often dislike, resent, and feel jealous of youth—its spontaneity and values as expressed in its overt counter culture. Although these feelings are usually covert and subtle, they are more pronounced in the case of teachers because they continually work with youth. This teacher-student conflict is usually obvious at the secondary school level when students are no longer considered cute and nice but wild and "hot blooded"; this is a period in the students' lives when they are forming their own culture and peer groups, when the distinction between youth and adults is emerging. Consequently, the students often must be manipulated and coerced by teachers and other adults.

The common adult dislike and fear of youth is compounded by the teacher's fear—fear of losing control in the classroom, fear of losing one's authority or having one's ego diminished in front of a group of ungrateful and uncontrollable students. To be sure, the process of coercion and manipulation is more overt, and the fear of losing control in the classroom is more common, in ghetto schools than in middle-class schools.

In ghetto schools the youth culture is also being judged by middle-class norms, and, therefore, the ghetto student is often considered more deviant by his teachers than his middle-class counterpart. The student's so-called deviancy clashes with the school's norms and values; for example, the school's formal language clashes with the ghetto child's dialect; the school's punishment of students who are caught fighting, with the ghetto child's value of and environmental necessity for using physical strength and force; the school's puritanical attitude toward sex, with the ghetto child's early sexual activities and lack of knowledge or unwillingness to use contraceptives.

The beginning of a solution is to cease accepting almost anyone and everyone into the teaching profession, especially now that there is an oversupply of teachers, and to develop rigorous standards and qualifications. The armed forces and industry have had personality and attitudinal tests devised to determine the aptitude of men and women in various fields of endeavor. Surely it can benefit education to follow this lead. It then becomes the problem of experts in the field of testing to devise suitable and expedient methods to measure aptitudes. Although psychological and attitudinal tests lack absolute reliability and validity, they can still serve as an important measurement and tentative source of evaluation to indicate projected strengths as related to positive attitudes toward teaching, especially toward disadvantaged youth and the ability to successfully teach these youth. Similarly, it is important to determine what kind of traits are necessary for a person to become a successful teacher at the various grade levels and socio-economical settings.

In the meantime, no one should be forced to teach in a ghetto school. The situation becomes a trap in which both teacher and students suffer. Rather than cajoling or forcing teachers to work in ghetto schools, we should screen candidates who volunteer.[1] Similarly, no one should be

---

[1] Perhaps an extra $1,000 differential might be necessary to interest these volunteers and select only those whose values, attitudes, and personality characteristics seem to coincide with desirable teaching models or styles, prototypes based on research data. Although it might be argued that the extra money would seemingly attract candidates with the wrong attitudes, it is time that we stop talking in terms of the outworn concept of dedication and speak in terms of reality. The profit motive should attract and reward qualified personnel.

forced into a training program geared especially for teaching the disadvantaged. Many institutions of higher learning, in their attempt to solve the educational ills of the ghetto, now offer preservice training only for teaching the disadvantaged. Not only is this an overreaction to the problem—a problem linked in part to the previous lack of such programs—but it also discriminates against future teachers who wish to work with middle-class or suburban students.

Career Plan for Training Teachers [2]

The Sophomore Year. Prospective teachers often fail to see the relationship and relevance of foundation courses to contemporary education. Foundation courses need to be revised and integrated with practical school experiences. The foundation courses envisioned by this author consist of a two-course sequence which, in part, provides the prospective teacher with experiences in the school as an observer for at least one morning per week. These experiences should help result in the prospective teacher learning if he really wants to teach and if he wants to work in a ghetto school, or at least provide the groundwork for such discussion at the college. These kinds of experiences and questions should not be postponed until the student teaching experience, when the individual is at the terminal point of college and it is difficult for him to change his field of endeavor unless he is willing to postpone his graduation for six months or a year, or when it is too late for the professor to discourage the student from entering the profession.

For the first semester, discussion should be based on current problems and trends which challenge teachers and schools. Topics on teacher militancy, professional organizations, accountability, criteria performance, voucher plans, school integration, decentralization, and community control should be discussed. The prospective teacher should be taught to cope with the explosion of general knowledge, as well as with educational knowledge. He should be required to invent solutions to current educational problems, to understand the organization of schools and what good schools should be like, especially when he begins to teach. Also, the young teacher needs to learn to respond effectively to the changing climate and to cope with the problems anticipated in the future. He should gain experience in becoming a change agent; he should gain background for becoming a future constructive critic of education, one who seeks

---

[2] The career plan for the prospective teacher starts at the sophomore year, and not the freshman year, so as to give students an opportunity to take their required subjects while thinking about a career.

reform and can bring about viable change without resorting to irresponsible sloganism and political anarchy.

For the second part of the foundations sequence, adequate preparation for the prospective teachers necessitates an interdisciplinary course in sociology and psychology taught by a sociologist and psychologist. This aspect of the program should be concerned with (1) developing insight into the dynamics of disadvantaged subcultural groups; (2) requiring an understanding of deviant and delinquent behavior, group behavior, child development and motivation; and (3) requiring an understanding of research findings in the social sciences, as the data relate to the diminution of group stereotypes and a more accurate view of the phenomenology of minority youth.

Teachers should be made aware of how the disadvantaged struggle with their environment and how their culture and learning style can enhance the teaching-learning processes. For example, the disadvantaged often learn best when instruction is visual, concrete, practical, and physically oriented—involving movement, excitement, and freedom of expression.

The prospective teacher should become acquainted with the often overlooked positive qualities of the disadvantaged, that is, their vitality, spontaneity, creativeness, frankness, individualism, informality, humor, friendliness, and group cohesiveness. Many people talk about respecting the disadvantaged without really knowing much that is positive about these youth, merely because it is the "right" thing to say.

Teachers should be made aware that middle-class values often leave something to be desired, and they should not try to change the child's life style and values or impose an alien, middle-class standard on these children. Teachers need to recognize the differences in cultural values without viewing one as right or better. Instead of trying to reshape the disadvantaged child, teachers should accept his life style and improve him within the scheme of his own values. Teachers should be taught to maintain their system of values, but, at the same time, respect and enhance the child's own values in order to reach him. The teacher should not expect to gain the students' respect merely because he is a teacher; he must earn it; he must show that he accepts and respects these children.

The Junior Year. At the junior year, a three-course sequence in research, curriculum, and instruction is suggested, with required readings supplemented by independent study which is related to the topics being discussed. Again, the prospective teacher should have real classroom and school experiences one morning per week, this time, however, serving as a tutor both on an individual and small group basis as well as helping the teacher in the classroom and performing some clerical duties so as to help the teacher while gaining insight into clerical aspects required of a teacher. For these reasons, the prospective teacher might be called an "assistant teacher" while in the school.

At the college, the prospective teacher should become familiar with (1) basic statistics, research concepts, tests, and measurements; (2) a background of the history and culture of minorities in America; (3) methods of diagnosing and aiding reading and language problems along with the ability to use these methods in his respective subject and grade level; (4) techniques of discipline appropriate to personality and group factors; (5) teacher behavior theory and classroom practice; (6) learning and motivating principles, as well as methods to foster student creativity; (7) curriculum organization and behavioral objectives; and (8) special methods in his subject.

Although most of these suggestions are important for the training of all prospective teachers, they are necessary for those who will work with the disadvantaged, since these students depend heavily on good teachers. The first four suggestions are specifically important for teaching the disadvantaged. It it important that the prospective teacher be familiar with statistical and research procedures not only so he will not reject research as irrelevant but also so that he will be able to interpret the research on the disadvantaged. Similarly, the teacher needs skills in tests and measurements for interpreting IQ and standardized tests and improving his own tests. The teacher should be knowledgeable of the history and culture of various minorities and able to integrate this knowledge into his lessons for purposes of enhancing the children's essential dignity and integrity. By the same token, every teacher of the disadvantaged should be a teacher of reading and language, since too many disadvantaged children are deficient in these communication skills for reading and speech specialists alone to cope with the problem.

Since discipline is often considered to be the number one problem, it is discussed here in greater detail than the other suggestions. To what extent the teacher is successful will largely depend on his classroom management and discipline techniques, that is, the rules and routine he establishes with his students. In middle-class schools it is possible to get along without good classroom management, but in ghetto schools it is not. The teacher, therefore, establishes order and routine immediately before he attempts to teach, so the children know what to do and what is expected of them.

Ideally, the prospective teacher learns to be understanding but not overly sympathetic; firm, but not inflexible; careful, but not exacting. He is not prejudiced. He has an intense commitment to his role, wants to teach, cares enough about these children to teach them, and is convinced that they can learn. It is pointed out that these children have many problems that middle-class children do not have or do not display in class. He accepts the fact that sometimes the children need to hate him, that the children express anger easily, that they resent authority figures, and that their language is vocal and expressive. This does not mean that the teacher accepts any behavior, but that he expects hostility and does not get upset or feel that it is a sign of his own inadequacy or that the children really mean to be at variance with him.

Disadvantaged children elicit from many teachers scorn, resentment, antagonism, but worst of all fear. To be sure, the prospective teacher must learn not to lose confidence or express fear. Of course, size helps, but the teacher's personality and the rapport he establishes with these children are more important. A thin, small woman teacher may be more effective than a big muscular man.

The Senior Year. The training sequence of the prospective teachers' senior year should consist of a two-course sequence at the schools, where professors and cooperating (master) teachers will hold classes together and work on an individual basis with the prospective teachers. Assignments should be made where vacancies will exist for the following year so that upon graduation prospective teachers can be assigned to the same schools if they elect to remain there. Successful introduction of a beginning teacher to the school is enhanced when the teacher has been given the previous opportunity to teach in the school or at least trained in a situation which corresponds to his teaching situation.

For the first half of the year, the prospective teacher might be called an "associate teacher" and for the second half he might be called a "practicing teacher." His program would be flexible and based on his own needs and specifications, and he would advance at his own pace and according to his ability to take on greater responsibility. Merely fulfilling the prescribed number of hours should not suffice; teaching competence, corresponding to standards set up by the professors and master teachers and eventually by the teaching profession itself, should be required.

In the beginning, the associate teacher should be given the opportunity to study and work with several teachers in his area of specialization and grade level. (For example, for every prospective junior high school science teacher, there will be an experienced junior high school science teacher.) A rotation system should be developed around the master teachers' programs so that each school day the prospective teacher would work with another teacher. Instead of learning with and seeing only one cooperating teacher, the prospective teacher would acquaint himself with several different successful teaching styles and classroom approaches and could adopt those that coincided with his personality. The idea of several cooperating teachers working with each associate teacher increases the chances of the latter assimilating a variety of viewpoints. Attention would be given to varied teaching techniques and curriculum methods. The prospective teacher would assist the teachers with tutoring and clerical work, as well as hall patrol, grading papers, preparing materials, writing lesson plans, and working with small and large groups in the classroom. While the prospective teacher would become familiar with the operation of the school, the working conditions of the teachers would be somewhat improved.

In addition, the school should help the associate teachers to learn how specialized members of the staff, such as the dean, guidance counselor, and attendance teacher, can help the teacher. The cooperating teachers would train the associate teachers to use and operate a variety of audio-visual equipment, since the colleges do not provide such instruction, and students, especially the disadvantaged, learn more effectively when they are able to see or manipulate what they are studying. The prospective teacher should be required to work in at least one community and social agency for at least six hours weekly, to learn the dynamics and problems of the ghetto community. It is hoped that this requirement could be eventually extended so that the teacher lives in the kind of community (for the entire term) where he will eventually teach. Besides reading about black history, and other related subjects, the prospective white teacher needs real experience in ghetto living to better understand and reach ghetto children.

Classes should be held at the school and taught by professors, cooperating teachers, and community guest speakers. Hopefully, discussion would help the prospective teachers to share their own ideas and experiences, as well as to evaluate their specific problems and approaches to the varied activities. Demonstration lessons, simulation teaching, microteaching, curricular materials, audiovisual media, and reading and language techniques would be presented and analyzed. Since college courses would be held at the school and since the cooperating teachers would be working closely with the professors, the prospective teachers would have the opportunity to test ideas in the classroom right after they are introduced in the lecture. This should make the courses more relevant. There should also be opportunity to bring students to participate in the discussions, providing the prospective teachers with a more realistic idea of the students' needs and interests. Although a part of the readings would be required, a greater part would be individualized according to the prospective teachers' needs and interests.

After a predetermined date, based primarily on a joint decision between the professor and cooperating teacher, the prospective teacher would work with one teacher with whom he felt most comfortable. His role would change to that of a "practicing teacher." The cooperating teacher would remain in the class as an observer and guide, but the practicing teacher would have complete responsibility for planning and teaching the lessons. When the cooperating teacher believed it was appropriate, he would leave the classroom and the practicing teacher would be completely on his own. To be sure, the practicing teacher would make mistakes and would have problems, but he would evaluate what goes on in the classroom with the cooperating teacher as well as in the post-session class with the professor and the other cooperating and practicing teachers.

Although T-groups have no preplanned agenda or rules by which they must operate, the object of these groups should be to help each prospective teacher to know himself, to become an honest, self-actualizing individual. The prospective teachers should be given the task of evaluating their own teacher performance and progress among themselves, as well as discussing various techniques and styles they have witnessed and are experimenting with. It must be made clear that what works with one teacher does not always work for another. Indeed, there is danger in trying to adopt a teaching style that does not coincide with one's own personality. Not only do disadvantaged students recognize the phonies right away, but they take offense at such deceit; moreover, the practicing teacher will never really be at ease, since what he is attempting does not come naturally. Practicing teachers should learn there is no one teaching style; it depends on the individual's personality and his ability to evaluate his own personality. Although understanding one's own personality helps establish an appropriate teaching style, everyday control is enhanced by good classroom management and rules and routine which are germane to one's style of teaching. While these techniques are generally basic, they should be subjoined to the individual's style of teaching, and the methods of implementing them in the classroom should vary, too, depending on the teacher's personality. Hopefully the T-groups will give the prospective teachers the opportunity to understand their own teaching style and personality.

Practicing teachers also should learn to evaluate their own feelings and attitudes. "Why do I want to teach?" "What am I doing in the classroom?" "How do the students perceive me?" "How do I feel about the students?" "How do my varied attitudes affect my teacher behavior?" In these groups, they are confronted with unexpected feelings on the part of the others, either in reaction to their behavior and teaching styles or to the activities of others. They recognize that it is natural to fear, even resent, difficult students or classes. The problem is not solved by pretending such feelings do not exist or covering them up or justifying oneself by explaining that the disadvantaged are hostile or alienated. The future teachers learn to evaluate themselves through their effects on the classroom situation. In order really to know themselves, teachers also must be willing to assess their own weaknesses and strengths and be willing to accept themselves and others in order to adopt realistic teaching styles appropriate to their own personalities—and the chance is given within the T-groups. Of course, there should be opportunity to extend these sessions to private conferences with staff members and preferably with consulting psychologists. To overlook these private conferences may be harmful for a person who is just becoming aware of his personal or teaching problems and who is trying to work them out.

This training period should also include films of practicing teachers in action and role playing as teacher and student. Viewing videotapes of themselves will give the practicing teachers the opportunity to see what they look like in front of their classes. By listening to and watching one another's films, they should become aware of teacher-student behavior patterns. Movements, mannerisms, and methods should be examined. Approaches to discipline and maintaining good mental health should be compared and changes should be made according to individual personalities.

Role playing should help prospective teachers gain insight into predictive understanding of their students' feelings and behavior. Predictive understanding is essential for maintaining discipline and a mentally healthy atmosphere; it is the ability to recognize what a student is about to do and why. This understanding cannot be gained through reading books but can be developed through novel and challenging situations which demand that an individual cope with and later analyze what is happening.

Only those practicing teachers who show concern, competence, and potential should be asked—not forced—to remain to teach the following year. This would improve the current method of assigning teachers who have had little or no previous contact with the disadvantaged and who are often reluctant, afraid, or incompetent to work with these students.

Beginning Two-Year Period. For many beginning ghetto teachers, inservice education comes too late—at a time when many are overwhelmed by insurmountable problems and have already given up or are thinking of transferring to another school or leaving the profession. Therefore, besides special preparation at the undergraduate level, it is worthwhile to request beginning teachers of the disadvantaged to participate in a two-year training and advanced program of graduate education during which the teachers will be called "intern teachers."

As previously mentioned, beginning teachers, usually abandoned by colleges as soon as they graduate and start teaching, would now be assured adequate assistance and continuous training through the combined efforts of the local institution of higher learning and school personnel, with the assistance of professors and cooperating teachers. Part of the graduate program would consist of a seminar extended over the two-year period, to be organized around the problems encountered by beginning teachers. These problems would be analyzed and used as a springboard to examine related issues.

Rather than being given a full teaching load and the most "difficult" classes, as is the general practice, beginning teachers would be assigned to "teachable" classes for only fifteen periods per week, with the rest of their time devoted to preparation, on the job training and assistance, and graduate education at the university.

The intern teacher would have the opportunity to exchange classes during the first few weeks, if need be, with the master teachers, who, as mentioned earlier, would be teaching the most "difficult" classes. In the event that some of the interns could not cope with a particular group, it would be beneficial to provide this "safety valve" rather than discourage them with one or more classes they could not handle or might have difficulty with. Indeed, there would be time for them to become familiar with and to learn how to teach a "difficult" group. The intern teacher should be paid a full salary, and after two years of part-time graduate education he could be awarded a master's degree in teaching the disadvantaged. By the beginning of the third year, the individual should be expected to carry a full teaching load.

Sometime near the end of each of the first two school years, the intern teachers should be given the opportunity to decide whether they wish to remain or transfer to another school. With this choice they would not fear becoming trapped in a situation they might dislike or be unable to cope with. Also, by this time, the beginning teachers would have an idea of what it is really like to teach in a ghetto school. No one would be coerced or forced to remain. The experienced teachers and administration should also be allowed to recommend transfers for anyone who they feel is not suited for the sterner task of teaching disadvantaged youth. This method could help serve as a "safety valve," too, and eliminate some of the future incompetents of the profession—many who wind up working with ghetto students.

Continuing Inservice Education. Because of the limited supply of teachers, large-scale inservice education, previously, was only feasible on a part-time basis. Today, because of improved salaries, fringe benefits, and teaching conditions, the teachers now are remaining in the profession for twenty to thirty years. There should now be required full-time inservice training. Through state and federal funds, the teachers should spend one year, every five or six years, improving their skills and "catching up" in their respective fields; otherwise, as in the past, they will become less effective with time.

For example, secondary school teachers need continuous education in their areas of specialization. The history teacher should be aware of current history in Southeast Asia, Africa, and the United States. The science teacher should keep up with the latest discoveries and theories, especially in the fields of chemistry, physics, and space technology. All teachers could probably benefit from periodic courses in child or adolescent psychology, human relations, racial dynamics, curriculum, and instruction. Similarly, they would benefit by reading and discussing the latest innovations in education, with the hope that some of these innovations could be utilized in the classroom situation. (Practical application of ideas and innovations could be worked out in the classroom if the teacher-training institution adopted the idea of the teacher educational center, as previously described.) Ideally, three or four teachers from each school should be trained together in one group and return as a team, sharing materials and ideas when working with their colleagues. This type of inservice education should be mandatory. Experienced teachers should also be given paid leaves of absences for such study.

As for the other years when the teacher is working in the schools, he should be exposed to a different inservice education, including instruction during school hours, preferably during two consecutive teacher-administrative periods—one that is closely connected to the needs of the individual teacher and school. The best way to develop a sound, practical inservice program at the schools is to allow teachers to express their interests and general objectives and to determine which consultants they need from the university or community. If teachers do not see these sessions as meaningful and appropriate to their work, they will look upon them as just another phase of administrative work or time-consuming activity. Therefore, they should prescribe the general design of the program. Discussions could center about activities that grow out of the teachers' work in the classroom and school; for example, applying techniques of using new materials and media in novel ways, pooling extensive reading lists for the students, devising methods for improving tests and student achievement, working out plans for improving community relations. An offshoot of this idea has mushroomed in England and Wales since 1965. Today there are approximately 500 teacher centers in the United Kingdom. Effective change and reform are implemented from the teachers, not from their critics, administrators, or professors. The teachers themselves are responsible for defining and solving their own problems. The teachers exchange ideas, receive assistance, and learn from one another. The rationale for the centers is that change and reform can be brought about mainly through those directly responsible for teaching.

Experienced teachers also need to attend professional conventions and meetings to learn about the latest ideas and trends and to report back to their colleagues. The school system should not only encourage but pay for such travel. Similarly, experienced teachers need to be encouraged to visit other school systems, even to teach in another state under an exchange program—to learn different approaches and to broaden their perspective.

From Theory into Practice

The above suggestions need not be implemented *in toto*. The suggestions are more important than the details, and the details can be modified according to local needs and changing times. In the past, however, similar suggestions have been set forth on paper but, for the greater part, not implemented in practice. Thus, the apparent reason for the failure of traditional training programs is not that the reasoning was unsound. It is because those charged with the responsibility for organizing and managing the programs did not state the objectives in precise terms or determine whether the various aspects of the program were being accomplished or if modification was needed. So long as people did not voice discontent, the assumption was that things were going well. More often, the intent was to ignore reality and merely suggest something that sounded workable on paper or that could be funded by an outside agency. The current problem, then, would appear not to be the need for the new teacher-training models or theories, as propounded by the current literature on teacher education, but the refining and implementing of the program outlined above—or a similar program.

Basically, the idea is to make the program more precise and reliable, to regulate the input variables so that the output can be better predicted, or at least favorably controlled. For example, the teacher's attitude is an input which can be measured with some degree of reliability and validity. But the teacher's general attitude is too vague; we need to focus on precise attitudes or traits. Similarly, it is useless to say that the ghetto teacher displays negative attitudes toward teaching his clientele without defining specifically what attitudes are negative.

Precise attitudes which are considered relevant for teaching the dis-advantaged should be defined initially by the training staff, for example, tolerance toward racial minorities, flexibility, and emotional maturity. These attitudes are subsequently set forth as objectives for teachers to attain. Then the attitudes can be measured by a standardized test given to the individual teacher and to the group as a whole. Activities are developed with the intention of improving these attitudes. Informal feed-back sessions may be provided (e.g., conferences or seminars) although, in some cases, they may be considered unnecessary. A post-test is ad-ministered; the new scores are compared with the old group scores, and the differences reflect, in part, how successful an activity or group of activities have been in improving these attitudes or accomplishing the objectives. This data is evaluated by the participants and staff members. The objectives are perhaps modified, or the activities are modified to meet the objectives. The procedures are repeated with another group of participants and, still again, with another group, and eventually it is learned what seem to be the best attitudinal objectives and corresponding activities; hence, this aspect of the program has a better chance of succeeding.

At this point, it might be beneficial to describe the basic procedures for organizing and evaluating objectives for teacher training: (1) objec-tives, (2) activities, (3) measurements, and (4) evaluation.[3]

Objectives. The program can be no better than its objectives or goals. A few examples will suffice. There is such a wide range of possibilities that it is usually considered effective to set limits for at least the nature and scope of what is intended. Goals may be explicit but poor. Many ideas cannot be adequately developed without clear and consistent emphasis throughout the program. Definite objectives which are stated in advance and in concrete terms can be measured; deviations from what is expected can be removed. The intention is to avoid vague or broad ideas which have different meanings to different people, differences which are caused

---

[3] There are four optional procedures (pre-test, informal feedback before and after the exit test, and follow-up data) which will be indicated in the model which follows later. Since these are optional procedures and are not always considered necessary, they are not examined at this point of the discussion.

by the nature of our language and which are often unwittingly overlooked by those concerned. Any activity or experience that consumes the time of the participants and staff members should be justifiable as contributing to one or several sound objectives. If goals are unclear, how can one attempt to justify what is going on? (The trouble is, however, that the field of education is confounded by and noted for its vagueness, and the training programs merely reflect the vagueness of the entire field.) Precise objectives will provide direction in pursuing commonly understood goals, and everyone concerned will be better able to direct his efforts to carry out what he is expected to.

How are the objectives to be developed? Objectives will reflect the institution's philosophy and organizational norms and processes. They will reflect the influence and analytical arguments of specific individuals working alone or in a group, the character and interaction of the group, and the extent to which the opinions of participants, junior staff members, and school related personnel such as teachers and supervisors are valued. Economic and political factors will also influence the stated objectives.

Each objective should (1) inform the reader what the learner will be doing (intended outcome) when demonstrating achievement of the objective; (2) explain the conditions imposed upon the learner which demonstrate mastery of the objective; (3) communicate a terminal behavior or acceptable performance; and (4) indicate what the learner will be doing when demonstrating the terminal behavior. Three examples of behavior objectives related to teacher training are now listed:

> Objective No. 1: At the end of the term, the score made by the group will be 5 points higher than it was when they were pre-tested at the beginning of the term for _____ trait on the _____ test.

> Objective No. 2: Without the aid of reference or notes on the final examination about the disadvantaged child, the students will be required to correctly answer 80 out of 100 short-answer questions.

> Objective No. 3: By the fifth week, the prospective teacher will demonstrate to the observer improved classroom management abilities by a 25% reduction of the number of his students coming to his class after the late bell and by a 50% reduction of the number of his students walking around the classroom during the lesson without his permission from the number of offenders during the first week when observed by the same person.

Activities. The activities used in the program should be functional to accomplishing the objectives. The initial activities will probably reflect the staff members' knowledge and biases; however, revisions and changes of the activities should be based on the evaluation sessions of both the staff members and participants. Some activities for accomplishing one or more of the three stated objectives are delineated below. The list is by no means conclusive; moreover, many of the activities can be applied to other objectives besides the aforementioned ones.

1. Lectures by Visitors (professionals, nonprofessionals; adults, students)
2. Lectures by Staff
3. Small Group Discussions (seminars)
4. Large Group Discussions
5. Individual Conferences
6. Group Conferences
7. T-groups
8. Role Playing
9. Simulation Teaching
10. Microteaching
11. Module Instruction
12. Assignment with Community Agencies
13. Field Trips
14. Part-time Supervised Teaching
15. Observing Experienced Teachers
16. Participating Teachers Observing One Another
17. Videotapes with Feedback
18. Tutoring
19. Case Studies
20. Logs, Diaries
21. Informal Talks with Students
22. Textbooks
23. Committee Assignments
24. Independent Study
25. Preparation of Paper
26. Developing Own Materials
27. Subject in an Experiment
28. Observer of an Experiment
29. Own Research
30. Free Time for Socialization

Measurements. The evaluator or staff should determine that the test(s) used measure(s) the stated objectives and that each objective receives the appropriate emphasis on the test(s). How to test each objective will depend on the intended outcomes. Some intended outcomes are more easily assessed by a standardized (psychological or cognitive) test, while others are more easily assessed by a nonstandardized (essay, objective, oral) teacher- or staff-made test. Similarly, some intended outcomes are more easily assessed by a traditional test situation (i.e., the above standardized and nonstandardized tests), while others are more easily assessed by a "nontest" situation, a situation which employs informal methods for gathering data (i.e., written reports, anecdotal records, checklists, observations, and ratings). In particular, many aspects of teaching are best analyzed through observations and rating scales, though there are problems of reliability and validity with all the current methods used to assess the teaching act. Control groups should be used wherever they are necessary, often when working with empirical data.

As previously indicated, pre-tests and post-tests are not always necessary; however, this procedure tends to clarify gain scores and to measure the extent to which the objectives were actually accomplished. For example, with Objective No. 2 it is possible for someone to pass the final examination without any instruction. A retest might show that the student passed the examination with the same score, thus indicating that the objective was inappropriate, that the activities were unrelated to the objectives, or that the student should have been doing independent work since he already had considerable knowledge of the topic.

In the final analysis, proper matching of objectives with tests requires competency in the subject matter and sophistication in test construction. It is presumed that the staff has knowledge of the subject matter. However, one also needs to be aware of the advantages and limitations of the various tests and "nontests," and for this reason the test decisions should be primarily decided by a formal evaluator who has knowledge of tests. Briefly, tests may be classified as follows:

    I. Standardized tests
       1. Psychological
       2. Cognitive
   II. Nonstandardized tests
       1. Essay
       2. Objective
       3. Oral
  III. "Nontests"
       1. Written reports
       2. Anecdotal records

    3. Checklists

    4. Observations

    5. Ratings

Evaluation. Having outlined objectives, activities, and tests, we must next establish evaluation procedures (if possible, including informal feedback at several intervals during the program, especially prior to and after the exit test). Evaluation criteria should help determine whether the objectives are appropriate and are being carried out as expected, whether the activities and tests are appropriate to the objectives, and to what extent they need to be modified. Only by establishing evaluation procedures can it be determined whether the program is proceeding according to expectations. These procedures help make it possible to note discrepancies between actual and intended outcomes, to determine the reason for the deviations, and to institute corrective action. If there are no deviations, the stated objectives are being carried out. The evaluation aspect of the program should provide data which will permit greater precision in subsequent efforts to write objectives. Neglected variables may be identified. New objectives, activities, and tests may be discovered. Follow-up data, although not pertinent to the immediate success of the program (and therefore often considered optional), should eventually be included as part of or following the evaluation.[4] It is especially needed if worthwhile research data is to be forthcoming, and if educators expect to learn what programs and their various aspects seem to work. Suggested evaluation procedures are listed below.

  I. Evaluation from participants

    1. Written reports (profile sheets, logs, etc.)

    2. Discussion (individual, group; with staff, without staff)

    3. Weekend retreat (with staff, without staff)

    4. Self-evaluation inventories

    5. Data based on tests (standardized; nonstandardized; traditional test situation, "nontest" situation)

  II. Evaluation from staff

    1. Written reports (profile sheets, logs, etc.)

    2. Discussion (individual, group; with participants, without participants)

    3. Weekend retreats (with participants, without participants)

---

[4] See footnote 3. Although follow-up data is often optional, it should eventually be considered—and usually as part of or following evaluation. Therefore, follow-up procedures are briefly discussed in this subheading as an aspect of evaluation.

    4. Self-evaluation inventories
    5. Reports (informal or formal) from outside evaluator (summative or formative evaluation)

III. Follow-up data
    1. Personal communications
    2. Newsletter
    3. Letters or questionnaires
    4. Pre-test, post-test
    5. Class visitation, intervisitation
    6. Evaluation by principal or supervision of school
    7. Group reunion
    8. Post-training class or workshop
    9. Use of participants for inservice training in their schools
   10. Long-range evaluation (at least 5 years, preferably divided into specified and equal time periods)

Model 1

Model for Organizing and Evaluating Objectives

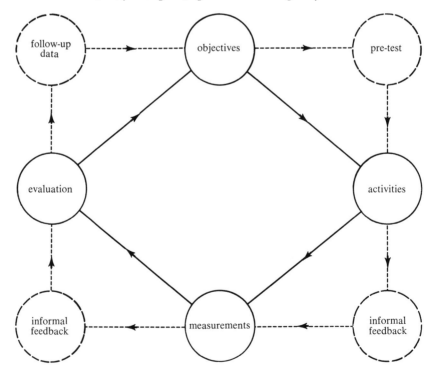

A Model for Organizing and Evaluating Objectives. To help conceptualize the above discussion, a model of the four basic procedures is indicated by the flow of connecting lines and circles. The dotted lines and circles show the secondary or optional procedures, or those which are not always necessary or crucial for the immediate success of the program. The objectives represent the beginning point, and eventually the flow of procedures return to this point; in turn, the objectives are considered accomplished or in need of being modified.

Limitations of Organizing and Evaluating Objectives

Having stated the potential use and some positive aspects of behavioral objectives and their related criteria references, we need to look at the other side of the coin. To be sure, no single change or innovation is adequate to cope with or completely erase all of the problems of teacher training. Furthermore, it is necessary to point out some of the possible hazards and problems inherent in developing objectives. Although the educational field is ready to embrace the principle of behavioral objectives, there is danger in a bandwagon approach; we tend to ignore reality and become seduced by imaginary promises without fully recognizing the limitations of what we are advocating. For this reason, some of the limitations of the four basic procedures for organizing and evaluating objectives are outlined.

Objectives
1. Some objectives may not be necessarily desirable or appropriate.
2. There is no guarantee that the objectives will be attained, even if precisely formulated.
3. There is no guarantee that good teaching and teacher-training programs can be defined in exact behavioral terms.
4. What constitutes good teaching and teacher training may not be limited only to what can be clearly defined, observed, or measured.
5. Formulating teacher-training objectives does not necessarily mean that they will coincide with the realities of the classroom.
6. Noncognitive behaviors which are difficult to formulate

and measure may often be ignored, thereby encouraging many educators' apparent disregard for learning in the affective domain (learning dealing with attitudes, feelings, and emotions).

7. Objectives may lead to trivializing the teacher-training program, reducing the program to small exercises.

8. Under the guise of educational competency and behavioral science, we may only be increasing our jargon and adopting an incomprehensible method of training teachers. Thus we may unwittingly devise a "scientific" method for disguising our poor teacher-training programs.

9. Behavioral objectives may become an *end* approach, rather than a *means* approach, for improving teaching and teacher training.

10. We may impose a rigidity on teaching and teacher education, thereby devaluating creativity and encouraging the mechanical and routine nature of what goes on in most classrooms and schools today. Young prospective teachers are already stifled and alienated by narrow teaching and learning. Must we further stifle and alienate them?

Activities

1. There is no guarantee that activities can be developed to accomplish all desirable objectives.

2. On the other hand, many activities may neither be applicable to objectives or suitable for enhancing intended outcomes but continuously advocated and modified because of our lack of knowledge of better activities.

3. Many staff members lack knowledge of appropriate activities, even with some of the activities listed above. What knowledge they possess is sometimes based on a sketchy idea of new innovations resulting from limited reading of the literature.

4. There may be too much stress on objectives and results, without fully assessing the activities. This may readily happen if the objectives seem accomplished.

5. It is difficult to determine whether one or several activities combined are germane to accomplishing an objective. Tests and informal feedback methods are not devised for computing this kind of data.

6. There is danger of limiting participants to the prescribed activities.

Measurements

1. There is always the problem of test reliability and validity.
2. Most tests, including standardized ones, do not have norms geared specifically for teacher-training programs, nor do they usually show reliable gain scores in small time intervals. Similarly, most tests measure relatively simple behavior. When measuring behavior that requires complex or demanding processes, such as teaching, tests provide less dependable scores.
3. Staff members are often reluctant to use informal measurements or "nontests," even when they may be appropriate for assessing objectives.
4. Staff members may give wrong interpretations, even subjective interpretations to test results.
5. There is a tendency to misconstrue results as "findings."
6. Staff members often have limited knowledge of the advantages and limitations of the different kinds of tests.

In connection with the last item, Stanley (1964, pp. 304–305) lists and summarizes the advantages and limitations of standardized (psychological and cognitive) and nonstandardized (essay and objective) tests. His outline is then supplemented with data on nonstandardized oral tests.

Table 1 [5]

Advantages and Limitations of Standardized and Nonstandardized Tests with Respect to the Criteria of Validity, Reliability, and Usability

	STANDARDIZED	
	psychological and cognitive	
Criterion	Advantages	Limitations
1. Validity a. Curricular	Careful selection by competent persons. Fit typical situations.	Inflexible. Too general in scope to meet local requirements, especially in unusual situations.

---

[5] Julian C. Stanley, *Measurement in Today's Schools,* 4th ed., © 1964. Reprinted by permission of Prentice-Hall, Inc., Englewood Cliffs, N.J.

Criterion	Advantages	Limitations
b. Statistical	With best tests, high.	Criteria often inappropriate or unreliable. Size of coefficients depend upon range of ability in group tested.
2. Reliability	For best tests, fairly high, often .85 or more for comparable forms.	High reliability is no guarantee of validity. Also, reliability depends upon range of ability in group tested.
3. Usability		
a. Ease of Administration	Definite procedure, time limits, etc. Economy of time.	Manuals require careful study and are sometimes inadequate.
b. Ease of Scoring	Definite rules, keys, etc. Largely routine.	Scoring by hand may take considerable time and be monotonous. Machine scoring preferable.
c. Ease of Interpretation	Better tests have adequate norms. Useful basis of comparison, equivalent forms.	Norms often confused with standards. Some norms defective. Norms for various types of schools and levels of ability are often lacking.
Summary	Convenience, comparability, objectivity. Equivalent forms may be available.	Inflexibility. May be only applicable to a particular situation.

NONSTANDARDIZED

Essay

Criterion	Advantages	Limitations
1. Validity		
a. Curricular	Useful for English, advanced classes; afford language training. May encourage sound study habits.	Limited sampling. Bluffing is possible. Mixed language factor in all scores.

Criterion	Advantages	Limitations
b. Statistical		Usually not known.
2. Reliability		Usually quite low.
3. Usability		
a. Ease of Administration	Easy to prepare. Easy to give.	Lack of uniformity.
b. Ease of Scoring		Slow, uncertain, and subjective.
c. Ease of Interpretation		No norms. Meaning doubtful.
Summary	Useful for part of many tests and in a few special fields.	Limited sampling. Subjective scoring. Time consuming.

NONSTANDARDIZED

Objective

Criterion	Advantages	Limitations
1. Validity		
a. Curricular	Extensive sampling of subject matter. Flexible in use, discourages bluffing. Compares favorably with standard tests.	Narrow sampling of functions tested. Negative learning possible. May encourage piecemeal study.
b. Statistical		Adequate criteria usually lacking.
2. Reliability	Sometimes approaches that of standard tests.	No guarantee of validity.
3. Usability		
a. Ease of Administration	Directions rather uniform. Economy of time.	Time, effort, and skill are required to prepare well.
b. Ease of Scoring	Definite rules, keys, etc. Largely routine. Can be done by clerks or machine.	Monotonous.
c. Ease of Interpretation	Local norms can be derived.	No norms available at beginning.

Criterion	Advantages	Limitations
Summary	Extensive sampling. Objective scoring. Flexibility.	Preparation requires skill and time.

	NONSTANDARDIZED [6]	
	Oral	

Criterion	Advantages	Limitations
1. Validity a. Curricular	Useful for testing student's depth of understanding of a topic or field of study. Able to assess student's conceptual skills and level of thinking, how student formulates hypotheses, implications, and conclusions. Tests student's reactions to different questions, how student organizes and expresses ideas.	Verbally glib person may bluff answers. Possible argument between student and examiner(s). Discussion may be sidetracked or become tangential. Personality factors may influence questions and responses.
b. Statistical		Unknown.
2. Reliability		Susceptibility to low reliability, generally unknown.
3. Usability a. Ease of Administration	Easy to prepare and give, flexible. Easy to create an informal and friendly atmosphere.	Questions are sometimes unprepared. Lack of uniformity. Time consuming, practical only with a small number of students.
b. Ease of Scoring		No rules, no keys. Sometimes influenced by the general impression of the student.

[6] This part of the table is organized by the author.

Criterion	Advantages	Limitations
c. Ease of Interpretation		No norms, usually lacks weighting procedures. Open to different biases and interpretations of the examiner(s).
Summary	Useful for testing student's depth of understanding where other tests seem inappropriate. Flexible.	Subjective, time consuming, no norms.

Evaluation

1. Many of the participants and staff members lack knowledge of sound evaluation procedures.
2. Most teacher education evaluation is based on informal methods, on opinions, and on suggestions.
3. Standardized tests are designed to discriminate among learners (participants), not necessarily to indicate the extent to which identifiable behaviors have been individually mastered, thus making it difficult to evaluate how much progress the individual learner has made with a given behavior.
4. Many important variables and relationships which affect the program may go unnoticed, because the evaluations are usually concerned with broad generalizations and suggestions.
5. Either because of politics or disinterest, staff members may support unsound views of the program director, and participants may support unsound views of the staff. On the other hand, there is no guarantee that the director will allow the staff and participants to help evaluate the program. He may simply ignore them.
6. The director or staff members who are responsible for evaluation reports may tend to be dishonest about obvious weaknesses or disguise them in order to protect themselves.
7. There is no guarantee that changes will be made as a result of the evaluation sessions.
8. With the exception of accreditation policies, teacher-training programs are rarely evaluated by an outside

agency. Outside evaluators may invoke suspicion among the participants or be considered a tool of the administration. They may also be dishonest so as to ensure future contracts.

9. Once a program is developed on paper and put into operation, there is little enthusiasm for making modifications unless there is a pending crisis or obvious problem.

10. Opinions are based on biases and knowledge. The results of evaluating the data may merely be consistent with the groups' biases and knowledge which are similar to those which originally interacted with the formation of the program. Thus necessary revisions may be overlooked.

11. There may be a premature evaluation of the program before it is fully operational.

12. There is a tendency to misinterpret tentative "findings" as "proof."

Conclusion

For the greater part, teacher training has failed to prepare teachers for the realities of the classroom. It is a failure in the eyes of most prospective teachers, experienced teachers, school administrators, professors of liberal arts, and candid professors of education. Although there have been some improvements through the years, the improvements have been piecemeal, slow, and ineffective with regard to the overall programs. Today there is an illusion that teacher training is being revitalized. New terms, new models, new R & D centers, and new research appear in the current literature. But few viable changes seem to be occurring, mainly because there is a gap between what educators say and what they do. Real change is an isolated phenomenon, occurring only in a few schools and institutes of higher learning. Perhaps the time may soon come for educators to be honest with themselves, to stop defrauding their colleagues and clientele, too.

As indicated earlier, the education field seems ready to embrace the principle of behavioral objectives. Good. But we should be aware of its limitations and problems; moreover, we should be prepared to go beyond the talking, reading, and writing stage in order to implement what we say we are going to do or what we claim to be doing.

V

Myths of Integration, "Liberalism," and Research on Blacks

This chapter examines some of the myths of integration, "liberalism," and research on blacks. The discussion is divided into four parts: (1) methods of organizational reform for implementing school desegregation, namely, (a) supersystem reform, (b) system reform, and (c) subsystem reform; (2) why school desegregation and integration have failed, with emphasis on (a) Northern hypocrisy and procrastination, (b) American race relations, and (c) the widening gap between blacks and whites; (3) the "liberals'" reaction to black power and black violence; and (4) false research on blacks, including (a) biases and limitations and (b) desegregation studies.

Methods of Organizational Reform

Supersystem Reform. Supersystem (some authorities use the term suprasystem) reform reflects change in society. From this viewpoint, the school is viewed as one of the many social systems which is dependent upon and reflects society; the school tends to change with society and in the same direction. From the standpoint of chance, total societal reform is rare, usually occurring during or after a crisis or revolution—either social, political, or economic.

The various Supreme Court cases involving school desegregation since 1954 may be viewed as supersystem reform or as an attempt to reform society. The main problem with these Court rulings is threefold: most of white society does not really want to take strong action to desegregate schools, the focus has been directed mainly at the South where *de jure* segregation existed,* and there have been escape clauses dealing with "rule of reason" and "reasonable time"—thus preventing meaningful integration. The major school desegregation cases decided by the Supreme Court were summarized in the *New York Times* (1971a): [1]

1. *1954, Brown v. Board of Education of Topeka, Kansas.* The Court rejected the "separate but equal" doctrine and decided that racial segregation in public schools was "inherently unequal."

2. *1955, Brown Case.* In a follow-up decision, the Court did not order immediate desegregation of public schools but required change "with all deliberate speed."

3. *1964, Griffin v. Prince Edward County School Board.* The Court claimed there was "too much deliberation and not enough speed." The Court declared that the closing of the public schools in Prince Edward County, Virginia, to avoid desegregation, was unconstitutional. Tuition grants to private white schools set up after the schools were closed were declared unconstitutional too.

4. *1968, Greene v. New Kent County.* The Court maintained that local school boards were required to plan desegregation proposals that promised to be effective.

5. *1969, United States v. Montgomery County Board of Education.* The Court ruled that a federal judge had the right to order school boards to integrate the schools' staffs according to specific ratios.

6. *1969, Alexander et al. v. Holmes County Board of Education, Mississippi.* The Court ruled that school districts must end segregation "at once" and integrate the schools "now and hereafter."

7. *1971, United States v. Charlotte-Mecklenburg County, North Carolina.* The Court supported bussing and other devices, e.g.,

---

* *Postscript:* In December 1971, the Boston schools were charged by the Department of Health, Education, and Welfare (HEW) to be in violation of the 1964 Civil Rights Act—the first leveled against a major city in the North. HEW threatened to eliminate federal aid, amounting to approximately $10 million annually, unless the school system ceased operating "two separate racially identifiable school sub-systems, one predominantly white and the other predominantly nonwhite."

Boston has 93,000 public school students. Of the 26,000 nonwhite students, 78% are enrolled in schools that are predominantly nonwhite. Boston school authorities have denied the charges but promise speedy reforms.

[1] © 1971 by The New York Times Company. Reprinted by permission.

racial quotas, pairing, and gerrymandering of attendance zones,
to remove the South's state imposed school segregation.

Although the larger society is generally unwilling to integrate the
schools, there are a few integrated residential communities in which the
white populace, even with children, is not fleeing to the suburbs; the
schools in these communities tend to reflect the community mix. In this
connection, we might stretch the concept of supersystem reform and assess the integrated community as if it were a society. The Hyde Park–
Kenwood area in Chicago is one such community in which the white
majority population (approximately 65%) is mainly stabilized—largely
due to the effects of the University of Chicago and its process of urban
renewal or black removal. The whites are atypical by most standards,
well above standard in income and education—intelligent, liberal, and
interested in progressive causes. Along with poor blacks, there is a high
percentage of atypical, middle-income blacks, as well as many Orientals
attending graduate school at the University and living in the community,
in managerial and professional occupations. Since the housing patterns
are relatively integrated, so are many of the community schools. Even
here, however, there is the beginning of out-migration of white home
owners, especially those who have daughters of high school age, and
some of the neighborhood schools are beginning to "change" or "tip"
beyond the fifty-fifty ratio.

System Reform. System reform encompasses the whole system in question
but not society. The system usually develops a set of codes and boundaries for blocking out alien inputs from the internal and external environment. Reform is based upon the nature of the system, according to
prescribed rules and criteria and through "proper channels" and compromise. These maintenance structures and norms tend to prevent
system reform; the system, in effect, seeks to perpetuate its own values
and philosophy—the *status quo*—and in doing so, it often fails to interact with the surrounding environment. For system reform to occur,
either there is new leadership at the top of the pyramidal authority, or
there is overt and ominous pressure from the environment to the extent
that its reputation or survival is at stake.

Methods for system reform can be summed up under an "engineering"
approach: the manipulation of students, schools, or school districts. As
of now, almost all attempts have failed. They include:

1. The construction of middle schools to extend the process of
   integration to grades five and onward through bussing. This

proposal is ineffective since the students usually attend neighborhood middle schools and high schools.

2. Redefining school attendance boundaries and changing feeder
   patterns of secondary schools, both of which are often demo-
   graphically unfeasible.

3. Open enrollment and free transfer plans allowing students to
   attend schools outside their neighborhood so long as there is
   adequate space; implementation of the plan usually leads to
   "tokenism."

4. The Civil Rights Act of 1964 by which funds may be withheld
   from the schools which do not comply with the law. Right now
   the law states that *de jure* segregation is unconstitutional; however, some lower courts—Massachusetts, California, and the
   District of Columbia—have ruled that racially imbalanced
   schools are illegal, too. In the meantime, the act is mainly
   directed at Southern schools, where *de jure* segregation was
   institutionalized, but there are increased efforts to focus on
   Northern schools that refuse to "engineer" their school boundaries. (Depending on one's interpretation, the act may also be
   viewed as supersystem reform.)

Subsystem Reform. Subsystem reform is the most common type of school
reform; it includes part of the system—usually in the nature of a model,
experimental, or pilot program. In prescribed, piecemeal fashion, the
system attempts to adapt to society or the surrounding environment. Or,
the system sometimes tries to show the public that it is innovative and
progressive. A few schools or school districts operate in accord with and
under the control of the larger system. The organizational framework,
control devices, and role prescriptions tend to remain intact. Organizational objectives and outcomes are implemented along intended behaviors. Occasionally, however, the subsystem deviates from intended
behaviors or worse, rebels against the larger system. This is what can be
called "muti" (mutiny) subsystem reform; it is noted here only for
purposes of distinguishing it from the usual system reform, which can
be called "supportive." [2]

Viable subsystem suggestions have been set forth by various school
systems, and, since these suggestions constitute a model or experimental
project, they are relatively more acceptable than the first two methods
of organizational reform. The fourth and fifth examples below are rela-

---

[2] Further reference to the concept of "muti" subsystem reform is in Chapter VI.

tively controversial and show how subsystem reform may be enlarged to system reform.

1. The proposal of a linear city includes a group of schools not located on a particular site but within their respective communities. The schools are connected by a transportation line and share educational centers which offer special facilities and personnel. Ideally, the educational centers would be integrated, the children being brought together for a few hours daily or days weekly to supplement their studies.

2. The joint occupancy scheme is a concept which combines public and private financing and ownership of a multipurpose structure. The plan is supposed to help cope with diminishing land resources and increasing real estate costs in large cities; it is supposed to reduce capital expenditures for acquiring and building new school sites, and it yields revenues from land that would normally be tax exempt. Hopefully, the structure would attract into segregated communities whites who wish to avail themselves of schools, jobs, and housing in one building.

3. The open air high school is an attempt to convert the city into a classroom. It is a school without walls, where the student can take full advantage of the business and cultural resources of the city. Its innovative quality and integrated setting should attract and maintain students of various ethnic and racial groups.

4. The educational park is a clustering of elementary and secondary schools located on one site and housing ten to thirty thousand students. The schools share central facilities such as a gym, library, auditorium, computer, etc., and personnel such as nurses, doctors, social workers, psychiatrists, etc. Given the special personnel and good teachers, it is assumed that quality education will result. The site of the cluster is a "neutral" area, and its very bigness and quality preclude future steps toward integration. While a small community may house its entire school system in such a setting, in its most imaginative form the educational park becomes a metropolitan school in which the inner city and the neighboring suburban communities construct and share educational parks around the periphery of the city. However, it is premature to expect suburban communities to combine their resources with the city's. Many of the suburban residents moved from the city to escape the black "invasion" and to send their children to "better" schools. Besides, several

black groups now view any form of metropolitanism as a ploy by whites to curtail their political and educational power. An offshoot of the educational park is Pittsburgh's Great High School concept—five "super" high schools, housing five to seven thousand students, which are expected to replace the system's twenty-three existing high schools. In effect, this is an example of how the educational park, or at least its facsimile, is transformed into total system reform.

5. Before the 1971 Supreme Court ruling, several cities and suburban communities had adopted the idea of bussing students across neighborhood boundaries. This plan often led to resistance from the white community. (In this connection, some educators had suggested that we put bounties on ghetto children, say $2,000 to $3,000 per child, so that whichever school enrolled them would obtain extra cash; white schools, even suburban schools, would find black children attractive.) Experimental bussing schemes which have had moderate success are the Boston METCO, the Hartford Project Concern, and the Rochester Triad Plan, to name a few. In smaller cities or suburbs where distance is minimal and in which there is a white "liberal," financially secure base, the bussing of students has been transformed into a total system approach. This has been true also in Berkeley, White Plains, Evanston, and Princeton (the pairing of schools). In almost all these earlier cases, the successful bussing of students took place in a setting which is in close proximity to a university—where a "liberal" atmosphere or the presence of such an atmosphere prevailed. At the present time, some state courts are declaring that segregated school systems in the North must be dismantled. This has resulted in forced bussing (a total approach or example of system reform), which in turn has caused explosive outbursts of anger and hatred—similar to the Southern reaction in the mid and late 1960s.*

Why School Desegregation and Integration Have Failed

Northern Hypocrisy and Procrastination. In general, the number of segregated schools throughout the country remains the same today as it was in 1954. Integration in Southern schools was delayed almost ten years after the Supreme Court decision in 1954. The Northern schools are

---

* *Postscript:* Outside the South, the most complex and massive bussing program taking place during the 1971–72 school year is in San Francisco.

more segregated now than they were in 1954. Thus, decreasing *de jure* segregation in the South is offset by increasing *de facto* segregation in the North. For the most part, we have "token" integration in the North, and in most cases no integration, only "changing" schools and communities. According to the 1971 government figures, there is a greater percentage of blacks in the South attending integrated schools than in the North and West together.[3] It should be noted, however, the method for reporting desegregation progress is by districts, a deceptive method which obscures widespread segregation of specific schools and especially classes within reported desegregated districts.

The North should not try to hide behind the difference between *de jure* and *de facto* segregation. The North finds it very easy to vilify Southern police dogs, bombings, or murders, but it continues to overlook subtle forms of prejudice and discrimination in its own back yard, e.g., segregated and inferior schools and houses, poor job opportunities for blacks, inadequate medical treatment and paltry health conditions which cause hundreds of unnecessary deaths of black infants, differential treatment of blacks by the police and courts, and the great number of riots and need for police control. (When a disturbance occurs in the black ghetto, the idea is to "seal it off" so it does not "spill over" into the white community.) Indeed, the North is just as bigoted and racist as the South. True, the North has several laws that prohibit discrimination and segregation and promote equality and integration in schools, housing, and employment; however, we should all recognize the gap between our laws and their implementation, and surely blacks recognize it.

The hypocrisy of the North is keenly illustrated by the rulings of the Supreme Court since 1954, which demand an end to *de jure* segregation of schools, a Southern problem, but ignore *de facto* segregation, a Northern problem. Most of the Court's procedures for ending state imposed segregation could easily apply to the North, too; yet the focus of attention has been on the South. Similarly, in 1971 the Supreme Court ruled that communities could block low-income housing projects— in effect, the Court saw nothing wrong with economic discrimination. However, since a large percentage of blacks are poor, and public housing is often the only kind of decent suburban housing blacks can afford, the ruling can be viewed as helping to perpetuate the country's dual racial practices by pressing for integration in the South and not in the North.

In Congress, Senator Stennis' 1970 bill was rejected, a bill which would have guaranteed equality of desegregation enforcement through-

---

[3] *Supra,* Chapter I, Footnote 9.

out the country, whether from *de jure* or *de facto* causes, in effect, meaning the equality of nonenforcement.[4] Similarly, Senator Ribicoff's 1971 bill was defeated in Congress, a bill requiring that all schools in an urban area (suburbs and city) have a percentage of minority students at least equal to half the percentage of minority students in an entire area. Thus, if 50% of the students in an urban area were black, 25% of the students in each school in the suburbs and city would have to be black. The bill gave the schools twelve years to achieve this level of integration but required substantial progress each year if the schools were not to lose their federal funds. Indeed, Senators Stennis and Ribicoff have good cause and are right to claim that the North is hypocritical; it is willing to shove integration down Southern throats but not willing to accept it in its states.

In the "liberal" North, school desegregation increases white migration to the suburbs. *En masse,* now, city whites are abandoning public schools or fleeing to suburbia; consequently, integrated schools change into black ghetto schools. The cycle raises the question of whether integration should be demanded or, for that matter, if it is feasible since the attempt to integrate tends to produce the opposite effect. Many of the city schools (e.g., Baltimore, Chicago, Gary, Newark, New York, Washington, D.C., etc.) already have more nonwhite students than white students and can no longer effectively integrate all their schools, even if the school authorities really wanted to. Granted, there is some talk of bringing students from relatively remote suburbs into city schools, as well as city students to the suburbs. It is doubtful, however, if such an idea will be implemented on a mass scale, as reflected by the Stennis and Ribicoff experiences. Indeed, no matter what the Gallup polls show, most whites reject the idea of bussing, and this has been overtly demonstrated in the few court orders that have affected the suburbs. Some of the reasons are motivated by outright racism. Other objections are linked with the white parents' fear that the buses will bring the problems of the ghetto to "their" schools and expose their children to the social ills that blacks have had to cope with and which have turned many of their schools into blackboard jungles. Many of the whites moved to the suburbs for the sake of their children's education and particularly will reject the idea of some judge they did not elect telling them they must send their children into ghetto schools, especially when the judge—if he has children—sends his own children to private (in effect, white segregated) schools.

---

[4] In 1971, the bill was approved in the Senate. However, the measure provided no basis for enforcement or legal action.

In this connection, the ban on funds to parochial schools will probably soon be lifted enabling them to receive a greater share of federal assistance and thereby leading to further withdrawal of middle-class whites from public schools. Similarly, there has been an increase of private segregated "academies" in the South. The federal government has permitted many of them to maintain a tax-exempt status, and many segregation-minded state legislators are beginning to support state aid to private schools because it would probably mean state aid to the academy phenomena, too. The flight of Northern whites to the suburbs and the growing Southern "academies," added with rising costs—ranging from teacher salaries, to electricity, to textbooks—and demands for reduced taxes and school budgets, and abbreviated federal aid to education, cause blacks to envision America sweeping the problem of the ghetto schools under the rug.

President Nixon has continually hinted that the interests of the country as a whole are not necessarily to be defined in terms of the interests of a racial minority, which is interpreted by many to mean that blacks must take a back seat again. Mr. Nixon prefers compliance by "good faith" rather than by "educational disruption," which means only one thing—especially in the Northern suburbs and in the great part of the American cities—segregation as usual. Before the 1971 Supreme Court ruling, he denounced bussing and other procedures that fit schools into a racial grid but were necessary to achieve desegregation. President Nixon previously has insisted that education must come first and desegregation must be accommodated to the principle of "neighborhood" schools. Similarly, he has distinguished between "integration" and "quality education," contradicting the previous Supreme Court rulings, and, rather than promoting integration, he has proposed to improve segregated schools.

The Court has now ruled that desegregation plans cannot be limited to the "neighborhood" school and that bussing is a legitimate tool of school desegregation. It remains to be seen just to what extent the President will modify his views. But this conflict between the judicial and executive branches of the government reflects the American dilemma over integration. The Supreme Court may interpret the law, but the President (and Mr. Nixon seems to represent the majority of white America) must enforce the law, and in some ways he has failed to do so. The President claims that he is for law and order; yet, he is reluctant to use all the power of the law vigorously against segregation, reflecting the majority of white America. There is no reason to believe that another president will be more "liberal," for the president reflects the majority view of the country, and white majority seems to be growing more conservative and anti-black. Also, it seems that the Supreme Court is becoming more conservative and some of the judges that Nixon appointed have a known distaste for racial desegregation.

The country believed in gradualism, not because gradualism was just or proper but because it permitted us to mask our real feelings. Gradualism still remains a virtue because integration *was* not and still *is* not the nation's primary concern. Most of the schools and society will remain segregated because the great majority of whites want to maintain the *status quo* and will formulate laws to maintain segregation, read the narrowest interpretation of Supreme Court desegregation rulings, or, if necessary, break the law to prevent it. Residual racism surfaces whenever blacks push for equality and integration—and now, for control of their own schools and communities.

Although recent surveys seem to reveal a decline in white prejudice and a willingness among whites to live next to blacks and send their children to desegregated schools, the increasing segregation in the North, the general racial polarization of the country, and the explosive outbursts of anger and hatred over recent bussing suggest that the polls may not reflect a true picture of white feelings toward blacks. White respondents may merely be influenced by social norms. The average white person seems to hold prejudicial feelings toward nonwhites, and especially blacks, but when queried he sometimes expresses nonprejudicial attitudes.

Although many whites feel inner resentment toward blacks, they now accord them equal treatment in their overt behavior because of social and legal pressure. Obviously, this type of phenomenon inflicts less harm on blacks; nevertheless, whites can easily be moved by new laws and norms which could be harmful to blacks and other minorities; the history of America's treatment of nonwhites is imbued with several examples— black slavery, Indian reservations and genocide, Chinese exclusion, and Japanese "relocation" camps.

American Race Relations. The reasons why whites do not want to integrate with blacks are rooted in American race relations. It is primarily based on a two-category system, a term first used by Warner (1953), in which whites are viewed as superior to nonwhites, where a "we-they" distinction is implied. To be sure, attitudes of white superiority and the desire to maintain the *status quo* are held by most whites—including average, decent, and honorable people.

The white power structure has resorted to one or more of the four methods (stages) for maintaining its relations with nonwhites: (1) prejudice, (2) discrimination, (3) segregation, and (4) extraordinary solutions (apartheid, exclusion, and extermination). This nation has often used one of these three methods in its relations with nonwhites and especially blacks; however, on occasions, the nation has resorted to extraordinary solutions, i.e., various forms of apartheid for blacks, Indians, and the Japanese; exclusion for the Chinese; and action toward Indians that comes close to complete extermination. Below is a table based on Daniels and Kitano (1968, p. 12), which illustrates these four methods of maintaining the two-category system.

Table 2 [5]

*The Four Stages of Maintaining the
Two-Category System*

	Stages	*Belief*	*Action-effects*	*Primary mechanisms*
	1	Prejudice	Avoidance	Stereotyping, informally patterned rules governing integration.
Ordinary solutions	2	Discrimination	Deprivation	More formal rules, norms, laws, and agreements.
	3	Segregation	Insulation	If the out-group is perceived as stepping over the line, there may be lynchings and other warnings.
Extraordinary solutions	4	A. Apartheid, concentration camps [6]	Isolation	A major trigger such as war is necessary; out-group perceived as a real threat or danger to the existence of the host culture. Ordinary mechanisms (for example, Stages 1, 2 and 3) have failed.
		B. Expulsion, exile	Exclusion	
		C. Extermination	Genocide	

[5] Roger Daniels and Harry H. L. Kitano, *American Racism: Exploration of the Nature of Prejudice,* © 1970. By permission of Prentice-Hall, Inc., Englewood Cliffs, N.J.

[6] Offshoots of concentration camps which also lead to isolation are reservation camps (used for the Indians) and "relocation" camps (used for the Japanese).

These methods (stages) are racist in the sense that they are originally based on assumptions of genetic inferiority of the target population and their effects help maintain such assumptions. These methods in various times have become accepted as laws, norms, and values; in effect, they have become part of the social order. And it is in the interaction of man's needs and fears with laws, norms, and values that institutions have been formed and have been adaptively shaped. Once the institutions have been formed, they acquire a life of their own, a functional autonomy; and henceforth, they play an important role in shaping individuals who grow up in their sphere of influence. "Man shapes his institutions but he is also shaped by them." By virtue of these racist methods and institutions the health, educational, social, and economic standards of the target group have become traduced and self-validating. For example, most blacks receive insufficient medical attention, attend inferior schools, live in depressed houses, are not well dressed, and have fewer job opportunities—all of which together become cyclical and freeze blacks into a second-class status. It is unnecessary to tell blacks they are inferior. Because of their status, most of them grow to feel inferior—to have self-doubts and weakened self-concepts—and in doing so accept the views of the larger society.

The process of acceptance starts at an early age—as soon as the child begins to interact with people at home and in the community, as soon as he has contact with the mass media and larger society. By the time the black child reads the current literature on black pride, it is usually too late. He or his older contemporaries may overcompensate with slogans, symbols, and names, but his personality has already been detrimentally affected—which is difficult to admit, and most blacks will not admit this to whites (especially now, with today's racial polarization) or even among themselves unless they are honest with their feelings.

On the other hand, most whites grow to feel superior and even arrogant toward blacks. The difference in status between blacks and whites reproduces and confirms the prejudicial image of blacks as something inferior; the myth becomes "self-fulfilling" and is used to justify the social order. By the time the white student hears the democratic slogans of equality, it is usually too late for him, too. Intellectually and emotionally, he is usually convinced that blacks are inferior; he sees it all around him —in school, in their jobs, the way they live, the clothes they wear, their different life style. Indeed, black popular rhetoric and white social science have little chance of success when they must battle against the social order, actual behavior patterns, and ingrained feelings. (This does not mean that the cycle cannot be broken. New laws which are enforced and preferential treatment would help reduce the problem.)

Keeping blacks down in a subclass keeps whites up, especially with regard to jobs, feelings of superiority, and general status. Granted, keeping blacks in a subclass is not all economically beneficial for whites; it increases welfare, mental health and crime costs which must be supported by taxes; it keeps down the GNP and the wages of unskilled white labor. In the final analysis, however, it keeps the whole share of the economic pie relatively larger for whites and insures a larger degree of white job security and promotions. As black demands become reality, there is a threat to white political power, too. Thus, the gains of one group involves the loss of power and prestige by another. Blacks cannot gain in power and prestige without some loss by whites.

Of course blacks have made considerable educational and economic gains within the last two decades, and an increasing number of blacks (disregarding the present economic recession and inflation) are entering middle-class status. However, the economic gap between blacks and whites is increasing as a result of the growing GNP. Blacks, although economically better off than ever before, are probably more psychologically deprived than in the past. Write Broom and Glenn (1965), "Negro Americans are on a treadmill. They must keep gaining on whites in education and occupation simply to stay the same distance behind in income [p. 119]." The problem is compounded by two additional factors. First, although job discrimination may be subsiding, the technological revolution discriminates against the poor educational and job qualifications of blacks. Second, black demand for equality is no longer a demand for "equal opportunity" but a demand for "equality of results." The trouble is, the white populace is at best willing to accept the former demand but not the latter demand because it would mean discrimination in reverse. Blacks, on the other hand, claim that preferential treatment is needed to make up for 200 years of slavery and another 100 years of discrimination.

Although many whites sympathize with the plight of blacks and may not be overtly prejudiced, still they are reluctant to have blacks move in next to them because of fear that the value of their property will decrease or that their children's schools will become inferior. Writes Glenn (1965), whites "do not want the problems of [blacks] solved at their expense. As usual, humanitarian motives lose faith in the face of threatened self-interest [p. 113]." For the greater part, then, those whites who support the black cause do so without great sacrifice or loss of self-interest. Democratic values and ideals, or what is right, are superseded by personal needs and interests. For example, there was Northern support for black rights in the South since the people had little at stake in the Southern way of life. Such people devoted less time for the black cause when it reached their home states and opposed their own life style and security.

Holding racist views [7] should be distinguished from actual racist behavior. All people, no matter what their color, hold such views—it is only the group in power who can freely act out its feelings if it wishes. Racist views vary from one individual to another and also from one situation to another. For example, a white person may get along with his black colleague at work, but, should the black person and his family attempt to move into an all white neighborhood where his colleague resides, the white person's attitude might surface and his behavior might change.

Lower-class and working-class whites are the most sensitive to the social and economic gains made by blacks, largely because of their own socio-economic insecurities; they are usually the first group to resist blacks. Middle-class whites are now becoming sensitive to the increasing demands made by college educated and middle-income blacks. The rich are still largely unaffected by black demands and still feel insulated and secure enough to be "liberal"; however, the rich who live in the cities are finding that their middle-class buffer zones are disappearing as the latter group migrates to the suburbs. These city rich are no longer as "liberal" as they were in the past. Of course, many white students now find it very easy to be "liberal" since they have no homes or property to protect, or their children's education to worry about. In short, while most whites are willing to concede that the law is right in demanding integration, they defer from implementing the law because it threatens their own interests. Even most white "liberals" who advocate integration run away from it or try to prevent it in their own schools and communities; where they do "accept" integration, it is not usually because they really want it but because of their guilt feelings or because they are "trapped" by their own rhetoric.

The Widening Gap. It is difficult for blacks to move out of the ghetto, and perhaps no black person has ever made enough money to completely escape the eye of persecution and discrimination. Rather than integrating blacks, the larger society has preserved segregation through legal and "accidental" arrangements. Despite words, recommendations, and new laws, the integration gap between blacks and whites may be so wide that, in effect, there are now, as the *New York Times* (1967) maintains, "two countries":

---

[7] A strict definition of racism would be linked to views based on the assumption of the genetic inferiority of the subgroup. The two-category system described above, and the laws, norms, and values that evolve from it, are rooted in this assumption and help perpetuate the assumption.

> There is a country of whites—relatively prosperous, unencum-
> bered for the most part by insurmountable social and economical
> barriers, free to shape its own destiny. And there is the country
> of the Negroes—a country whose capital is the ghetto, whose
> constitution states that "all men are created equal, but whitey
> comes first," and whose statistics still spell out a largely un-
> changing picture, despite new laws on the books . . . (p. 12).[8]

And, the U.S. Riot Commission Report (1968) begins with the following statement:

> Our nation is moving toward two societies, one black, one white
> —separate and unequal. Reaction to . . . [the] disorders has
> quickened the movement and deepened the division. Discrimina-
> tion and segregation have long permeated much of American
> life; they now threaten the future of every American (p. 1).

The division of the country is keenly illustrated by the white out-migration to the suburbs. From 1950 to 1970, as many as 35 million Americans moved to the suburbs, and the trend is increasing. Although several
factors affected this movement, the fear of black people and the continuous black migration from the rural South to the Northern cities were
the major factors. Thus, it is estimated that by 1985 seven of the ten
largest cities, and many of the smaller cities, will have a black majority,
and this is already true of the black student enrollment in eight of these
large cities. As the movement of whites continues to the suburbs, the
city governments are losing their tax base, industry, and political power;
in fact, in some cities the officials are purposely transferring new responsibilities to the state so as to avoid the eventual black control of
city-based institutions. Unless the white city out-migration to the suburbs ceases, the future of the American ghetto is extremely bleak. Writes
Downs (1968):

> . . . when Negroes become the dominant political force in many
> large central cities, they may understandably demand radical
> changes in present policies. At the same time, major private
> capital investment in those cities might virtually cease if white-
> dominated firms and industries decided the risks of involvement
> there were too great. In light of recent disorders, this seems very
> likely. Such withdrawal of private capital has already occurred
> in almost every single ghetto area in the U.S. Even if private
> investment continues, big cities containing high proportions of

---

low-income Negroes would need substantial income transfers from the federal government to meet the demands of their electorates for improved services and living conditions.

But by that time, Congress will be more heavily influenced by representatives of the suburban electorate. The suburbs will comprise 41 per cent of our total population by 1985, as opposed to 33 per cent in 1960. Central cities will decline from 31 per cent to 27 per cent. Under a present-policies strategy, this influential suburban electorate will be over 95 per cent white, whereas the central-city population in all metropolitan areas together will be slightly over 60 per cent white. The suburban electorate will be much wealthier than the central-city population, which will consist mainly of Negroes and older whites. Yet even the suburbs will be feeling the squeeze of higher local government costs generated by rising service salaries. Hence the federal government may refuse to approve the massive income transfers from suburbs to central cities that the mayors of the latter will desperately need in order to placate their relatively deprived electorates. After all, many big-city mayors are already beseeching the federal government for massive aid—including Republicans like John Lindsay—and their electorates are not yet dominated by low-income Negroes.

Thus the present policies strategy, if pursued for any long period of time, might lead to a simultaneous political and economic "confrontation" in many metropolitan areas. Such a "confrontation" would involve mainly Negro, mainly poor, and fiscally bankrupt larger central cities on the one hand, and mainly white, much wealthier, but highly taxed suburbs on the other hand. Some older suburbs will also have become Negro by that time, but the vast majority of suburbs will still be "lily white." A few metropolitan areas may seek to avoid the political aspects of such a confrontation by shifting to some form of metropolitan government designed to prevent Negroes from gaining political control of central cities. Yet such a move will hardly eliminate the basic segregation and relative poverty generating hostility in the urban Negro population. In fact, it might increase that population's sense of frustration and alienation.

In my opinion, there is a serious question whether American society in its present form could survive such a "confrontation." If the Negro population felt itself wrongly "penned in" and discriminated against, as seems likely, many of its members might be driven to supporting the kind of irrational rebellion now being preached by a tiny minority. Considering the level of violence we have encountered already, it is hard to believe that the conditions that might emanate from a prolonged present-policies strategy would not generate much more. Yet the Negro community cannot hope to defeat the white community in a pitched battle. It is out-numbered 9 to 1 in population and vastly more than that in resources. Thus any massive resort to violence by Negroes would probably bring even more massive retaliation by whites. This could lead to a kind of urban *apartheid*, with martial law in cities, enforced residence of Negroes in segregated areas, and a drastic reduction in personal freedom for both groups, especially Negroes.

Such an outcome would obviously violate all American traditions of individual liberty and Constitutional law. It would destroy "the American dream" of freedom and equal opportunity for all. Therefore, to many observers this result is unthinkable. They believe that we would somehow "change things" before they occurred. This must mean that either the present-policies [segregation] strategy would not lead to the kind of confrontation I have described, or we would abandon that strategy before the confrontation occurred (pp. 1354–55).

Downs goes on to point out that it is doubtful that the central cities will consist of a stable, well-to-do black citizenry capable of supporting its own community and government. Since blacks and other nonwhite minorities will form a larger share of the total city population than now, the percentage of central city people living in the midst of poverty or just above the poverty level will probably increase (to approximately 33%). Although it is possible that nonwhite incomes might increase faster than the forecast, the substitution of relatively poor blacks and other racial minorities for a middle-income populace will most likely counterbalance increases in the incomes of nonwhites. Thus, blacks and other racial minorities will be in the majority, but they will be just as poor, or poorer, as now in real terms. Moreover, the costs for running the cities and providing services will increase. Future cities will become larger ghettoes and will have higher costs, but fewer resources and income than now. In contrast, the suburbs will control the state and federal governments and will most likely become wealthier than they are now because of the increased middle-class tax base and the transfer of many businesses and industries away from the city. All these factors lead to the confrontation described above. Downs suggests that the only feasible strategy for avoiding such a confrontation is to provide massive aid and integrate the cities now—before it is too late. However, this seems unlikely in view of today's racial polarization and increased out-migration of whites, coupled by the Supreme Court's recent ruling which permits the suburbs to block low-income housing—in effect, which discriminates against blacks moving into white suburbs, in turn, making the suburbs more attractive to fleeing whites.

The confrontation that Downs mentions is happening now, on a piecemeal basis in the form of urban riots. Referring to these riots, the *New York Times* (1967) also paints a dim future:

> . . . in society, as in the world of physics, every action produces a reaction. As the trend toward violence grows among blacks so does its counterpart among frightened whites. More and more the voice of the racist demogogue is heard, and cries of Black Power invoke the echo of White Power. In community after community more and more Negroes and whites take advantage of the nation's insanely lax laws on firearms and buy rifles, pistols, and other weapons. . . .

> The American people are staring down a road that could lead to the ultimate catastrophe, in which the struggle would be not between the police and rooters but between masses of Negroes and whites engaged in war in the streets, the enemy defined only by the color of his skin.

> . . . the threat of confrontation between Negro and white in the United States today is the most serious problem this nation faces . . . (p. 1).[9]

Although the riots seem to have dwindled since the above statement was written, welfare benefits have recently been curtailed in many cities, the recession economy has cut into available jobs for unskilled blacks, and most businesses are unable to offer extra employment as in the late 1960s. Latest 1971 figures provided by the U.S. Labor Department show a 44.9% unemployment level among black teenagers in the poorest areas of the 100 largest cities, as against 18.1% for white teenagers. In the more affluent areas of these cities, unemployment for black teenagers is 27.9% compared with 16.6% for their white counterparts. (It is this teenage group that tends to have a low frustration tolerance and tends to riot, as indicated below. The black teenagers and the black Vietnam war returnees who are unemployed at the rate of approximately one out of five combine for a potential dynamite situation which could ignite, thus repeating, and perhaps becoming worse than, the summer riots of the late 1960s.) Even at the national adult level, the so-called narrowing job gap between blacks and whites is reversing. The government puts overall unemployment for blacks at 10.5% and for whites at 5.7%. To be sure, the

---

[9] *Ibid.*

growing frustration of blacks plus their villifying descriptions of whites as well as the growing backlash of whites have further divided the nation. As the ghettoes in the cities become larger and poorer, which Downs (1968) contends is a strong possibility, there is the hazard, as the *New York Times* (1967) states, "this country could be torn asunder [p. 1]."

Even if the white nation were willing to integrate with the black nation, or even if there were enough whites left in the cities to integrate with blacks (though the white percentage will soon be too small for genuine integration), integration as it has been carried out under the present black-white situation does not seem to be the answer. Integration now means to go through the motions of reform without real reform. Interracial contact alone is not the answer; the contact must be on equal basis where there is mutual cooperation. Otherwise, the present inferior-superior relationship between blacks and whites will continue, thus reproducing the same prejudiced social order. To be sure, blacks must integrate on an equal basis with whites, but they are not ready for this now. What blacks must first do is to gain control of their own institutions and upgrade their social and economic status. Because the color barrier prevents them from assimilating into the American mainstream, they must enter it on their own terms. As Carmichael and Hamilton (1967) maintain:

> ... black people must organize themselves without regard for what is traditionally acceptable, precisely because the traditional approaches have failed. It means that black people must make demands without regard to their initial "respectability," precisely because "respectable" demands have not been sufficient (p. 166).

Granted, there is no way blacks can operate as an independent island surrounded by a hostile and larger white community. Blacks still need white financial support, too, and they can improve their status only as much as the white power structure permits; it is actually in the white community where the power lies to change the social order. Change can possibly occur if whites leave the black country—unless welcomed by blacks. Indeed, it is time, now, to stop exploiting black people. Blacks have the right to control their own destiny, especially since they are for the greater part not welcomed now into white schools or society. It is time to stop the rhetoric about integration. The majority of whites do not want it, and perhaps it is not in the best interests for the majority of blacks to integrate while second-class to whites.

Blacks must be allowed to control their own institutions—just like other white minorities were permitted control over their communities before they assimilated into the larger society. The black educated and leadership class should remain in the ghetto, rather than divorcing themselves from their people and also failing to gain complete acceptance of the white community. In particular, it is this black educated group that should liberate itself from ideological dependence on white norms and life style; it is this black group that should manage black institutions and provide the leadership for the uneducated and lower-class blacks. The trouble is most educated and upward mobile blacks find the ghetto intolerable and prefer to leave it.

Blacks need to manage their own institutions not because they are isolationists or racists but because of their frustration resulting from their second-class status and from resistance to genuinely integrated schools and society. Black control of the schools and other social institutions does not necessarily have to lead to permanent isolation; it can mean that blacks find new ways to work with the larger society on a more equal basis so they can eventually become a part of the total system and not lose their identity or be frozen into a second-class position. Creation of independent black institutions would not represent a step backward, but permit the black community to integrate later with whites on a relatively more equal basis.

The "Liberals' " Reaction to Black Power and Black Violence

As for white "liberals" who have traditionally advocated school reform and integration, they are now confused and divided over the issue of black power and local control because it enhances political reform, or at least change, that is contradictory to the concept of integration. The "liberal" rejection of black power and black-controlled schools may become a greater problem than the opposition of the white conservative or overt racist, for the black revolution—despite the current rhetoric about whites being unwelcome—still depends on "liberal" acceptance and support. While it is fashionable among "liberals" to support progressive causes such as the black social revolution, and while "liberal" guilt over how white society has dehumanized blacks causes many to reluctantly support black demands and make a mockery of their goals for integration, many "liberals" are dissatisfied because they sense that they will not have as many job opportunities in the black community, nor will they be in the position to "save" the black man.

It must be recognized that "liberals" in America are relatively powerless. Although they are free to speak and write, they have little influence in shaping the power structure; they are not integrated with or "meshed" in the political, military, and business mainstream—as are European liberals. To some extent the "liberal" alliance with blacks is not only linked to guilt feelings and a sense of morality, but also to a drive for power. Yet black power demands the rejection of white influence, including the "liberal," which in turn adds to the "liberals' " dilemma. In a broad sense, it might be argued that all behavior, including the white "liberals' " behavior, is based on personal interests, i.e., preventing or relieving guilt, enhancing satisfaction, self-righteousness, and economical or political gain. If this is the case, and the white "liberal" is denied the opportunity to fulfill his personal interests because blacks reject his participation or threaten his economical security or his already limited political power, why should he continue to support the black cause? Similarly, the white community, in general, is against the black power movement, because it rejects white dominance and substitutes black control of black institutions. Whites would lose their economic profits from the ghetto, their land-holding interests, businesses, slum houses, etc.; some whites would lose their political power, and many whites would lose their jobs. Whites tend to feel comfortable with the present black-white social order and tend to feel that black control would mean a new set of norms and laws, possibly black reprisals. In fact, many whites fear, even have paranoia of, black dominance—dominance of their own ghetto.

While among many "liberals" it is hackneyed and trite to point out that white racism is a major cause for the black plight, this "wisdom" contradicts the feelings of the majority of whites, and, in the final analysis, power lies with the white majority, not the "liberal." This difference of opinion is illustrated by white America's reaction to the U.S. Riot Commission Report (1968), which condemns white racism as a major source of the urban riots and American racial distemper, a conclusion which is generally accepted by the "liberal" and rejected by the larger white populace. Most whites feel little or no personal guilt toward the black plight; in fact, the increasing black demands seem highly related to the growing white backlash. Although they may admit the guilt of their grandfathers, they are not willing to accept a collective or inherited guilt, and the feelings that whites owe a debt to blacks is rare, even among "liberals." For those "liberals" who accept a collective and inherited guilt for white sins committed against blacks, this is needless masochism. Here, Jonas' (1970) analysis is relevant.

> A large number of liberal whites and movement blacks accept the principle of collective and inherited guilt. Collective guilt means that every member of a group is guilty for the sins or crimes committed by a single member. Thus, every white man is guilty of the oppression committed against black men.

Inherited guilt means that the children of the guilty (and the grandchildren and so forth) are guilty of the crimes perpetrated by their ancestors.

There are some very practical problems with these theories. For example, if collective guilt is valid, are all Negroes guilty for the horrible deeds of those African chiefs who sold their fellow men into slavery? Since virtually all the slave traders were Arabs, are all Arabs today guilty of the crimes committed by a few of their forebears? Just where do we draw the line?

Similarly, with inherited guilt. Since a great many white Americans practiced segregation by day and integration by night during our history, a good many men and women today classified as Negroes have white ancestors. Are they partially guilty for the crimes of their white ancestors or does their black ancestry neutralize the guilt of their white ancestry? Do only the white genes transmit guilt?

The kind of guilt-ridden white liberal we have all encountered is often unstable, unpredictable and too prone to throw in his lot with those who will punish him the most to feed his masochistic needs. Unless you beat him regularly, at least with words, he is very unhappy. And those of us who are working in the freedom struggle simply haven't got enough time to accommodate him or his needs.

His instability you have already witnessed: after the flurry of liberal involvement in the movement in the early and mid-sixties, he moved on to other causes which became the fad—the "in" thing. When the war became the issue, he and his colleagues deserted the freedom struggle in droves, and so they have drifted from Vietnam to population control to the draft to Cambodia to Kent State to ecology to campus issues. Now all of these are valid issues dealing with real problems, but we believe there is only one major national problem, a single priority issue, and that is the historic racial injustice which still prevents the nation's 22 million Negroes from sharing equally in everything that is America. Until this is solved, nothing else matters as much. And if it isn't solved, nothing else will matter (p. 17).[10, 11]

---

[10] © 1970 by the New York Times Company. Reprinted by permission.

[11] Also, in a recent dialogue with James Baldwin, Margaret Mead pointed out that collective and inherited guilt have little meaning for her. For example, she was against the bombing of Hiroshima but had no influence on the decision and, therefore, cannot assume guilt for what was decided without her being a part of it. Such thinking can also be applied to the black-white history of this nation.

Although white America seems preoccupied with racial justice and equality, its methods of deferring real justice and equality have been through organizing proposals, programs, and conferences—mainly prating about race and poverty while debating the wisdom and extent of spending an extra million dollars on still another project. Inaction becomes the major action of the power structure; such people in authority are initially moved by violence and riots, or even the threat of violence or riots. In the long run, however, many recommendations are forgotten, much funds diminish, the illiberal reading of the law tends to prevail, and procrastination and the breaking of the law often resumes. In appearing before the U.S. Riot Commission (1968), Clark mentions this inertia. Referring to the reports of earlier riot commissions, he said:

> I read that report . . . of the 1919 riot in Chicago, and it is as if I were reading the report of the investigating committee on the Harlem riot of '35, the report of the investigating committee on the Harlem riot of '43, the report of the McCone Commission on the Watts riot.
>
> I must again in candor say to you members of this Commission —it is a kind of Alice in Wonderland—with the same moving picture re-shown over and over again, the same analysis, the same recommendations, and the same inaction (p. 483).

In the meantime, the black experience tends to make little improvement on a relative basis, and the existing projects affect only a small percentage of blacks who are in need of such services and assistance. Taking into account the increasing black population and the tightening job market and inflational spiral, the services which are available end up aiding a smaller percentage of black poor each year and have less of an impact on those who are assisted. The blacks who gain are often already middle class, moonlighting on second jobs or being promoted or asked to direct a special program—a high paying position which is often nontenured, based on special funding, often created on an emergency basis, accompanied with little power and authority, basically to handle the "black problem." Blacks recognize white America's reluctance to do anything more than talk, appease blacks with a few emergency programs, or permit a few black "exhibits" into the system. Of course, today almost every city governmental, educational, and social institution needs a "house black." In many cases the new position is somewhat related to youth or student unrest. For selfish reasons, then, some black leaders in the government, colleges, and social agencies seek to keep blacks agitated so as to insure their own jobs.

Among most white "liberals" and among white educators who advocate, in print and in speeches, racial justice and equality, black power, and community control, this author senses an underlying uneasiness, a sense of doubt, alarm, fear, even residual racism at certain times, in conversation with such "good" people. Behind closed doors and among white friends, many "liberals" who often profess to be the friend of the black community renege on their "principles," and blacks surely realize this hypocrisy (indeed, they have realized it since the Civil War ended and supposedly granted them full equality); therefore, they no longer trust well-intentioned whites.

The problem is somewhat illustrated by the anxious white "liberal" who, while working or socializing with blacks, either appears overly friendly or too careful in what he says or does or too desiring to be "educated" or told what to do. In his attempt to show how at ease and secure he is with his black "friend," the white "liberal" sometimes interjects stale "watermelon" or "tap-dancing" jokes, or has an urge to reveal his knowledge about the latest book on race. To be sure, blacks cannot escape from the topic of race among their well-intentioned white "friends," or, for that matter, among themselves. When talking with blacks, the white individual and even the "liberal" tends to subtly indicate that he feels he is talking to a different kind of human being. This is compounded and reinforced by the black individual who often tends to remain aloof or on guard and tends to over analyze what he feels is the subtle but "real" white attitude. Also, most blacks today are unable to envision whites as individuals who wish to work with blacks and who are concerned with helping minority groups. This black myopia often turns a potential white friend into an indifferent, even alienated, individual. Furthermore, many blacks unconsciously prefer and encourage white resistance and alienation, for then it is easier to rationalize their own failure and desire to be weighted down by the heroic cross of oppression.

Even at the colleges and universities, where liberalism is supposed to flourish, discrimination against black professors is a historical fact, as illustrated in the "liberal" North until very recently by the few full-time black faculty members, and especially black chairmen, deans, and other administrators. Today, there is a tendency for Northern institutions of higher learning to engage in preferential treatment in the hiring and promotion of black faculty members. With the exception of the white professors who feel secure in their position and field of study, most whites, including the "liberals," resent this preferential treatment. Thus, a promotion of a black professor is viewed by most whites as being racially and politically tainted—the need for an "instant exhibit." A promotion of a white professor in comparison is still taken for granted. Racial dissonance is perhaps more evident among recent white Ph.D. graduates who feel the job market squeeze and learn that blacks with master's degrees are filling many vacancies in the social sciences; moreover, the black degree is often considered watered-down, based on a recent trend to accept many blacks with an inadequate education into master's and doctoral programs and pass them on based on the criteria of color, not competence, rather than be accused of prejudice. The outcome is that many of these bewildered white graduates are being forced into teaching at the junior college or high school level, where they often wind up teaching a large number of black pupils who need good teachers, but who encounter a covert hostile instructor. And, those who are interested in academic credentials are becoming suspect of the black degree.

To make matters worse, many white professors, because of the fact they are white, have difficulty working with and accepting blacks on an equal basis, and especially on a black superior-white subordinate job-role basis. On the other hand, many black professors, because of the fact they are black, are usually caught within the web of suspicion and hostility. They view their new job or position as a white trick or concession; they often envision that they are promoted to perform as the powerless, functionless "exhibit" or good "nigger."

It is premature and unrealistic to expect black and white America to work together on an equal basis; they have not in the past and today the two races are more polarized. To claim that the two races can harmonize is counter rhetoric to the reality of the white whip and black fist; it contradicts historical facts and present reality. To talk about a black-white society of equality and justice is to refer to a utopia which in America is based on the fabrication of the melting pot, fading folly which does not apply to blacks, which should no longer sedate this now polarized nation. Besides, there is no guarantee that the federal government will continue to intervene for the benefit of blacks. The federal government reflects the interests of the dominant white group and institutions, and, as previously indicated, American history informs us that whites have often shown racist tendencies toward nonwhites, and whites today are becoming more conservative and alienated by black demands. Without trying to sing a dance of doom, this author believes fear and hostility engulf the land. We are already in the midst of a racial illness that may eventually lacerate the social fabric of the nation.

Campbell and Schuman (1968), in their study of fifteen cities across the nation, point out that most blacks believe that better employment and improved communication between blacks and whites, and an end to discrimination, would prevent future riots. However, most whites believe that more repressive methods are needed, e.g., police control. Whereas most blacks point to discrimination and poor living conditions as the major causes of the previous riots, most whites see militants and undesirables as the major causes. While more than 33% of the blacks interviewed feel there has not been much real improvement since the mid 1950s, more than 95% of the whites believe that such progress has been made.

Since many of the younger blacks interviewed did not experience the more overt forms of discrimination characterized in the early 1950s, it is assumed that black youth would not say there has been much progress in eliminating racial discrimination. Also it is this young group that tends to be more militant and feels that violence gets more results. Campbell and Schuman show that the majority of blacks (at least on the questionnaire)* reject the use of violence both as a strategy and as an approach they would take part in themselves; they prefer nonviolent protest, e.g., picketing, boycotts, and appeals to civil rights organizations. However, the mass media tends to focus on the violence of blacks which, in turn, feeds the original prejudicial feeling of whites toward nonwhites. Hence, although the majority of blacks reject the use of violence, it is safe to assume that many whites feel that blacks hate them, and every time they see a black fist in papers or on television or hear a black power slogan they become anxious.

A small minority of vocal and extremist blacks are threatening urban riots and revolution; foolishly, they contend that the black-white conflict cannot be resolved without violence. According to Campbell and Schuman, although the percentage of blacks who advocate violence is about the same percentage of whites who advocate counterviolence, the numbers add up to about a 10:1 difference because of the difference in the black-white population.[12, 13] It is reasonable to argue that a small percentage of black extremist thinkers should not be taken seriously; this

---

* *Postscript:* Blacks have had to learn to deal with the "man," and one way to deal with him is to provide the "right" answers or those deemed proper. Even if the interviewer were black, he is often considered a tool of the white establishment, someone not to be trusted.

[12] Fitting into the common assumption that youth is less conservative and more prone to advocate violence, the authors show that there is a strong consistency between age and those respondents (both black and white) who advocate violence. Thus, what is interpreted as a racial phenomenon seems more associated with age and youth masculinity; however, the racial aspects are exaggerated by the mass media, which adds fuel to black rhetoric and white fears.

[13] The riots can also be viewed as a primitive means of mass rebellion against the white "colonialists." In this connection, the police are seen as doing the work of the white dominant group—restricting the movement of blacks, harassing and attacking them, shooting to kill them for alleged criminal acts, and controlling ghetto uprisings.

small percentage may only represent approximately 10% (or less) of the black population, but this adds up to as many as 2.2 million people who are easily able to interchange thoughts and possibly unify their strategies because of modern facilities in communication, mass media, and transportation. It is this type of group—small, determined, and well-organized—that often creates national trends and influences political policy because the mass of people are indifferent.

In their study, Campbell and Schuman indicate that only 6% of the black respondents advocate a separate black nation; however, they too contend that a small percentage of blacks represents large numbers and can have an influential impact on the nation; they write:

> The study . . . counts only Negroes in the 15 cities, there being an unknown but undoubtedly large number of individuals with similar beliefs in other American cities. Thus when we say that six percent of the sample advocates the formation of a separate black nation, we are implying that some 200,000 Negroes in these 15 cities feel so little a part of American society that they favor withdrawing allegiance from the United States and in some sense establishing a separate national entity.
>
> Unlike election polls where it is usually correct to focus on majority or at least plurality figures, "small" percentages in this study must not be disregarded as unimportant. In a formal election six percent of the vote means little, but in a campaign to change minds and influence policies, six percent of a population can represent a considerable force. This is particularly true when the six percent represents deviation from a traditional position, since it is likely that many of those who hold to the majority position do so with little thought or commitment. To deviate from a very widely held norm probably requires more conviction than to hold to it, and if we could estimate this extra factor and weigh it into the results we might well find the force behind black nationalism to be considerably greater than its numbers suggest. Finally, the high degree of residential and general social segregation in these cities promotes communication and association among such individuals, and provides them with easy access to just the audience they wish to reach (p. 17).

The authors conclude that an assassination, war, or race riot could radicalize these black separationists. The outcome, of course, would be disastrous.

Although there is no official policy of mass suppression of blacks, white individuals, and some of whom are in governmental and military positions, may already be contemplating this as the "solution." The white power structure is willing to make limited concessions, in part because of violence or the threat of violence. But there is a tipping point where violence leads to repression. Increased Black Panther and terrorist tactics, even though by a tiny minority, only increase the weight of the police club and, even worse, could drive the *haute monde* of Congress and the Pentagon to employ "total measures." Every government, to be sure, no matter what its political gestalt, must react to violence and terrorism or else it will cease to exist—and many governments in the past have overreacted. Under normal circumstances a black-white compromise would be expected, but racism does not lead to normal behavior and the discord between both races is probably too wide. To prevent a worsening situation, perhaps the only solution is for whites to leave the black country.

We must recognize that racism is a global, human phenomenon, soiling even the idols of various racial, social, and political groups; affecting all people—black, white, red, and yellow; poor and rich; new left to ultra right; average, decent, honorable people. Also, we must recognize that any group which possesses power tends to keep the other group(s) subordinate. If the dominant and subordinate groups are divided along race, then the dominant group also tends to exhibit racist behaviors. In terms of power, in this country whites are the ruling group and blacks are the subject group. If the dominant-subordinate groups were reversed, the direction of the racist behavior probably would be reversed, too.

The best we can do is to control our racism, to be sensitive and honest about it. It is necessary to stop deceiving ourselves into believing that our racial attitudes can be changed on a mass scale. To change attitudes requires structural change, but the populace is unwilling to accept such change because it possesses racist feelings. Thus, the barrier that causes the problem and the problem itself are reinforcing. Many readers may feel that they are not racists; such "good" people are most likely deceiving themselves. The individual can perhaps be made aware of his own feelings by the way he reacts to a mixed racial couple or the discomfort he feels and the overt or imaginary hostility he senses if he rides on a bus or train filled with people of the opposite race.

On an individual basis, of course, some blacks and whites can work together as equals, even with the white being in a subordinate job position; they can be genuine friends and accept each other as human beings. Surely, many readers can personally verify this type of relationship. Yet, there is, at best, a little *arteigen*—what the Germans refer to as the Nordic mythical racial soul—in all of us, and this collectively emerges as part of the social order. Now is the time to be honest with ourselves and stop mouthing third-grade slogans about the social order. Away from the quiet offices and libraries, away from the desks and cubicles—wherever this chapter is being read—is the real world, and it is time that we recognize its social order, as well as our real attitudes and behaviors. Also, at times we are probably all victims of our rhetoric, racism, and emotions, and this author and the reader, as well as the white "liberal" and black militant, are not exceptions to these human weaknesses.

False Research on Blacks

Biases and Limitations. Some critical comments will be offered concerning the biases and limitations of research on black families and culture; most of these methodological weaknesses lead to false research (which can also be applied to poverty groups). "Facts" often support myths and stereotypes, and myths often magnify the "facts." The usefulness of this false research is that eventually no sound evidence is needed to prove a point, or better yet, everything is evidence, whatever fits into the stereotypes and myths. For example, any unpleasant variable or event occurring within the subject population can be used to prove a point. After a while there is little need to even look for negative behaviors; "conventional wisdom" and folklore tend to prevail and there is little need to prove the "obvious." (A reinterpretation of the data is possible but this usually proceeds at a slow pace and often must first be accepted by most of the authorities in the field.)

1. *Problems of reliability and validity.* Social science research is often weakened by problems and limitations of reliability and validity. Enough has been written about these weaknesses to make reiteration redundant. It need only be pointed out that these weaknesses are also germane to research on blacks, and perhaps more obvious and blatant.

2. *Hypotheses.* Research is usually limited to specific hypotheses or basic questions of the design. The investigator, therefore, often misses important variables and new data unless he is willing to change his original hypotheses to correct the distortions inherent in the original design. The social scientist rarely makes the necessary changes because of lack of time, money, manpower, or knowledge— or, in most cases, because of practicality.

3. *Researcher's expectations.* The researcher's expectations contaminate the study by interacting with the results, but to what extent is difficult to determine. There is a tendency to overlook or underemphasize data that does not support preconceived hunches.

These problems are perhaps greater with research on race because of strong attitudes, biases, and possibly even emotionalism regarding the topic.

4. *Sample population.* Most research on blacks is based on a comparison with whites. Investigators are often content with finding subjects without going through methods of systematic sampling. Rarely are the samples representative or randomized from the larger population because the investigators have problems obtaining willing subjects and consent from parents, practitioners, and, now, community participants. Just as the quiet child in class often receives little attention from the teacher in comparison to the noisy child, the black child (or adult) who is mentally healthy, "normal," or "average" receives less attention by the social scientist than blacks whose psychological and cognitive development seem impaired. Finally, generalizations of the results are unwarranted except as they are made in reference to similar populations.

5. *Statistical methods.* Many of the commonly used statistical methods employed for assessing differences and relationships between and among groups (black and white) or subgroups (within black and white groups) are fully applicable only when random samples from a defined population are used. Since randomization is rare, the conclusions drawn from these statistical procedures are questionable, perhaps even invalid.

6. *Misleading literature.* There is a tendency among social scientists to refer to original reports and studies without reading the entire document itself but rather relying on secondary sources and other authors for interpretations and conclusions. For example, how many social scientists have actually read the Coleman Report, the U.S. Commission Riot Report, or the Jensen study? Yet social scientists constantly refer to these documents, quote them, and support or criticize the findings of these documents by relying on someone else's interpretations and conclusions. In other cases, the social scientist merely reads the conclusions of a specific study, without reading the design and procedures of the study. The outcome of this practice is that misleading data and false interpretations can easily be promulgated by the fact that few social scientists or writers actually read the original or complete source. Closely related to this problem is the fact that some social scientists, and especially doctoral students, have a tendency to refer to and elaborate on the research which supports their own hypotheses, conclusions, or the implications of their studies while overlooking contradictory data. This practice tends to transform into "conventional wisdom" research which

should be qualified and which should be subject to opposing views.
7. *Soft data.* There is a tendency to draw conclusions from an inadequate sample, inadequate descriptions of the sample, and an
inadequate number of studies. Some of the research on blacks, and
especially on the poor, are based on observational and anecdotal
data as well as interviews—all of which are highly susceptible to
the biases and knowledge of the investigator conducting the study.
Indeed, there is danger in making statements or generalizations from
the descriptions by popular but dubious researchers, i.e., Oscar
Lewis, *Children of Sanchez* or *La Vida,* Herbert Gans, *The Urban
Villagers,* and Robert Coles, *Children of Crisis.* Assumptions about
an individual, family, or interest group should not be applied to a
larger group. The individual is a member of several subgroups (as
are families and interest groups) and has his own unique personality
which differs from the larger reference group. Except for the value
of suggesting hypotheses or perhaps encouraging new concepts, the
above studies have little social science value for purposes of generalizations and conclusions.

8. *Variables and relationships.* Most research on blacks report
casual relationships of variables and ignore cause-effect relationships of variables. The outcome is that the social scientist often
talks about broad associations and not causes of problems or specific remedies to counteract these causes. Variables often are not
controlled, and even when they are controlled, they often overlap
and couple to produce still other variables which are not controlled.
Many of the findings break down as soon as new variables are introduced. Since in real life a host of variables affect the individual or
group, the results never tell the whole story because all of the
variables (some of which we may not even know) are not controlled.
Indeed, the students' attitudes and behaviors depend on their
"whole" environment; abstracting part of the whole, or measuring
a few variables, is bound to distort reality and be misleading. A
well-designed study may show certain variables are related; nevertheless, it is unlikely to reveal other variables which influence, or
are more important in determining, the results.

9. *Income.* Income is perhaps the most important variable to control when conducting studies on blacks, or between blacks and
whites. Most of the data on blacks focus on the lower class; therefore, it cannot be generalized to blacks in other income brackets. In
some cases, lower-class blacks are unwittingly compared with
middle-class whites. In the cases where the income variable is controlled, there is rarely careful differential between the various layers

of poverty (ranging from chronically poor to short-term poor) and between the lower-lower, lower, and lower-middle groups and working-class families. Inconsistency among poverty research findings may be due to the differences in subgroups within the general status of poverty—differences which have not been controlled.

10. *Examiner's and examinee's race.* Both the examiner's and examinee's races interact to affect the results of the study. The examiner's attitude toward and rapport with the respondents or subjects, which is in part affected by their racial and social characteristics, may retard or increase cognitive scores or affect attitudes in an undetermined way. For example, black subjects usually score higher on cognitive tests with black examiners. Also, the subjects respond to the racial and social characteristics of the examiner, which in turn affects the results of the study. Subjects often withhold information from examiners or interviewers perceived as members of another group.

11. *White, middle-class norms.* The instruments used for research are almost always based on white, middle-class norms. Not only is this unfair and invalid when testing blacks or the poor, but it obscures the dynamics of black and poverty culture. To be sure, attitudes, behaviors, and cognitive scores cannot be accurately assessed with regard to "normality" and "abnormality" or "average" and "below and above the mean" unless assessed in terms of the subjects' cultures. What is considered "normal" by the larger society may be considered "abnormal" by the subculture and vice versa. When comparing blacks with whites or the poor with the middle class, the instrument used should first be standardized on the populations being tested. Otherwise, a white middle-class yardstick is being employed to measure nonwhite, often nonmiddle-class groups, subsequently, comparing them with the larger society on foreign terms.

12. *Black-white differences.* Most of the research is in terms of the differences between blacks and whites. This trend is based somewhat on the orientation of the investigator who looks for significant differences or on the orientation of the author who compares these two groups for writing a manuscript. In effect, the differences between the two racial groups are usually exaggerated and the similarities are usually ignored or underemphasized. Because social scientists tend to work with these group differences, they often fail to consider within-group variations and differential subgroups within the larger black group, e.g., sex, age, education, and income.

13. *Implications of significant differences.* The social scientist often ignores the implications of significant differences. In most cases, he

does not point out that, although a specific group does exhibit charactertistics which are significantly different in other groups being compared, this does not necessarily mean that the total population exhibits these differences. Results are usually based on small samples. Even if the sample groups are randomized, there is no guarantee that the biases are operating in the same direction and to the same extent with the total population. There is no guarantee that a few extreme cases are not causing the observed differences between or among the different groups. Even when there are significant differences, in most cases the majority of the individuals in the various groups being studied are more alike than different.

14. *Interpretations.* There is a tendency to be careless about the interpretation of the findings—to interpret without giving due regard to the limitations of the study and without making necessarily qualifying statements. Often, sweeping generalizations are made which are based on tentative findings and unwarranted inferences. The assumptions and interpretations about blacks, or for that matter about any group, are partly true and partly false depending on the context of the statement and proper modification. For example, research shows that a larger proportion of boys from fatherless homes than from two-parent homes engage in delinquent acts. But it is also true that fatherless homes tend to be poor and black, and the poor black are apprehended and convicted more often than the middle class and the white for similar acts.

15. *Need for replication.* Before an original research becomes accepted as knowledge or folklore, the study should be replicated by other investigators. Failure to replicate the study makes the findings suspect. The trouble is that many social scientists are willing to act in haste—both the person who obtains significant differences and the person who reads the findings and accepts them without proven replication—so long as the data correspond to their own biases and knowledge. In the past, the problem of lack of replication was probably more evident in the research results which purported black inferiority because these findings coincided with "conventional wisdom."

16. *"Conventional wisdom."* The social scientists' hypotheses, conclusions, and implications are influenced by "conventional wisdom," which is often based, in part, on distortions and overgeneralizations about the black family and culture. New findings which are incompatible with "conventional wisdom" are sometimes ignored or underemphasized because the data are not easy to explain and fit into the folklore. There is often the continuous acceptance of

previous "findings" as valid even though contradictory data exist. For the most part, only secure or prominent investigators of the research establishment are willing to challenge "conventional wisdom."

17. *Attitudinal surveys.* The social scientists have not been completely successful in developing instruments that accurately reveal real attitudes and forecast concurrent behaviors. Thus, despite surveys which show that white prejudice and discrimination toward blacks is decreasing, or despite surveys which show that blacks do not strongly resent whites or do not wish to repeat the same mistakes of white racism, real attitudes are not necessarily reflected in surveys. We cannot necessarily believe what people say when questioned in surveys, because respondents tend to give socially acceptable answers. People tend to reserve their real feelings for their families and friends.

18. *Unreality.* Many studies on blacks are conducted under unreal and artificial situations. Real life factors are sometimes ignored because they are intangible, too complex, or too difficult to control. Thus the following variables are often ignored: effects of prejudice and discrimination, racial intergroup contact, color variations within groups, regional attitudes toward blacks, and contemporary history —and these variables are important. For example, as a result of the recent increase in black pride, the research on blacks which directly or indirectly affects self-concepts and self-images may have to be revised.

19. *Lack of relevance.* For the greater part, the black community feels that it has been "surveyed and studied to death" and that little good has occurred. Consequently, the black community tends to view research as irrelevant, meaningless, or even harmful to them. This problem is compounded by the fact that when social scientists look for problems to study they usually turn to their colleagues or peruse the professional journals, rather than ask members of the black community or their subjects what might be troubling them or what phenomena are relevant to them. For example, there is little research on how to combat white racism or the growing black racism. The social scientist must learn to consider the relevance of the study and its applicability to the population being studied.

20. *Research v. practice.* While the social scientist is concerned with research and knowledge for its own sake, the practitioner is concerned with service and the application of research and knowledge. The researcher usually is not concerned with practical problems because what is appropriate in one situation is often not

applicable to other situations. On the other hand, most research is impractical for the practitioner who is working not with generalizations but with individuals, not with mean scores but with individual variability. The gap between the social scientist and practitioner is perhaps even wider in the black community because the problems of the practitioner are more difficult, and he feels the research is less applicable to his situation. Furthermore, the practitioner in the ghetto is often concerned about covering up the inefficiencies and problems that he is confronted with; therefore, he views the social scientist as a possible threat who may uncover the truth or expose the present conditions of the school or social agency.

21. *Community concern.* The social scientist sometimes forgets that his subjects are human beings, not rats or statistics to be manipulated. He is not always as concerned with the subjects' interests and welfare as he is with the productiveness of his own research.[14] This factor, along with the fact that the black community feels the research on blacks is irrelevant and used to publicize negative aspects of their community and culture, is encouraging the black community to establish rigid controls and checks on the social scientist, which detrimentally affect the validity of the studies and make it nearly impossible to obtain representative samples. These rigid controls and checks are compounded by the fact that the white social scientist is often no longer welcomed by the black community and often no longer receives cooperation for his research. The general hostility toward the white social scientist is also linked to the political ambitions of community black militants who view the social scientist as a potential outsider and threat to the control of information from ghetto areas. The community black militant would prefer complete control of communication in order to have people come to him for information and his opinion. He would also prefer to have his own "inside" social scientist who would slant the findings to accommodate his interests.

22. *Need for greater involvement.* Few social scientists attempt to test their ideas and theories; they are more interested in conducting their research—a step-in-step-out approach which alienates both the practitioner and black community. Similarly, by virtue of his

---

[14] For example, subjects' consent in the absence of full information is often damaging; personality tests often induce subjects to reveal more about themselves than they intend. Is it proper to ask children about the education or income status of their parents? Do investigators have the right to use the students' cumulative school record, extracting such data as psychological and cognitive scores? Do school authorities have the right to give consent *in loco parentis?* Is it right to use one-way mirrors without the subjects' knowledge?

academic credentials, the social scientist often builds a wall between himself and the practitioner, himself and the black community. The latter become sensitive and defensive to what they interpret as academic snobbism; they reject him as insensitive, irrelevant, and even incompetent. The social scientist needs to show a greater commitment to the needs and interests of the clientele he serves and to become more deeply involved in eliminating the barriers to social change. If the social scientist fails to respond to these new trends, much of his research will continue to be considered irrelevant.

23. *Negative viewpoint.* The social scientist tends to look for problems, emphasizing negative traits and behaviors and viewing differences from the norms of the larger society, or white middle class, as "problems" or "abnormalities." Studies are more likely to focus on the pathologies of blacks than on the people and institutions that have caused them. Since the focus is negative, few strengths and positive traits are pointed out.

24. *Positive viewpoint.* In reaction to the negative portrayal of blacks, there has been a recent tendency to present a glowing and romantic image of black life and culture. This "underdog" research (and commentary) often transfers the blame from the individual and family to white racism and society. This viewpoint is just as invalid as blaming blacks for all their problems and pathologies.

25. *Individual vs. situational factors.* The social scientist tends to view the individual subject or group as the independent variable, and the situational factors (environment) as the dependent variable —thus overlooking the importance of society and its effects on the individual. Pathologies of the individual are usually stressed without considering situational factors. The individual's psychological development is pointed to as the contributing factor to his present condition, while social realities such as racial and social discrimination are often ignored.

Behavior is functional to individual personality and environment. Behavior of the individual (e.g., delinquency and premarital sexual experiences) can be interpreted as reflecting the personality traits of the group (an independent variable) or it can be viewed also as behavioral attributes linked to the pressure of environment (a dependent variable) that would produce similar effects on most people living under such conditions. Indeed, social scientists can no longer deny the existence and effect of situational factors.

26. *Racial and ethnic sensitivity.* Closely related to the positive portrayal of blacks is a new trend of sensitivity, at times even

hostility and paranoia, on the part of blacks and other ethnic groups and minorities (including homosexuals, women's organizations, etc.) toward being described by the dominant culture. Minority-group Americans are today quite aware of belonging to an ethnic minority and are often extremely defensive and belligerent about it. These feelings sometimes carry over to the white social scientist who refuses to pretend that there are no differences among racial and ethnic groups and who is, in turn, put on the defensive inviting criticism, harassment, and even the possible threat of violence from various members of the college community and racial groups. The trend is reaching the point where there is a lack of tolerance toward controversial findings and where the oppressed minority is becoming the oppressive minority. Granted, racial and ethnic minorities have been discriminated against and, at times, oppressed; however, hypersensitivity and other reaction to racial and ethnic differences (some real, some imaginary) can only impede frank discussion and legitimate reform—and transform the social scientists' tolerance to hostility.

27. *"Self-fulfilling prophecies."* The social scientists who research and describe black children and adults often contribute to negative "self-fulfilling prophecies" which operate in school and society. Social scientists, in their attempt to educate the public, usually paint a negative description of blacks which becomes a part of the "conventional wisdom." Thus, they must bear some of the blame for causing these prophecies that they and their partisans direct toward others, and particularly toward practitioners—teachers and social workers.[15]

28. *White social scientists.* The great majority of social scientists are white and obviously middle class; they unwittingly reflect the biases of their own culture and tend to view blacks in relation to white middle-class culture which can be and has been harmful to blacks and has helped perpetuate false data. Not only has the contribution of black social scientists and authors in the social science disciplines been scanty, but whites have been considered the experts on black families and culture and are likely to review reports and books on blacks.

29. *Black social scientists.* A large portion of the recent research and books written by blacks and reviewed by either blacks or whites are suspect. Most black social scientists and reviewers tend to be promoting a political cause or cultural movement and seem

---

[15] Also see Chapter III.

to be less interested in honest research or reviewing. On the other hand, today, there is a reluctance on the part of many white social scientists to criticize the black community or black social scientists openly. Perhaps only recognized black social scientists (e.g., Kenneth B. Clark, Allison Davis and Hylan Lewis) can be trusted by the research community for their presumed scholarship on blacks or criticized by whites without charges of irrelevancy or racism.

30. *Division among black and white social scientists.* The white social scientist resents and is becoming alienated by the black community's disapproval of his work and of him as an individual. He resents the new rhetoric that is replacing reason and threatening academic standards and interest in research. Moreover, he resents the favored treatment afforded to his black colleagues at the college or university campuses. The division between the black and white social scientists is widened by the fact that the recent black studies departments in many institutions of higher learning often reject white participation and organize themselves as a separate entity from the rest of the predominantly white faculty. On the other hand, blacks resent being treated as convenient pawns to "handle the black problem." Charges of racism and unfair practices are now sometimes made by both black and white faculty members; the atmosphere in some institutions of higher learning is covertly strained and there is a growing lack of communication between the few black and majority white social scientists.

It is important to recognize that the research concerning the black community is characterized by public visibility and emotionalism. The findings can be threatening either to the black community or to the white practitioner working in the ghetto, or to the white power structure. The social scientist must recognize his role and responsibilities, as well as the potential impact and the dysfunctional outcomes of his research. He must be cognizant that he is often considered an authority, sometimes even by virtue of his degree, affiliation, and the jargon he uses, and what he says often influences public policy and social change.

Although the reader may resent or deplore the findings of a specific study, the social scientist has the right to free inquiry so long as his research does not degenerate into systematic distortion or propaganda. A study may be criticized or rejoinders may be written, but no one has the right to subject the social scientist to harassment or threaten him because the findings do not agree with popular rhetoric.

The social scientist must go where the current problems are, and he must be allowed to investigate all facets of society; otherwise, his work becomes irrelevant. He must not be denied access to the black community on the grounds of race, for he can do more good than harm for the black community—especially in helping to effect social change. On the other hand, the black community has the right to know the overall purpose of a specific study and the right not to cooperate if its people or spokesman feel that the social scientist is intent on conveying a negative image of blacks or doing harm to the community. The black community must recognize that the research controlled by them will be rejected by most of the research community as invalid and dishonest. To reach some kind of compromise with the black community, the white social scientist should be willing, at least, (a) to include members of the black community as participants in the research wherever possible; (b) to control the variable of investigator's or examiner's race; (c) to select social scientists from the same minority group that is being researched—at least whenever possible; (d) to make research more relevant to the black community and the practitioners working with the black community; (e) to explain the basic ideas of the research to the black community without contaminating the validity of the study; and (f) to allow for a rebuttal in the form of a minority report or statement which will be attached to the original study—if the black community desires it. There is also a need for social scientists to give serious consideration to the complaints of ghetto dwellers. In fact, the pressure of contemporary events is forcing social scientists to look at the character of the social order and to reevaluate the theoretical concepts and models by which they have explained black Americans and race relations in the past.

Desegregation Studies. Most educators maintain that school desegregation and academic achievement are related, and that only by desegregation will blacks receive an "equal educational opportunity." Their reasoning is based on the current research; however, the research suffers from a number of methodological limitations which are listed below:

1. *Confusion over terms.* There is no commonly agreed upon meaning of words (e.g., racial imbalance, desegregation, interracialism, and integration) among the investigators and social scientists themselves.[16] For example, in some cases the social scientist is concerned

---

[16] For our purposes, we will confine the discussion to "desegregation" and "integration." "Desegregation" is a legal term referring to the elimination of racial segregation within a school or school system; it includes a transitional stage, having diverse effects on minorities, and especially blacks, and whites (Katz, 1968). The term, although first used with regard to *de jure* segregation, now may include a situation dealing with *de facto* segregation. "Integration" follows "desegregation"; the elimination of racial segregation becomes an accomplished fact—at least for the time being.

that the school mix corresponds to the community mix. In other cases, the concern is over specific percentages—percentages which vary among social scientists and regions. Also, there is a difference between forced, token, and voluntary desegregation. Thus, linguistic usage, conflict over terms, and interchangeability of terms cause confusion over operational definitions and generalization of the data.

2. *Design of the study.* Little, if any, of the research on desegregation has adequate sample sizes, random samples, pre- and post-tests, or equated control groups (dealing with ability, age, sex, residence, school attendance, size of family, income status, and parental education) of similar students attending segregated schools. Even when a group approaches randomization, staff selection and parental consent are usually biased factors; the experimental group is thus selected or loaded for positive characteristics. Similarly, there are few longitudinal studies, most are cross sectional.[17] For example, the scores of black children in integrated schools are not traced throughout their school careers but compared with those of a segregated group after a short interval—say one or two years. Long-term effects are therefore ignored.

3. *Hawthorne effect.* Since the studies on desegregation consist of relatively short time intervals, student achievement may interact with the Hawthorne effect. In effect, the students realize they are a special group; teachers reaffirm this point, examiners test them, community and government people visit their schools, etc.; thus, the students try harder than usual.

4. *School characteristics.* Gains in the scores of blacks attending a predominantly white school may not be specifically related to racial or social mixing per se but may be due mainly to improved school facilities; teacher morale, attitudes, and experience; and ambitious programs in the school. It seems that almost none of the studies attempts to measure and compare the quality of education in desegregated and segregated schools with student achievement. The increase in academic achievement of blacks in desegregated schools might be matched by that of blacks in segregated settings if both schools offered the same quality of education.

---

[17] The Coleman Report is the most impressive cross sectional study which suggests that desegregation is related to improved academic performance of minority groups. A discussion of the limitations of the design is pointed out in the Winter 1968 issue of the *Harvard Educational Review*. Also, see Ornstein (1972) and St. John (1970).

5. *Selected groups.* The studies that purport to establish the "positive" effects of desegregation are mainly based on nonrepresentative black populations. In the North, most blacks who attend desegregated schools are middle class; their parents often live in interracial or "changing" neighborhoods or are highly motivated to send their children to predominantly white schools. On the other hand, lower-class blacks are trapped in the ghetto, and most attend segregated schools. In the South (and in some pilot programs in the North), a small number of highly selected blacks have been transferred to previously all white schools. Consequently, in both the North and South, these black students are often middle class or have been selected on the basis of potential achievement, motivation, and adjustment. Most likely, they would have succeeded wherever they were enrolled; thus, the "positive" findings associated with desegregation may be masked by the initial variations of student abilities, income, and parental interest.

6. *School vs. classroom.* The racial composition of the school and classroom rarely coincide. Student achievement scores are usually correlated with school percentages; the classroom composition is ignored even though the classroom percentage of white students has a strong effect, and possibly stronger effect, on black students than school percentages do. Since most schools still use some form of tracking or homogeneous grouping, it is likely that in many desegregated schools, black students find themselves segregated in their classes.

Although the research, on the whole, purports the desirability of school desegregation, there appear to be too many limitations in the research to allow us to draw firm conclusions. Although the findings tend to confirm that the achievement scores of blacks are higher in desegregated schools than in segregated schools, the results are unconvincing and seem to be distorted or masked by inadequate research designs and procedures.

Educators often fail to take into account that blacks undergo a great deal of psychological and cognitive stress when they attend desegregated schools, enough stress to possibly do more harm than good. In fact, there is a growing body of literature (Armstrong & Gregor, 1964; Gottlieb, 1964; Hodgkins & Stakenas, 1969; Katz, 1968, 1969; Proshansky & Newton, 1968) that shows that, under many circumstances, the more insulated black children are from white schools and society, the less anxiety, deviant behavior, and forms of mental illness are expressed. The reasons are sixfold:

1. *Alien world.* Desegregated schools are run by white adults and reflect the values of white, middle-class society. The black child will find himself engulfed in a different culture—ranging from the books he will read, the curriculum content, the people in power and authority, the predominantly white teaching staff, and the food in the cafeteria. Segregated black schools have recently adjusted or are in the process of rectifying such problems, but there is little motivation for predominantly white schools to change their white orientation. The desegregated schools that are more sensitive to the concerns of the black child are those which have a larger percentage of black students—in effect, most of them are "changing schools" and soon they will be predominantly black or segregated.

2. *Black students vs. white students.* The black student comes to class with justifiable, as well as sometimes paranoic, hostility toward white society which is expressed toward white teachers. The student is often suspicious of the teacher and over-reacts to slight and sometimes imaginary signs of discriminatory teacher behavior. Other black students voice their slogans of power and violence and eventually "turn off" or make their white teacher defensive—even hostile. On the other hand, many white teachers come to class with several prejudices toward blacks. Some of these feelings are subtle, the tendency to be more critical of black students or to react to differences in achievement by black and white students. Some of the feelings are more overt, outright rejection of the child based on race. The black student reacts to the teachers' prejudices (real or imaginary), and the white teacher reacts to the student's hostility—reinforcing a vicious cycle which makes for a brutal atmosphere and a nonlearning situation.

3. *Black students vs. white students.* In predominantly white schools, the black student will find that white students have most of the status and belong to the "right" clubs. Perhaps more important, the attitudes of most black and white students toward each other—especially at many secondary schools—is one of mutual unacceptance, resentment, suspicion, and in some cases hostility, all of which reflect the recent racial polarization in the country. The outcome is that both groups to varying degrees tend to segregate themselves from each other in the cafeterias, study halls, school yards, and clubs.

4. *Intellectual inadequacy.* Most blacks are not prepared to match the scholastic standards in predominantly white schools; this inadequacy is partially based on the acceptance of the white group's image of blacks and their own previous inadequate education and

lack of early childhood stimulation at home. When the average black student is put into a class with middle-class whites performing on or above grade level, how can we expect white students—even from "liberal" families—to feel there is really no difference? If the classroom is grouped according to ability, the black student will most likely find himself in a segregated (segregated by ability, not race) classroom, thus reaffirming his own image of black intellectual inferiority.

5. *Reaction to white competition.* Confronted by white academic standards, the black student often develops low task motivation and increases his expectancy of failure. Similarly, strong unconscious feelings of hostility are usually directed at the individuals—students and teachers—from whom the negative evaluation comes. The black students often desire to escape from the situation, escape from the white student and teacher. In the past, the black student had to suppress this desire, return to a segregated school, or drop out of school. Today, the black studies programs are, in part, developed to fulfill the black need to escape from white competition. White students are usually barred from such programs or accepted in limited numbers; the instructors tend to be black, and the grading system is questionable.

6. *Sense of control.* The student's sense of control of the environment is positively related to academic performance. Although there is research that tends to show that the black student's sense of control increases in an integrated school, there is other research (Gottlieb, 1964; Katz, 1968, 1969) which seems to indicate the opposite. In this connection, the black student's sense of control will most likely decrease because he will find hostile white students and teachers; he will find that white students are in a more favorable academic and social position than he is; he will perceive few blacks in positions of authority and power with the exception of perhaps an "exhibit." Finally, his parents will have less opportunity to engage in decision making than in a black community controlled school.

Conclusion

It should be noted that failure will often be more harmful and success will often be more rewarding for black students in a desegregated school than in a segregated setting. In the former school, their failure or success will largely depend on their actual abilities, expectations, and the amount of white hostility. The main problem is that most black students are unprepared to compete with white students. Not until the educational standards of blacks are raised in their own schools to the level of white schools, by the controlling black community, or not until white schools are willing to provide adequate tutorial services and teachers who can teach basic reading and English to students is it wise for blacks to be thrown into desegregated schools on a mass scale. To desegregate, under the present conditions, is to surrender to politics and pressure; it overlooks genuine reform.

VI

Decentralizing Urban Schools[1]

Introduction

I will admit that when integration was the "liberal" thing, I believed in it and advocated it. Now it is becoming fashionable to call for school decentralization, and perhaps I have been misled and seduced by the literature, or perhaps I am reflecting my "liberal" guilt or the current rhetoric, for I, too, now call for decentralization. In advocating school decentralization, I realize that I may, unwittingly, become an ally of the white and black racists who make it difficult to unite America. Having thus cautioned the reader about my biases, I will proceed with the discussion, which may be divided into five parts: (1) a socio-historical overview, (2) the New York City school controversy over decentralization, (3) school decentralization plans of other urban school systems, (4) arguments for and against decentralization, and (5) a model for reorganizing urban schools.

A Socio-Historical Overview

Although most surveys show that blacks still prefer integration, investigators fail to recognize that many blacks do not seek integration per se but wish to send their children to white schools because they are "better"

---

[1] For purposes of this discussion, the author contends that the issues of decentralization and community control although not synonymous are theoretically commingled and should not be separated. Granted the schools can be decentralized without providing community control; however, in order for the community to gain control on a large scale, the schools will probably have to be decentralized.

or wish to live in white communities because life in the ghetto is often painful and ugly. A considerable number of black people, especially in our Northern ghettoes, have repudiated the ideology of integration as a farce, a honkie hoax. Two hundred years of slavery and another hundred years of being second-class citizens have taught many blacks that the methods used by Dr. George Washington Carver and Dr. Martin Luther King are impractical. Rather than work within the system, many blacks seek to create their own system and educate black children in black schools with black teachers and administrators—teachers and administrators who are accountable to the black community, too.

Black power demands that the school curriculum not only include black history and culture but that history be reinterpreted so that students realize that George Washington, the father of White America, used to tell lies and that he owned slaves; that the Constitution of White America considered a black as three-fifths of a person, etc. Rather than black students learning about the "contributions" of Negroes and seeing the Negro as part of American history, there is a demand for the study of the germinal heritage of black culture—Nat Turner, W. E. DuBois, Marcus Garvey, Frantz Fanon, etc. Rather than the black students having to seek self-realization through defensive polemics and discussion of Negro heroes who are "acceptable" to whites, the students are given the opportunity to assert their own identity and shift discussion to whatever they wish to pursue, or to what is valid according to blacks. They are given the opportunity to view not themselves but the white power system as a major source of their problems, and they discuss possibilities of rectifying the situation.

Traditionally, the schools have been responsive only to the dominant white power structure. Subordinate groups that were once considered apolitical or indifferent are now demanding that the schools be responsive to them, too, that power be transferred to them—the consumers. The pending crisis is keenly described by the U.S. Riot Commission (1968):

> Ghetto schools often appear to be unresponsive to the community ... and parents are distrustful of educational officials.
>
> The consequences for the education of students attending these schools are serious. Parental hostility to the school is reflected in the attitudes of their children. Since the needs and concerns of the ghetto community are rarely reflected in educational policy formulated on a citywide basis, the schools are often seen by ghetto youth as being irrelevant....
>
> In the schools, as in the large society, the isolation of ghetto residents from policy-making institutions of local government is

adding to the polarization of the community and depriving the system of its self-rectifying potential (pp. 436–37).

Most black teachers welcome school decentralization and community control; they envision it as an opportunity to bolster local black power, as well as their own "green power" through administrative promotions which they have generally been denied. Indeed, it is legally and morally justified for black controlled school boards to hire or promote qualified principals or superintendents on the basis that the individual is black, BLACK.

Our laws have permitted other groups a degree of separatism, permitting them to establish their own schools in order to maintain their customs and religious beliefs. Catholic and Jewish parents have the opportunity to send their children to parochial schools; the rich have the option to send their children to private schools. The white "liberals" who belong to the NAACP and move to suburbia are often seeking "better" schools for their children; in effect, they establish their own school systems and tend to favor individuals of their own ethnic groups in their employment and reward practices.

Much of the present demand for local control must be viewed in the context of the present unrest in the ghettoes which is partially due to frustration arising from the fact that blacks have not been permitted to shake loose the albatross of dependency which has historically hung around their necks. Now the pendulum is beginning to swing the other way; blacks are beginning to get their way too. For many whites, however, local control of the schools by the black community is construed as a black victory and white defeat. Also, whites cannot accept the feeling of being out-numbered or out-voted by blacks. The exodus of whites from the inner cities and their bewildered statements such as "They want everything their way," "What do they expect from us?" "Will they ever be satisfied?" illustrate to some degree the whites' discomfort and their desire to maintain the luxury of supremacy.

The apprehension by whites is increased by the fact that a large number of black people no longer are committed to educational reform within the existing educational structure. They are not only questioning but opposing its legitimacy. They have lost confidence in the white, middle-class educational leadership and seem no longer willing to accept the "wisdom" of the professionals. Bitter failures of compensatory education and integration, coupled with the current demands of black power, have resulted in new and growing demands of blacks for the redistribution of power and control of their own schools. For many blacks, meaningful educational reform can only come about through black controlled schools. A new dimension of "equal educational opportunity" is developing, the equal right to exercise control and make decisions concerning public education.

The New York City School Controversy
Over Decentralization

Although the New York City schools have always been noted for reform (e.g., "The Demonstration Guidance Program," one of the forerunners of compensatory educational programs; More Effective Schools; curriculum reform in reading and teaching English as a second and third language; special high schools for talented students; classroom sizes reduced to less than thirty students; teacher unionism and concurrent teacher benefits; teacher accountability; etc.), the sheer size and bureaucratic nature of the system had created almost a hopeless situation for reform in which power was limited to an inside select group of administrators at the central board.

Gittell's (1967) analysis of the bureaucratic and power arrangements were keenly described in her study of the city's schools, an analysis which tends to correspond with other large city, overcentralized school systems: (1) the board of education had major power in formulation of almost all policies; (2) the superintendent had nominal powers and was unlikely to take a position which differed from the central bureaucracy; (3) local school boards had almost no power; they served as community buffers and rubber stamped the policies of the board of education; (4) district superintendents had risen through the system and had only limited powers; they served as buffers between parent dissatisfactions unresolved by principals in their districts; and (5) the teachers' union mainly limited their issues around personal interests (e.g., salaries and job conditions) which were defined as "professional" interests. In general, attempts to reform the system were stifled by bureaucratic complexities and poor communication.

Shapiro's personal description, which was reported by Hentoff (1966), of how the system operated was equally depressing: "All the way up the chain of command in the school system were people with a vested interest in keeping the truth away from the person on the next rung. By the time anything came to the top . . . conditions were reported as being fine [p. 39]."

Similarly, as a former teacher in New York City, this author remembers several teachers and parents trying to get in touch with someone in authority at the central board. If the communication was through a letter, there was either no reply or it was a form answer which indicated that it was not the person's responsibility; invariably, it was someone else's responsibility. If the communication was via the telephone, it meant being switched from one office to the next office until you were accidentally disconnected or you ran out of patience or nickels. If the individual personally tried to see someone at the board who had authority, he was met by a host of secretaries, clerks, and career people who would inform him that the possibility of seeing this administrator was at the present impossible and that the best thing to do was to write a letter.

Stage I: The Bundy Report. In 1967, the New York Board of Education became committed, at least in words, to a policy of decentralization (Chapter 487 of the New York Law of 1967) and directed the mayor to prepare a decentralization plan. With the "green light" from the mayor and the New York State Legislature, a committee headed by George McBundy, president of the Ford Foundation, and the committee members representing the black and Puerto Rican communities as well as the educational establishment, formulated a comprehensive and controversial proposal for school decentralization and community control. The plan was entitled, *Reconnection for Learning—A Community School for New York City*—better known as the Bundy Report. The plan was endorsed by the Ford Foundation and suggested that:

1) New York City schools be reorganized into thirty to sixty community school districts, ranging from 12,000 to 40,000 students.
2) A central board of education—either nominated by the mayor or in part by the mayor and the community school boards— and a superintendent of schools have responsibility for determining city-wide school policies and adhering to state regulations.
3) The community school districts be governed by a local board of education, selected in part by the mayor from a city-wide list of candidates and selected in part by the community.
4) The local board of education have control of all elementary and secondary education within its boundaries; they would have control over the budget, curriculum, and personnel, including the right to hire, fire, and promote personnel, but all policies and personnel would have to meet state standards. In the meantime, all tenure rights of teachers and supervisors would be retained.

Stage II: The Ocean-Hill Brownsville District and the 1968 New York Teachers' Strike. Based on the recommendations of the Bundy Report, and with the approval of the New York State Board of Education, three demonstration sites (I.S. 201 school complex, Two Bridges District, and the Ocean-Hill Brownsville District) were created by the board of education in June 1967. These sites were symbolic of the trend toward decentralization and community control, and the Ocean-Hill District eventually became the focal point of the 1968 New York City Teachers' Strike, which saw the black community, supported by the mayor's office and Ford Foundation, aligned against the predominantly white teachers' union and supervisory association, with support from labor unions.

The board of education created the position of "administrator" of the Ocean-Hill Brownsville District for which Rhody McCoy was nominated by the local board. The board also created the position of "demonstration elementary school principal" and assigned three people who were chosen by the local board to these positions. The board made these appointments without regard to the requirements of the school system and without regard to the eligibility list of the board of examiners which was set forth by the New York Constitution and Educational Law concerning civil service provisions.

The persons eligible for appointments as principals sought to restrain the board from making these appointments. The New York Supreme Court recognized the need for local control.[2] The court also pointed out that since the position of "administrator" was a new position, it did not impinge on the law intended to maintain the merit system. However, it ruled that the position of "demonstration principal" was in no way different from the regular elementary principal; therefore, these appointments were declared illegal since they were made without regard to the eligibility lists.[3]

The governing (or local) board sought unlimited power over personnel. Their argument was based, according to Flynn (1969) "on the fact that effective local control could only operate apart from the bureaucratic laws which served to perpetuate the present, nonfunctional system [p. 397]." The court answered that the appointments were nevertheless illegal, and it could not see how the experiment would be hindered by the governing board nominating and appointing people from eligible lists. Thus, Flynn points out that while the court recognized the need

---

[2] *Council of Super. Ass'n. of Public Schools* v. *Bd. of Educ.* 56 Misc. 2d at 34, 288 N.Y.S. 2d at 138 (1968). Also see Footnote 13.

[3] *Ibid.,* at 141 (1968).

for local control it was unwilling to provide "the power and authority to employ it [p. 398]."

The court's decision was a setback for advocates of community control, and the majority of the members of the governing board, with the support of militants from the community and city, decided on a confrontation—in line with the philosophy of black power. The local board proceeded to dismiss thirteen teachers and six administrators. Contradictory and vague charges were brought against these educators. The local board refused to submit the dispute to binding arbitration; to submit it to arbitration would mean the end of the confrontation. The local board claimed to have the support of the community; however, Shanker (1969) asserts that a Harris poll was taken in the spring of 1968, a few months before the beginning of the confrontation, and it found that the community was dissatisfied with the performance of McCoy (44% of the responses were negative and 29% were positive) and the local board (47% were negative and 38% were positive), and only 29% of the respondents supported the decision to remove the eighteen teachers and administrators. Furthermore, during the summer of 1968, a petition signed by more than 2,000 community people demanded new elections for a local board, which, according to Shanker (1969), was "twice as many people as had originally voted the previous summer" for the members of the local board (p. 457).

During the summer of 1968, the black Judge Francis E. Rivers invalidated the dismissal charges against the eighteen educators. The Ocean-Hill Brownsville board refused to budge from their position; moreover, the local board added approximately eighty-five additional teachers to the dismissal list. The teachers' union viewed this as a threat to its rights and security; the union assembly voted to strike approximately 1,900 to 250, and the membership followed suit approximately 12,000 to 1,800. The strike began on the first day of school but only lasted for two days. The local board eventually agreed to allow the now 100 disputed teachers to return to their schools, but the teachers were repeatedly harassed and threatened by militants (many who were not members of the community), and the police were needed.

The union's reaction was swift. Three days later they struck again, and this time the union demanded the dismissal of Rhody McCoy and the Ocean-Hill Brownsville Board. The second strike lasted two weeks. It ended when the union was guaranteed by the local board, with the official observers and the police insuring compliance (which was supposed to be the case according to the Rivers' decision and the local board's agreement which ended the first strike), the rights of the disputed teachers who wished to return. In turn, the union dropped its demands for dismissing McCoy and the governing board. As many as eighty-three teachers returned, but they were not allowed to teach; they were given nonteaching jobs and continually harassed. Community people and militants collided with the police and J.H.S. 271, which was the focus of attention of the school district, was closed for days. The harassment, now followed with violence, continued, and after three weeks the union went out on strike again for yet another month. Throughout the strike, the Ocean-Hill schools and the schools of the other two experimental sites remained open.

It should be noted that it was the dismissal of the teachers and not the principle of decentralization and community control which brought on the strike, and the harassment of teachers that continued the union's strike policy. The teachers allied themselves with the supervisory association, for both groups believed that their rights of tenure, security, and their right to defend themselves at hearings were threatened. The UFT stated repeatedly that it favored decentralization, a plan which included the right of the local boards to decision-making power over curriculum and personnel and guaranteed funds over the mandated costs for use as the local board saw necessary to implement new programs. The union also wanted to establish a city-wide review board to which parents could bring complaints against teachers and administrators and which, in turn, would guarantee these educators a fair hearing.

Although the strike finally ended, there were repercussions in other black and integrated schools. The relations between white teachers and black students and the black community in general have continued to worsen since the strike, which in turn has intensified the black-white polarization of the city and the decline of "liberal" support for the black social revolution. This trend is reflected in part by the steady increase in school violence—ranging from stabbings and rapings of teachers to the use of mace and Molotov cocktails. The violence steadily drives more white teachers out of the schools and brings in more police, a vicious cycle which for the last ten or fifteen years has been a part of the New York City School System and many other large city school systems, and which has snowballed in New York City since the strike.

Stage III: The Decentralization Act of 1969. Hope to achieve a strong decentralization plan was reduced as a result of the racial tension between the black community and predominantly white teachers' union and supervisory association, as well as the accompanying conflict with the mayor's office, Ford Foundation, board of education, and the labor unions. The Decentralization Act was passed on the last day of a delayed session of the state legislature. The influence of the Bundy Report and a series of compromises are clearly observed in the basic regulations of the act; the law can be summarized as follows:

1) District school lines should be established so as to create between thirty and thirty-three local school districts (thirty-one school districts were eventually created), each with its own community board of education and each with at least 20,000 students.

2) The central board of education should consist of seven members, five to be elected from each borough and two to be elected by the mayor.[4]

3) Local school boards may be elected by registered voters and parents of students enrolled in schools of each district.

4) Local school boards can hire their own superintendent so long as he meets state education requirements. Supervisors and principals may be hired, too, from city-wide qualifying lists. However, before a future list of administrative eligibles is prepared, the present list must be exhausted.[5] For those schools whose students fall within the city's lower 45 percentile in reading, local school boards may hire their own teachers from various qualifying lists—based on the board of examiners' tests or a passing score on the National Teacher Examination.[6] Teachers' rights will be safeguarded through an appeals procedure and protection of tenure.

5) The local school boards may control the curriculum, but it must be in accordance with state regulations. The local school boards can select textbooks from a list approved by the central board and city-wide chancellor (superintendent).

6) The central board still retains control over most of the budget.[7]

---

[4] Since the populace of Manhattan and the Bronx is predominantly black and Puerto Rican, it is not unlikely that with a "liberal" or black mayor the central board would consist of a majority of blacks and/or Puerto Ricans, two elected and two appointed, and rightfully so since the majority of the public school students consists of these two racial groups.

[5] For a few years, then, this limits the appointments of black administrators.

[6] It should be noted that the NTE does not require a written essay; some educators claim such essays discriminate against most minorities whose education is perhaps limited.

[7] This last point is critical. For the community to gain real control of the schools, it is essential that it acquire control of the purse strings. Economic power is related to political power. As long as the local community is dependent on the goodwill of the central board, the local community does not have a complete independence or authority; theoretically, the larger system is still in a position to sabotage the local board's operation.

Local school board budget powers are generally advisory;
however, their unamended requests can be submitted to the
mayor's office for review. Local school boards can enter into
contracts for maintenance and repair up to $250,000 per year.
Site selection and costs of new schools are decided both by the
central and local boards.

7) The high schools will remain under the administration of the
central board of education.

The Decentralization Act can be viewed as an example of system
reform. In view of the earlier discussion on school reform,[8] the Ocean-
Hill experiment may be classified as an example of subsystem reform
which transformed into a "muti"-subsystem, that is, it deviated from
the intended behaviors of the central board or "mother system." Although the Ocean-Hill Brownsville District was submerged into a larger
school district (#23),* the school "muti" was successful—to the extent
that the "mother" system was reformed. Of course, the reader can
dispute the extent of reform; nevertheless, the school system did change;
concessions were made to the communities, and many of the powers
of the central board were reduced and transferred to the local boards.[9]

---

[8] *Supra,* Chapter V.

* *Postscript:* One of the chief critics of the Ocean-Hill experiment was Samuel D.
Wright, a community resident, black lawyer, and New York assemblyman; he was
elected president of district #23. During the summer of 1971, the local school
board (comprising nine members, each with an equal vote) fired five principals
and put as many as four others on probation. Four of the ousted principals rose to
their position during the controversy over the Ocean-Hill experiment.

Questions about the representation of district #23 and other local boards also
arise. During the first school board elections, only 15% of the eligible voters
bothered to go to the polls and only 5% went from district #23. In districts #13
and #15, located in Brooklyn, and district #3, located in Manhattan, local boards
with white majorities were chosen to govern schools that were overwhelmingly
black and Puerto Rican. The author is not questioning the possibility of a white
person serving the interests of the minority communities, but that the idea of
community control means that the local board should reflect the community mix
so that it can identify with and carry out the wishes of the residents and the parents
of the children who attend the community schools. If the eligible voters remain
indifferent, then the people do not have the right to lay the total blame on the
teachers and administrators.

Writing in the August 15, 1971, issue of the *New York Times,* Shanker pointed
out that most of those who did vote in the school elections were members of
organized groups: affiliated with churches, political clubs, unions, and anti-poverty
agencies. "When the voters were counted," wrote Shanker, "parents and minority
groups found themselves with less power in the schools than ever before." After
pointing to the poor turnout of eligible voters, illustrating the same percentages
above, he concluded: "Obviously, the advocates of community control had grossly
exaggerated the size of the demand for participatory democracy [p. 11]."

[9] The opposite conclusions are reported by Fantini and Gittell, both who have
written extensively on this subject.

Other Urban School Decentralization Plans

It is wrong to assume that New York City is unique and that its school problems have little relevance to other large cities. Successful protest strategies of the civil rights and black power movements have quickly spread in the past from city to city. Also, the growing demands of black power and the inability of the white-controlled school systems to reach black students are basically the same in other large urban areas. Judging by past experience, events and reform measures in New York City schools usually spread to other school systems. Although conflict in the school system and in the city of New York may be more intense, because of the size and multi-ethnic nature of the schools and city, it has a habit of promulgating across the country.

Other large city school systems, either because they view decentralization as a viable reform measure or, more likely, because they are trying to avoid conflict, have developed their own models for decentralization. Below is a summary of several different urban school decentralization plans, those of Los Angeles, Chicago, Detroit, Philadelphia, as well as those of Louisville-Jefferson, Kentucky, and Hyde Park–Kenwood, Chicago. The extent of community control varies with each plan.

Los Angeles. The Los Angeles schools, the second largest school system,[10] consist of more than 60,000 staff members, 750,000 students and 620 schools. During the 1968–1969 school year, the system decentralized its administrative operation by the:

1. Elimination of the divisions of elementary and secondary education and their related attendance area offices.
2. Creation of four geographic zones with K-12 responsibilities, each headed by a zone superintendent who was made in charge of the district areas within his boundaries and who was made accountable to the director of instruction and upward.
3. Reorganization of the four central board divisions (personnel, budget, controlling, and school planning), with emphasis on providing services. The division superintendents were lowered in rank and were made accountable to the deputy superintendent.

In November 1970, a task force on decentralization was established by the superintendent of the schools. Based on a series of eight public hearings as well as hearings with various staff organizations and com-

---

[10] New York City is the largest school system in the nation, consisting of more than 70,000 staff members, 1 million students, and 950 schools.

munity groups, and supplemented by a city-wide survey of the professional staff and by interviews of the professional staff in thirty-two selected schools and the four zone offices and central board, the task force made twenty-six recommendations which centered around the eleven themes below:

1. Individual schools should have the authority to organize the curriculum and determine elective courses.
2. Individual elementary and junior high schools should receive a budget for textbooks rather than requiring them to use books approved by the state.
3. Individual schools should have the authority to plan their budget.
4. School principals should be delegated the authority to supplement district purchasing up to $1,500.
5. Individual schools should have the flexibility to convert a limited number of unfilled teacher positions to dollar equivalents to employ additional personnel.
6. Principals of each school, the teachers, parents, and students (in the secondary schools) should mutually decide upon a school-community organization. Options could include a (a) parent-teacher association, (b) school-community advisory committee, (c) boosters' club or parents' club, or (d) "other forms of organizations."
7. Ten regular and three experimental administrative areas should be established at the beginning of the 1971–72 school year.
8. Each of the new administrative areas should be headed by an area superintendent, along with appropriate ancillary personnel that were listed in the report.
9. The field service centers of the four present zones should be realigned to better serve the thirteen new administrative areas.
10. Three experimental areas located in different (white, black, Mexican-American) sections of the school system should be supported by the state legislature for one year of planning and three years of experimentation. (The policies envisioned in these three experimental areas tended to correspond with a slightly stronger position toward community participation, not local control, and with emphasis on innovation, experimentation, and research.)
11. The present system of electing seven members to the central board should be increased to eleven members, thus corresponding to each of the eleven electoral districts of Los Angeles.

The recommendations of the Decentralization Task Force (whc se members were selected by the general superintendent), reflect the present philosophy of the central board and administrative personnel. There is greater opportunity for community participation, but with little opportunity for community control. The orientation is clearly toward administrative decentralization, with some increased professional power. Actually, responsibilities of the principal are enlarged, but the principal is selected by the central board. The following words of the task force keenly illustrate its position on decentralization and local control:

> Despite the lack of clear evidence that local control of schools necessarily compensates for the complex problems associated with public education in large urban centers, elements of the community have advocated turning the school system to locally elected school boards in the name of decentralization. . . . Despite the fact that in cities where this has been tried (notably New York City) the evidence to date seems to indicate that this approach can have the effect of driving white parents out of integrated (mixed) neighborhoods, white children out of public schools, and white teachers out of the city altogether. If such were to take place in Los Angeles, it is clear that decentralization could certainly result in inferior education for minority children in the Central City as experienced white teachers move elsewhere. Paradoxically, all this would be accomplished in the name of "decentralization" and "neighborhood" self-government— which, based on the experience of other great cities, could mean that school boards polarize and intensify all latent racial and potential conflicts in any particular section of the City (*Educational Renewal,* 1971, pp. 27–28).

In March 1971, the Los Angeles Board of Education voted on the task force's recommendations. The outcome was as follows:

1. Recommendations one, two, three, and five were approved basically as stated above.
2. Recommendation four was modified so that each school can spend up to $2,000 of its budget for materials rather than going through prescribed school system purchasing procedures.
3. Rather than setting up thirteen administrative areas, twelve areas were organized, each with an area superintendent and the appropriate ancillary personnel. Each of the areas will have three to five high schools under its jurisdiction, as well as the feeding elementary and junior high schools.
4. In approving the concept of field service centers, each center (a

total of four originally corresponding with the four zones) will
serve two to four of the new twelve administrative areas.

5. The task force's recommendation calling for three experimental
areas was modified to establish twenty-six demonstration
schools, two in each of the twelve areas, and three model school
complexes in different parts of the school system. The demonstration schools and model complexes are given the freedom to
experiment with new techniques to improve the teaching-learning process. By modifying the original "experimental" school
recommendation, the board provided a greater amount of local
autonomy. Although the demonstration-model schools were established by the board, the state legislature did not grant the
necessary funds.

6. The board of education vetoed the recommendation to enlarge
the board membership to eleven, pointing out that the main idea
was to concentrate on improving the local school and enhancing
community participation.

In June 1971, the board of education mandated the establishment of
advisory councils. This was the last of the decentralization recommendations to be acted upon. Each of the new councils are to have no less than
eleven elected members. The majority of the members shall be parents
of the children enrolled in the school, and the other members are to be
representatives from the community, teaching staff, and students (secondary school). The function of the councils is advisory, to serve as "a
resource to the principal who remains responsible for [the] decisions."
Thus, the control of the schools still remains in the hands of the professionals.*

Chicago. Chicago is the third largest school system in the nation, consisting of approximately 27,000 staff members, 576,000 students, and
570 schools. In 1966 the Chicago public schools commissioned a private
consulting firm called Booz-Allen and Hamilton to survey the school
system and provide a plan for school decentralization. In May 1967, the
company made recommendations that the central board should:

1. Retain responsibility for setting policy and deliberating major
issues.

---

* *Postscript:* In a telephone conversation on December 20, 1971, with Mr. Jerry
Custis of Public Information at the Los Angeles City Schools, this author learned
that the board of education is presently considering the recommendation of permitting the councils of each of the schools to determine how to spend ESEA
money, totaling up to $200,000 per school.

2. Establish three standing board committees (facilities, finance, and community relations) to identify key issues and present them to the central board.
3. Establish the position of deputy superintendent who would be in charge of system-wide services and departments. The deputy superintendent would be accountable to the general superintendent and central board.
4. Divide the city into three major areas, each headed by an area associate superintendent. The area associate superintendent would be in charge of field organizations and programs within their school districts (approximately nine school districts per area) and would be accountable to the deputy superintendent and upward.
5. Assign line responsibility for the schools to district superintendents. They would have direction over the schools within their districts and would be accountable to their respective area associate superintendent and upward.

The Board of Education of Chicago adopted the above major recommendations and proceeded to divide the system into three areas and twenty-seven smaller districts. However, under this plan the local board was merely a discussion forum. The local superintendents (area and district) had authority and power but their orientation was upward to their administrative superiors, not to the community or people.

In 1969, the Illinois legislature created the Commission on Urban Education to study the problems of decentralization and local control. The commission began its work in October 1969, and terminated its work in February 1971, issuing a document commonly referred to as the Peterson Commission Report. The commission's basic recommendations are stated below:

1. Legislation be enacted to implement decentralization and local control in designated urban areas of the state, including the city of Chicago.
2. Legislation be enacted to support experiments in urban school decentralization.
   a. The suggested experimental design consisted of six districts in Chicago. Four of these would be experimental districts; two would have complete control of curriculum, personnel, budget, and pupil policy, while two would share authority with the central board. The other two control districts would function under the traditional authority of the central board.

b. The six districts would be matched by class and race; three would be predominantly black (75% or more) and three would be predominantly white (75% or more). The average income would be similar in all the districts.

The commission also suggested the following principles for school decentralization and local control:

1. Recognize the diverse needs of the city's population.
2. Insure increased community awareness and participation.
3. Elect local boards by members of the respective communities.
4. Identify and define powers that belong exclusively to the local community, those that belong to the professionals, and those that should be shared.
5. Establish a position of educational ombudsman to serve as a liaison between the central and local boards.
6. Insure local control in the following areas: (a) curriculum, (b) personnel, (c) budget, and (d) pupil policy.
7. Embody decision-making provisions and necessary resources for implementing: (a) periodic evaluation of the total program, (b) standards for evaluating professional's performance—and holding them accountable, and (c) criteria for teacher transfers.

The commission (1971) also summarized that the people living in suburbia "must pay for the cost of 'unequal' education needed to provide equal opportunity to oppressed children in the inner city" and that "the schools and teachers . . . be made accountable to the communities . . . [p. 53]."

It should be noted that the above guidelines and conclusions reflect a strong position in favor of local control of the schools, in part reflecting the influence of the black militant educators who served on the commission (i.e., Rhody McCoy, the former "administrator" of the Ocean-Hill Brownsville District; Barbara Sizemore, director of the Woodlawn Experimental School District in Chicago; and Calvert Smith, formerly a member of the Center of Inner-City Studies in Chicago and now affiliated with the University of Cincinnati). Also, many of the objectives and ideas correspond with the Bundy Report.

Detroit. Detroit, the fourth largest school system in the nation, with a staff of approximately 20,000 people and with approximately 300,000 students and 300 schools, decentralized its schools as a result of Public

Act 48, enacted into law by the state of Michigan in 1970. The act called for the following:

1. Creation of eight regional school districts.
2. Establishment of a regional board for each regional district, consisting of five members elected by the residents of the regional district who are registered voters.
3. Election of a chairman for each regional board, on the basis of the largest number of votes received during the regional board elections, who also serves on the central board.
4. Expansion of the central board from seven members to thirteen members. Five members are to be elected at large and eight members are to come from each of the eight regional districts, one person per region, that is, the chairman.
5. Undertaking by the regional board of the following responsibilities: (a) selecting personnel, including the regional superintendent, from a pool of eligibles established by the central board; (b) discharging, assigning, and promoting all teachers subject to review by the central board; (c) determining curriculum and testing procedures; and (d) requesting funds, with the central board determining the need and allocation of the money.
6. Maintaining control of the following by the central board: (a) central purchasing, (b) payroll, (c) contract negotiations, (d) property management and maintenance, (e) bonding, (f) special educational programs, (g) allocation of funds, and (h) determination of guidelines for regional boards.
7. Securing of the rights of retirement, tenure, and seniority of employers transferred to a region by the central board or between regional boards. These rights are not impaired or abrogated.

In general, the Detroit plan for decentralization is administrative in nature; nevertheless, in theory it provides a reasonable degree of community control. The central board would most likely work with the regional boards, since the majority of the members of the central board are also on the regional boards. Because of the sizes of the city and school system, the eight regional districts established in Detroit are smaller in area than the more than thirty-one school districts established in New York City.

Philadelphia. The Philadelphia school system is the fifth largest in the nation, consisting of approximately 15,000 staff members, 290,000 students, and 275 schools.[11] In December 1968, the Philadelphia Board of Education resolved to appoint a study commission on decentralization, called the Commission on Decentralization and Community Participation. The commission met throughout 1969 and early 1970 and eventually submitted in July 1970 three options for decentralizing the schools which should be voted on by parents where their children are enrolled and by adults who are not parents but who reside in a designated school community. No one plan was recommended for the entire city, rather each school community would be given the opportunity for choosing one of the three options below.

Option I: Informal Community Participation.

1. Many communities may wish to retain their present relations with the schools. With this in mind, school-parental groups generally remain the same, but the principal and present school associations evolve different patterns of informal community participation in school affairs.
2. The principal may arrange for community participation and consult the school association in the areas of curriculum, personnel, and finance. However, decision making remains with the principal who is subject to the policies and regulations of the district superintendent and central board.
3. For certain positions, i.e., vice principal, department heads, and team leaders, the principal may make selections from a pool of eligibles determined by the central board.

Option II: Advisory Participation Through an Elected Committee.

1. School communities may choose to have a school advisory committee or designate the school association to advise the principal and make recommendations concerning curriculum, personnel, and finances.
2. The school advisory committee or school association serves in a consulting capacity. Decision making is still with the principal who is accountable to the district superintendent and central board.
3. The principal makes the final selection of the various leadership positions from a pool of eligibles determined by the central board. The school advisory committee or school association may

---

[11] Although the city of Philadelphia is larger than Detroit, the former has a large parochial school system (more than 150 schools); therefore, the Philadelphia public school system is smaller than Detroit's.

recommend candidates for principal from a pool of eligibles, but the final selection is based on the approval of the district superintendent and central board.

Option III: Shared Authority and Responsibility.

1. School communities may choose to have a school board or designate the school association to share decision-making authority in the areas of curriculum, personnel, and finances.
2. If a school board is elected, it should consist of nine elected adult members of the school community. At the secondary level, the school board should also consist of two students, bringing the total membership to eleven.
3. If the school association is designated, it should determine the organization of its body.
4. The school board or school association, after hearing the recommendations of the principal, has the authority to modify them in the following areas: (a) courses in addition to required ones, (b) books, and (c) instructional materials and media.
5. The school board or school association has the right to (a) select the principal, from a pool of eligibles, so long as he is approved by the district superintendent and the central board, and (b) testify before the central board or state legislature for purposes of obtaining funds.

In general, all three options reject the idea of community control but encourage a limited and safe degree of community participation. Under Options I and II, the principal retains his power and is accountable to the district superintendent and central board; only under the second option does the community have the right to advise the principal. Under Option III, the principal is, to a limited extent, influenced by the school board or school association. However, he is still accountable to the district superintendent and central board. In all three plans, the central board retains its authority and power, although the commission recommended that the central board be elected rather than appointed.

Louisville-Jefferson County Plan. Plans for school decentralization and community control are not limited to large cities or reflect only the demands of the minority community. In the case of the Louisville-Jefferson County Plan, the trend toward decentralization is linked with metropolitanism—with considerable autonomy at the community level. Although the plan was defeated by the Kentucky legislature in 1968, the basic ideas are listed below.

1. Creation of a Metropolitan Educational District
   a. The Metropolitan Educational District would have control over (a) finances, (b) school construction, (c) and research and planning.
   b. The district would be headed by a chief administrative officer.
   c. A Metropolitan Educational Commission, comprised of citizens from the metropolitan area, would be responsible for the operation of the schools in the district.
2. Creation of local community, semi-independent subdistricts.
   a. The community school districts would possess the authority to extend an additional but limited tax on property within their boundaries to pay for school programs. (This would benefit wealthy school districts.)
   b. Each community school district would have authority over (a) curriculum, (b) personnel, (c) inservice education, (d) evaluation of the school program, and (e) the design of new programs.
   c. Each community school district would be run by a local board, consisting of seven elected members.

Hyde Park–Kenwood, Chicago. As previously mentioned, the Hyde Park–Kenwood area is a predominantly middle-class, white community. Besides being politically sophisticated and socially active, the people possess a genuine sense of community pride and participation. With this in mind, the people have established the Hyde Park–Kenwood Community Conference, a community organization which coordinates various social and educational programs (dealing with youth employment, tenant unions, real estate, ecology, health maintenance, women's rights, racial discrimination, parks, and schools). The community conference coordinates, provides information and services, and serves in an advisory capacity to the eight school boards—called local councils—of the respective schools in the community.

Procedures vary for electing members to each local council. Their authority and power vary, too—in part, depending on the extent of militancy of the members of each local council and the parents of each school. As with the other councils in the city, the local councils in Hyde Park–Kenwood have managed to obtain the right to select their own school principals. However, the local councils in Hyde Park–Kenwood also share decision-making responsibility with the district superintendent (#14) and individual school principals in the areas of curriculum, textbook selections, limited finances, and pupil policy. At the present, the "Council for Local Control," a committee of the community conference has drafted a plan which will also delegate to a local school board the authority to (a) hire teachers and paraprofessionals, (b) evaluate the faculty, (c) formulate and supervise objectives, (d) supervise maintenance and construction of buildings, and (e) have complete control of the budget.[12]

In sum, it is misleading to compare the different versions of decentralization among large cities. The difference in sizes, even among the five large school systems, is wide. For example, as previously mentioned, the eight regional districts established in Detroit are for the greater part smaller in area than the more than thirty-one school districts established in New York City or the twelve administrative areas established in Los Angeles. Definitions are confusing, too. For example, the concept of region in Detroit is equivalent to the concept of district in New York City and administrative area in Los Angeles; the concept of area in Chicago is equivalent to zone in Los Angeles. When referring to large cities, the extent of community control, even community participation, is usually limited; decentralization generally refers to administrative procedures. Also, it is misleading to conclude that the demand for decentralization and community control is only limited to large cities and minority groups, as indicated by the Louisville-Jefferson County Plan and the Hyde Park Community Conference in Chicago.

Legal Issues of Community Control. The growing trend of black parents seeking decentralization and local control represents a departure from the present majority point of view of the inferiority of segregated schools since the Brown decision and the subsequent court cases to desegregate the schools. On what legal grounds can the black community present their case? Although the courts are not clear on the exact extent of the parents' right to control the education of their children, they do agree that parents have the right to a personal choice.

In the first court case directly involving the issue of local control *The Council of Supervisory Association of the Public Schools* v. *The Board of Education of the City of New York* (1968), the court recognized the need and effectiveness of local control; it stated:

> . . . in certain communities, specifically disadvantaged areas, the performance of pupils in those schools [is] far below the level of pupils in other communities and that there [is] a definite

---

[12] The above is based on interviews with Mrs. Arlene Rubin, chairman of the "Council for Local Control," Hyde Park–Kenwood Community Conference and Herschel Rader, the major author of the plan to increase local control of the schools in Hyde Park.

correlation between the schools' performance and parents' involvement in the subject schools.[13]

In this connection, Lopate, Flaxman, Bynum, and Gordon (1970) reviewed several studies which showed a high or significant relationship between parent participation in school affairs and their children's heightened ego development and academic progress. Similarly, Jablonsky (1968), the associate director for the ERIC Information Retrieval Center for the Disadvantaged which monthly accumulates and disseminates a vast amount of research data on the disadvantaged, concluded that the schools where parents and communities were actively involved "have greater success in educating children [p. 6]."

In the *Hobson* v. *Hansen* Case,[14] the court extended the scope of "unequal educational opportunity" to the track system, also pointing out that the Washington, D.C. Public Schools, or the "power structure," paid little attention to the interests of the powerless minority. Although the school system did not exhibit a discriminatory intent against minorities, Judge Shelly Wright weighed the "adverse effects" of the track system and concluded it was unconstitutional. This interpretation was primarily based on the doctrine of "equal educational opportunity," which is linked to the "due process" clause of the Fourteenth Amendment and the "critical right" court cases which justify intervention when the rights of minorities are threatened.[15]

Although the Ocean-Hill Brownsville local board [16] lost its court case in trying to establish the legality and independence of its schools, the previously stated New York and Washington, D.C. courts' interpretations have special application to future legal issues of community control which were apparently ignored in the *Ocean-Hill Brownsville* case. It may be argued that: (1) centralized large city schools are bureaucratic, impersonal, unresponsive to ghetto residents, and are unequal to suburban schools in terms of measurable criteria such as economic and plant resources and teacher and administrator characteristics, resulting in "inequality of educational opportunity" for minorities, even if the intent is nondiscriminatory; (2) decentralization and community control is a "critical right" for minorities in order to correct the inequalities of ghetto education; (3) community control of schools by minorities, balanced against the "adverse effect" and limited results of centralized education,

---

[13] *Council of Super. Ass'n. of Public Schools* v. *Bd. of Educ., op cit.*
[14] *Hobson* v. *Hansen.* 269 F. Supp. 401 (D.D.C. 1967).
[15] *Ibid.* Also Flynn (1969) and *Hobson* v. *Hansen* (1968)
[16] *Ocean-Hill Brownsville Gov. Bd.* v. *Bd. of Educ.* 56 Misc 2d at 37, 294 N.Y.S. 2d at 138 (1968).

assumes the character of a constitutional right; and (4) although segregated schooling legally connotes inferiority, the law is based on the supposed fact that the effects of segregation are detrimental to black children; however, this fact may not be absolutely true.[17]

The idea is to pursue the words of the *Hobson* case which asserted that a "power structure" may deny "equal educational opportunity," regardless of racial imbalance; thus, if the "power structure" denies "equal educational opportunity" or has failed to promote it, the school system should allow greater participation in local control of the schools. Community advocates need to focus on the inequalities of centralized school systems through objective measures, then show how decentralization and local control may reverse these inequalities—all of which have already been suggested by the *Council* of *Supervisory Association* court case and the review of literature by Lopate *et al.* (1970).

Arguments For and Against Decentralization

Twelve arguments for and against decentralization and local control now follow. Most of the discussion is favorable, reflecting, of course, the author's own biases.[18]

1. *Decentralization will impede integration.* Those who make this claim —mainly the white power structure of the schools and cities and the "average" white parent—have often tried to maintain the *status quo.* This meant being against integration when blacks demanded it and now keeping them from gaining control over their own communities and schools. Integration demanded that blacks be admitted into the system; they were never allowed entry, and now they seek to change the system. Whites no longer have to decide what to do with those "niggers"; many of those "niggers" have decided that integration is no longer feasible or in their best interests. Integration connotes assimilation into the WASP system, being socialized by an environment and a school that the black child has little control over. The majority of blacks now demand an open and free society which recognizes their identity. Rather than being assimilated, a process where the dominant group enforces certain norms and values on a subgroup, minorities seek cultural pluralism, a process

---

[17] *Supra,* Chapter V. See problems inherent in the research on blacks and with the desegregation studies.

[18] Fantini and Magot (1968) examined eight points in favor of decentralization, six of which appear in this subheading; however, their analysis is different since they have stronger biases in favor of decentralization and local control.

where there is give-and-take between the dominant group and subgroup and there is a relative degree of equality and respect among all cultures. To be sure, every reader who is a member of a religious, ethnic, or racial group recognizes that the process of assimilation in America, or anywhere else, was at times psychologically harmful to him—especially during childhood and youth.

In any event, the Northern schools, as previously mentioned, are more segregated today than they were prior to the Supreme Court decision in 1954. Most educators contend that schools cannot be integrated unless the communities are integrated, and it is unrealistic in the foreseeable future to expect white communities to welcome blacks. Most whites never really wanted to integrate; many blacks no longer want it, and it doesn't seem feasible—with or without decentralization. Indeed, educational reform and redistribution of power should be implemented in relationship to reality, and the reality of the racial situation connotes that genuine integration is infeasible. Since blacks are unwelcome in white communities and schools, unless in some cases the percentage of blacks is kept at a minimum or unless there is coercion, they have the moral right to control their own communities and schools.

2. *Decentralization will balkanize the cities.* The myth of the melting pot no longer exists. Communities and schools are already balkanized, especially along ethnic and racial patterns. Although the school system did not create ghettoes or enclaves, it often gerrymandered school districts around them. Since the great majority of schools and cities are not willing to support integration, or even to respect ethnic and racial differences, minority groups should have power—at least control—over their own destinies in their communities and schools. Decentralization and community control do not necessarily have to lead to isolation; it can mean that minorities find new ways to work with the larger community on a more equal basis so they become a part of the total system, without losing their identity or surrendering their culture. Giving local power to various subgroups means that various ethnic and racial groups can possibly exist together with justice and equality. It will mean that the American twentieth century concept of a nation of many nations and races can work.

3. *Decentralization is the return to the myth of "separate but equal."* Most blacks have always wanted better schools for their children. This meant trying to attend integrated schools (especially in the South where the white power structure puts the most money and best equipment into schools attended by white students). However, this did not always mean

integration for the sole purpose of integration. If the black schools were made superior, or at least as good as the white schools, the black community (even Messrs. Kenneth B. Clark, Robert L. Carter, and Bayard Rustin) would probably be satisfied.

Most black people recognized long ago that integration in the North, due to racial attitudes and demographical trends, was fast becoming infeasible. They demanded integration partially because they were trapped by their own rhetoric and partially because it pressured school systems to try to improve ghetto schools. Decentralization and community control is based on the belief that blacks can improve their own schools better than the system can—or will, under normal circumstances.

The difference between *de jure* and *de facto* segregation is "conventional wisdom." The latter type of segregation, in fact, is common in American society; perhaps it should not be misconstrued as unequal or nihilistic; in part, it merely reveals that different culture and ethnic groups prefer to live together and send their children to the same school. This practice is the basis of an open and free society, as well as the neighborhood school.

4. Decentralization is a scheme for alleviating the pressure from the black community. Decentralization and community control connote local involvement and thus a reduction of alienation between the schools and community. No matter how well-chosen and how well-intentioned the members of the central board in a large city, they cannot possibly be as adequately informed as a local board about the interests and needs of the schools in each neighborhood—with its own ethnic and racial differences and with its own student-teacher-administrator-community problems.

In the past, city schools have excluded lower-class and minority groups from policy making. This is smug contempt toward the poor and nonwhites; it is contradictory to participatory democracy. The middle-class suburbanite would not tolerate a school system run by an outside agency, especially one that failed to educate or recognize the needs of his children. In effect, we permit whites who can afford to move to suburbia to set up and run their own schools, while we exclude poor and nonwhites from controlling their own city schools. If the schools are to be relevant to ghetto children, their parents should have a voice in decision making.

5. Ghetto parents, with little formal education, are unable to effectively run public schools. There is no proof that ghetto people are unable to run their schools since schools in the city, suburbs, or rural areas have been customarily controlled by the middle and upper classes. Past experience reveals that most "experts," whether they come from Harvard University, a central board of education, or the nation's capital, are unable to solve the educational ills of the ghetto. Most professional educators—teachers, administrators, etc.—have failed to educate the black poor, too. Decentralization and community control is an attempt to cope with this failure; it is an attempt to increase parental participation in educational decision making. Black parents want the opportunity to fail for themselves—or the opportunity to succeed. Since they should be aware of their own problems and the problems of their children, they should be able to make good use of their new responsibilities.

At any rate, the parents will not run the schools but rather vote for a local school board that will hire teachers, administrators, and consultants to make the professional decisions and run the school on a daily basis; the school personnel will be accountable to the local board—not to a remote city central board which is usually unable to grasp local problems and which usually seeks to maintain the *status quo*. To question the feasibility of giving the poor and/or ghetto residents the right to elect their own local board is analogous to questioning the fundamental concept of democracy—the right of the people to elect their own representatives to city hall and Congress. Since the democratic process is dependent on popular education, there is a relationship between ghetto parents controlling their own schools and the democratic process.

6. *Decentralization will enhance black racism.* Charges of racism are sometimes exaggerated and, in many cases, connote white fear of and racism toward different racial groups, a twin enigma which is rooted in American history. In the few cases where blacks are teaching white hate, this enmity is better for the students than the customary process of learning to hate themselves—a more "refined" racism, subtle but inherent in our texts and curricula, as well as indicated by adult feelings and gestures which are communicated to the students—and over a period of time is more destructive to the students' selfhood than is the "unrefined" rhetoric of "pigs," "honkiedom," "whitey," etc.

The schools are a product of society—WASP society—which has injured most black children. If charges of racism are leveled, they should first be directed at white society and their schools which have defined blacks, at best, as inferior or "invisible" second-class citizens. Black parents want to control their own schools to stop this injury to their children. Their children also need an education that will help them cope with white discrimination and racism. Indeed, there is justice in the demand for black pride to replace white mythology; however, it should be noted that there is a tipping point, where black pride begins to duplicate the errors of white racism and racial narcissism. Blacks, rather than becoming infatuated by slogans and myths, hopefully, will seek to reform their schools.

7. *Decentralization will foster "vigilante" groups which will harass white teachers and supervisors.* Middle-class whites do not have to resort to such groups because they do not experience the same intense frustration; moreover, they generally have enough influence so that dissatisfaction with the schools and staff is minimal. So long as blacks are discriminated against and refused the right to control their own schools, self-appointed groups or black militant groups will sometimes try to change the system —and most white teachers and administrators are part of the system, or at least help perpetuate it. Once blacks gain control of their own schools and once the rhetoric ceases, there will be no need for black groups to harass white school personnel; moreover, the parents can be trusted to stop this harassment because their children's education is at stake. The group that probably cannot be trusted is the school personnel—black or white—whose first interests are to themselves, and not their students. This is also one reason for the need for professional accountability. If, however, "vigilante" groups persist, it behooves the teacher or administrator, white or black, to try to deal with the problem, rather than run from it. Acquiescence to racism, black or white, spreads racism and, in turn, polarizes the black and white communities even further.

8. *Decentralization will reject white participation.* Blacks recognize that decentralization largely depends upon the white taxpayer paying for it and the white power structure permitting it. They are a minority group and can go only as far in improving their schools as whites allow. Granted, there is talk about only black teachers and administrators being qualified to work with black children, but blacks recognize the need for and help of capable and concerned white professionals. Nevertheless, it behooves the white teacher to answer these false pronouncements and demands for white exclusion. Most white teachers refuse, however, to speak out because it invites confrontations and charges of racism. Yet not to deal with these pronouncements is to invite future confrontations and the loss of many competent ghetto teachers.

Presently, the black community is basically ruled by white business and political interests; the black schools are run by white educators. Black pride and power reject white domination, but not white participation. White controlled schools have failed to educate black youth. Decentralization and community control permits blacks to run their own schools, to decide who they want to hire to teach their children. Most blacks are not saying they do not want to have anything to do with white teachers and supervisors; they are saying they should have a voice in the affairs of educating their own children.

9. *Decentralization means the professional standards, especially the merit system, will be lowered.* Although the examination system for promotion has helped reduce corruption and patronage in city schools, it has unwittingly created inbreeding and has discriminated against ethnic groups different from those in control of the system. For example, in Boston the teachers, administrators, and central board barons are predominantly Irish. In New York City, they are predominantly Jewish. In Milwaukee, they are predominantly German and Scandinavian.

The examinations are also designed to discriminate against professionals from outside the "mother" system. Participating in a supervisory test usually involves traveling to specific test centers on several occasions over a six-month to one-year period. Answers to questions are largely based on local "wisdom," not state or nationwide professionalism or philosophy. Rigorous test procedures make test candidates study for years and memorize monographs on index cards. Those who pass these tests prove they are good test takers and have facility with the English language; there seems to be little or no correlation between high scores on their tests and successful leadership.

The black community no longer accepts many values imposed by middle-class educators. In particular, objective tests and procedures are viewed as an old-style method of maintaining middle-class standards and limiting minorities from becoming administrators. Thus, these factors are viewed as contributing to the failure of educating the disadvantaged. The present promotion system needs to be modified and replaced by one that is more flexible and allows for diversity, outside leadership, and minority advancement. New hiring and promotional standards which allow for such flexibility, while maintaining literacy and competency standards, need to be established, and professionals need to be held accountable.

10. *Decentralization will weaken the teachers' and supervisors' organizations.* Large city school systems breed and perpetuate administrative bureaucrats—school personnel who seek to maintain the *status quo*. The only group to successfully challenge the bureaucrats' control has been the teachers' union, and its major concern has been to improve teacher salaries and conditions—and rightfully so, since the function of a union is to further the interests of its members.

Decentralization and community control mean a loss of professional or teacher and administrator power, at best, a sharing of power with the community but, at worst, complete accountability to the community. The growing threat to the teachers' and supervisors' organizaions was reflected in the fact that during the 1968 New York City teacher strike the three experimental school areas remained open and 85 percent of their staff crossed the picket lines. Also, black teachers and supervisory organizations are growing across the country—a potential threat to the present AFT and supervisory associations.

For the community to demand control of their own schools means they must challenge those who are now in power. Unfortunately, conflict, sometimes force, should be expected from those who seek to change the power structure, especially if they are continuously denied power.

11. *Decentralization is inefficient and creates duplication and extra costs.* The battle against school bigness is part of a larger social trend in our country against institutional bigness in government, industry, universities, churches, etc. Bigness usually creates institutional complexity and problems in communication and decision making. Bigness makes the system unresponsive to the needs of the community and local schools. Pilot programs and special projects are implemented at a great cost; they are often ineffective but formulated to maintain the *status quo* and to create the facade that the system is responsive to the consumers. Bigness alienates the average citizen and ignores "grass roots," which is tantamount to ignoring participatory democracy. Such alienation either leads to apathy or action, and the latter often leads to overt conflict with professionals which cannot be measured in dollars but has a detrimental impact on teaching and learning. Finally, any cost of duplication should be offset by the cost of school bigness.

12. *Decentralization does not change the system; it merely changes the size.* Decentralization is also part of a social process of change in the cities. Redistribution of power is in itself an aspect of change. Passing the responsibility of education from the bureaucrats to the people is a change, and considering how very far from their promise and potential the schools have failed to educate the poor, they cannot get much worse and hopefully they should get better with community participation and control. School decentralization and community control connote a change in personnel practices and in the curriculum, as previously mentioned, and simultaneous motivation for publishers to print more objective materials, as well as to present a more favorable reinterpretation of black literature and history.

Decentralization means the schools belong to the people, making it possible for the schools to relate to the parents and their children. The community-controlled school is certainly more aware of the needs and interest of local residents, including the adult population, thereby serving as an innovative force in meeting their recreational, cultural, and educational needs. The closer bond between school and community permits the school to become a center for coordinating community problems and policies (among them housing, welfare, employment, health, and legal aid) and community social institutions which are related to the urban setting.[19] The fact that the schools, one of the social institutions of the community, will be controlled by the people can help restore a sense of community and foster educational responsibility and accountability.

In most large cities, the schools have become overcentralized and organized as monolithic power configurations. The context and implications of this type of power arrangement is clarified by the figure and explanations below.

Model 2

Continuum of Power Configurations [20]

Monolithic	Factional	Coalitional	Amorphous

Model 2 illustrates a continuum of power, ranging from the monolithic level (defined, monopolistic) to the amphorous level (vague, powerless).

A brief description of the power configurations are:

1. *Monolithic.* Monopolistic, single or cohesive group.
2. *Factional.* At least two people or groups have power.
3. *Coalitional.* Leadership and power varies with the issue and consists of fluid coalitions.
4. *Amorphous.* Absence of any persistent pattern of power.

Decentralization is an attempt to reduce the monolithic power of the central board of education and redistribute the power to the community. With power belonging to the community, there is no guarantee that the power configurations would change; however, it would most likely become factional or coalitional, and, hopefully, coalitional, which seems to be the closest to the democratic ideal.

---

[19] *Supra,* Introduction.
[20] Based on Carver and Crowe (1969).

A Model for Reorganizing Urban Schools

Whether decentralizing the school system and permitting local control of the schools will actually lead to more effective education for black children and other minorities is no longer the real issue. The fact is trends across the country suggest that decentralization and varying degrees of community participation and community control will increase in the 1970s and eventually become a permanent facet of urban education. The redistribution of power and the subsequent changes in the schools provide the opportunity for improving the education of the disadvantaged as well as that of *all* children.

Below is a model which outlines characteristics of the traditional urban school as well as the ideal urban school and can serve as a broad guideline for reorganizing the schools. The model suggests that the schools are social institutions which can be defined by basic characteristics. Of course, the characteristics represent hypothetical dimensions; they are not conclusive, and they reflect the author's knowledge and biases. Another author would most likely present a varied model.

In general, the traditional school is machine oriented while the ideal school is people oriented. Whereas the former organization reflects a micro approach and closed system, the latter organization attempts a macro approach and open system. The traditional organization usually is restricted, advocates a collective norm, and functions with little reference to the individual; the ideal organization is more diffuse and concerned with intra-relationships and calls attention to different aspects of individual behavior.

Model 3

Selected Characteristics of Traditional and Ideal Urban Schools

MAJOR COMPONENTS

Characteristics	*Traditional School*	*Ideal School*
Central Board	Mandates directions to local schools Patronizing attitude of central board administrators toward local school personnel Resentment of local school personnel toward central board administrators	Cooperative teamwork between central board and local schools Mutual respect and communication between central board administrators and local school personnel

Characteristics	*Traditional School*	*Ideal School*
Administrative Subunits	Manifold, uncoordinated	Limited, coordinated
School District	Large size	Reduced size
	Central board exercises major control	Central board and local board share control
	Distant from community, unaware of needs of the local schools	Sensitive to the needs of the local schools
Community	Indifferent, powerless	Active, influential
	Alienated toward the system and school	Cooperation with and trust in the system and school
Parents	Same as community	Same as community
District Superintendent	Machine oriented, views himself as part of the management team	People oriented, leadership in instruction and community organization
	Divorced from the community and school	Community and educational leader
	Status quo approach	Reform minded, change agent
	Tenured, product of the system	Contract for a (three year) period which may be renewed by the local board; responsible to the community, and his job depends on making sufficient reforms
Principal	Same as district superintendent	Same as district superintendent
Teacher	Treated as a machine part	Treated as a person and respected as an individual
	Subordinate, and relatively powerless	Decision-making influence
	Divorced from community	Community change agent
	Little rapport with students	Good rapport with students
Students	Treated as a machine part	Treated as a person and respected as an individual
	No say in decision making, powerless	Decision-making influence, new responsibilities
	Limited rights	Rights are respected

ORGANIZATIONAL NORMS AND STRUCTURES

Characteristics	Traditional School	Ideal School
Ideology	Machine oriented, closed	People oriented, open
	The *status quo* approach, threatened by change	Adaptable, innovative, accepts change
	Rigid, narrow minded	Flexible
Criteria of Norms	Traditional	Progressive
	The school system's norms dominate	Consumers' (parents' and students') norms dominate
Types of Values	Pragmatic	Moral, ethical
Socialization Process	Assimilation	Cultural Pluralism
	Conformity	Individualism is encouraged
Power and Authority	Vertical	Horizontal
	Visibility of power relations	Power is diffused, shared, and reciprocal
	Closeness of supervision	Supervision is limited
	Impersonal Rules	Personal feelings are considered
	Interpersonal tension	Socializing, give-and-take relations
Executive Office	Authoritarian	Democratic
	Control vested solely with top echelons	Control shared, checks and balances at various echelons
	Ignores subordinates' needs and interests	Consultation with subordinates
Behavioral Distances	Factions, cliques	Overall loyalty to school
	Subgroups among staff— based on race or age, department, position or power	Few, if any, subgroups
Roles	Incompatability, conformity	Expectations are mutually supporting
	Prescribed, concerned with attributes of people	Flexibility, concerned with relationships and interdependence of people
	Student-teacher-administration distinctions and conflict	Student-teacher-administration dialogue and rapport

Characteristics	Traditional School	Ideal School
Career Patterns	Limited	Several entry points, including paraprofessionals and teacher aides
	Promotions based on "payoff" system, inbreeding	Promotions based on merit and objective criteria, diversity
Norms of Reciprocity	Individual is isolated	People are mutually dependent on each other
	Limited teamwork	Teamwork, people help each other
Energy	Disregards external environment	Continuous inflow of energy from external environment
	Fails to recognize that it is functional, in part, on external environment	Changes with or ahead of external environment
Information Input	Hides and ignores its problems	Recognizes and corrects its problems, small groups organized to solve problems
	Limited and ineffective procedures for solving problems	Variety of procedures used to find solutions
	Screens out new data, reluctant to change	Unenclosed, willing to accept new ideas and change
Research	Describes problems	Geared toward solutions
	Dissonance between researcher and practitioner	Communication and rapport between researcher and practitioner
	Research rejected by practitioner as impractical, practice considered anti-intellectual and mechanical by researcher	Researcher and practitioner see the value of each other's work
Innovation	Hit-or-miss, is based on hunches and sentiment	Scientific, based on feasibility and success factors
	Wasted cost, effort, and time	Cost-effectiveness criteria
Implementation	Based on mandates from higher authorities	Based on research findings and evaluation, revisions, and re-evaluation

Characteristics	Traditional School	Ideal School
Cycle of Entropy	Organization becomes outmoded, runs down, and moves toward disorganization and decline	Organization accepts and stores new input, thus acquiring a negative entropy

TEACHING AND LEARNING PROCESS

Characteristics	Traditional School	Ideal School
Teacher Training	Training institution is generally divorced from school, contact is limited to training student teachers	Close relationship between training institution and school
	Training is based on acquiring credits	Training includes proven performance
	Training is unrelated to school and classroom situation	Training is related to school and classroom situation
	Gap with preservice and inservice teacher training	Continuous teacher training
Curriculum	Past and future oriented	Immediate, as well as past and future, oriented
	Nonessential, trivial information	Relevant data
	Prescribed guidelines are followed	Guidelines are modified to meet students' needs and interests
Teaching Style	Related to system's and school's philosophy of what is "good" or "proper"	Many styles are acceptable, attempt to match the teacher's style with the students' learning style
Teacher Expectations	Stereotyping and classifying students into positive and negative learning categories, achiever-nonachiever	Students are perceived as potential learners, limited classifications
Grouping	Homogeneous	Heterogeneous (if feasible)
	Large student-teacher ratio	Small student-teacher ratio
	Classroom is organized as one group, teaching directed at "average"	Several groups formed in classroom, teaching is individualized

Characteristics	Traditional School	Ideal School
Classroom	One method is acceptable, usually formal classroom	Several methods are acceptable, formal-informal range, including experimentation with "atypical" methods
Media	Bought whenever funds are available	Evaluation of instructional worth of media
	Unused by most of staff	Inservice training for using new media
Learning	Teacher is purveyor of knowledge	Teacher is counselor and resource person
	Cognitive orientation	Cognitive and affective orientation
	Knowledge, memorization of data	Concepts, hypotheses, generalizations, implications
Grading	Cognitive tests are stressed	Cognitive test scores are supplemented with students' creativity, motivation and effort
Accountability	Students are held accountable	Students, parents, teachers, and administrators are held accountable
	Students' home and environment are considered major learning factors, used to alibi failure	Students' home and environment is considered as only one learning criterion. School assumes its responsibility, too

Conclusion

Some basic principles for school decentralization emerge from this chapter. These principles are based on the review of issues by Smith and Hazard (1971),[21] because of their similar views with this author.

1. Result in a realignment of the parties involved in the process of educational decision making, giving parents and community residents an increased voice in policy making.

---

[21] Calvert H. Smith and William R. Hazard, "On Decentralized School Systems," *Illinois School Journal,* © 1971. Reprinted with the permission of the *Illinois School Journal,* published by Chicago State University and of Calvert H. Smith and William R. Hazard.

2. Open the educational system to a far broader base of talent than the conventionally prepared career educator.

3. Foster the respect for and the preservation of diversity.

4. Insure increased community awareness and participation in the development of educational policy closely related to the diverse needs and aspirations of the city's population.

5. Afford the children, parents, teachers, other educators, and the city at large a single school system that combines the advantages of the finest suburban and small city educational system.

6. Strengthen the individual school as an urban institution that enhances a sense of community and encourages close coordination and cooperation with other governmental and private efforts to advance the well-being of children and all others.

7. Define and identify those powers that belong exclusively to the local community, those properly held by the professionals, and those that should be shared. Insure the hiring of an educational ombudsman to serve as an independent review office of all local and central board decisions.

8. Build into the local community the skill and competence to develop and establish educational policy and to acquire the skills to measure the effectiveness of the educational program.

9. Insure local control over key policy decisions in four critical areas: personnel, budget, curriculum, and pupil policy.

10. Vest decision-making power in community representatives. Technical resources must be made readily available to the community to be used at their discretion.

   a. Local governing bodies [should] be locally selected and mechanisms for encouraging broader community participation should be thoughtfully developed.

   b. Local boards [should] make provisions for periodic evaluation of the total program. Chief administrators, principals, teachers, and community workers should be evaluated along with the program.

   c. Standards for evaluating professionals' performances must be spelled out specifically and known in advance by administrators, teachers, and parents.[22]

---

[22] Teachers must also have the right to appeal negative evaluations and be guaranteed a right to a fair hearing by a city-wide review board.

    d. Criteria for teacher transfer must be made explicit, and such criteria must be expanded to include standards of effectiveness.

    e. Local boards [should] have complete control of their budgets, with their own bank accounts, the right to hire and fire, and the right to make their own contracts for building maintenance and repair.

    f. Parents and community residents [should] have the authority to select from among a variety of sound educational alternatives which have been outlined by professionals serving the community. The professional staff should be agents of the community by helping it reach its goals (pp. 25–26).

The schools have always been controlled by the middle- and upper-middle class society. This went unnoticed because the gap between the poor and affluent was not always so wide and the black-white conflict had not yet surfaced. Previously, there was more hope, too, among the poor for entering the American mainstream and among blacks for experiencing the promises of integration.

However, the schools have always failed to educate most of the poor, for the great majority dropped out of school or graduated as functional illiterates. This went unnoticed for so long because the labor market absorbed these educational waste products; moreover, most of these school failures were white and did not face continuous job discrimination; they were able to assimilate in one or two generations whereas the new poor—many of whom are nonwhites—no matter how many generations are considered, find assimilation difficult, if not impossible.

If it were not for the school systems' monopoly of the education of the poor, the schools probably would have gone bankrupt long ago. As of now a large number of parents send their children to parochial schools, and the population that can afford to send their children to private schools or flee to the suburbs do just that—and, in doing so, forsake the city public schools.

Decentralization (and community control) is an attempt to change the bureaucratic and impersonal nature of the schools and to remedy the present educational crisis in the ghetto. It is a crisis that has been growing since the large city schools started to become overcentralized and blacks began their exodus to the "Promised Land" across the Mason Dixon line. Since the civil rights movement and the War on Poverty, the crisis has become more evident. Many blacks are now claiming that their children can receive an equal or superior education in their own communities, rather than in a white school that doesn't really want them. Educators who prefer to maintain the *status quo* are perhaps inviting disaster by default. School decentralization is in part fuelled by the black power movement; both trends seek to expose the system and create a new one—viable, innovative, and related to the needs and interest of all youth and especially black youth. It has more potential for good than for evil. We should at least give it a try and, in doing so, seek a new coalition among students, parents, teachers, and administrators.

REFERENCES

Allen, Dwight W., & Mackin, Robert A. "A Revolution in Teacher Education." *Phi Delta Kappan,* 1970, *51,* 485–88.

Allen, Vernon L. "Theoretical Issues in Poverty Research." *Journal of Social Issues,* 1970, *26,* 149–67.

Alloway, David N., & Cordasco, Francesco. *Minorities in the American City.* New York: David McKay Co., 1970.

American Association of Colleges for Teacher Education. *Realignments for Teacher Education.* Yearbook 1970. Washington, D.C.: AACTE, 1970.

American Civil Liberties Union. *Academic Freedom in the Secondary Schools.* New York: American Civil Liberties Union, 1969.

Andrew, Dean C., & Roberts, Lawrence H. *Final Evaluation Report on the Texarkana Dropout Program.* Magnolia, Arkansas: Regional VIII Education Service Center, July 1970.

Armstrong, C. P., & Gregor, A. J. "Integrated Schools and Negro Character Development." *Psychiatry,* 1964, *27,* 69–72.

Berry, Brewton. *Race and Ethnic Relations.* Boston: Houghton Mifflin Co., 1958.

Berry, Brian J. L., & Meltzer, Jack. "Introduction." In B. J. L. Berry & J. Meltzer (Eds.), *Goals for Urban America.* Englewood Cliffs, New Jersey: Prentice-Hall, 1967.

Berke, Joel S., Bailey, Stephen K., Campbell, Allan K., & Sacks, Seymour. "The Patterns of Allocation of Federal Aid to Education." Paper Presented at the Annual AERA Meeting. New York, February 6, 1971. (Research Grant No. 690–0506)

Bettelheim, Bruno. "Obsolete Youth: Towards a Psychograph of Adolescent Rebellion." *Encounter,* 1969, *33,* 29–42.

Billingsley, Andrew. "Black Families and White Social Science." *Journal of Social Issues,* 1970, *26,* 127–42.

Blauner, Robert. "International Colonialism and Ghetto Revolt." *Social Problems,* 1969, *16,* 393–408.

Booz-Allen & Hamilton. *Organizational Survey: Board of Education—City of Chicago.* May, 1967. (Mimeographed)

Broom, Leonard, & Glenn, Norval D. *Transformation of the Negro American.* New York: Harper and Row, Publishers, 1965.

Brown, Jr., Roscoe C. "How to Make Educational Research Relevant to the Urban Community—The Researcher's View." Paper Presented at the Annual AERA Meeting. New York, February 5, 1971.

Bryant, Barbara E. *High School Students Look at Their World.* Columbus, Ohio: R. H. Goettler, 1970.

Bureau of the Census. *U.S. Census of Population, 1960.* Vol. 1. Washington, D.C.: U.S. Government Printing Office, 1961.

Bureau of the Census. *U.S. Census of Population, 1970.* Vol. 1. Washington, D.C.: U.S. Government Printing Office, 1971.

Burnett, Calvin W. "Urban Education in Low Income Areas: An Overview." *Catholic Educational Review,* 1969, *67,* 105–22.

Campbell, Angus, & Schuman, Howard. *Racial Attitudes in Fifteen American Cities.* Supplemental Studies for the National Advisory Commission on Civil Disorders. Washington, D.C.: U.S. Government Printing Office, 1968.

Carmichael, Stokely, & Hamilton, Charles V. *Black Power.* (Vintage ed.) New York: Random House, 1967.

Caro, Francis G. "Issues in the Evaluation of Social Programs." *Review of Educational Research,* 1971, *41,* 87–114.

Carter, Barbara. *Pickets, Parents, and Power.* New York: Citation Press, 1971.

Carver, Fred D., & Crowe, Donald O. "An Interdisciplinary Framework for the Study of Community Power." *Educational Administration Quarterly,* 1969, *5,* 50–64.

Chestler, Mark A. "Shared Power and Student Decision Making." *Educational Leadership,* 1970, *28,* 9–14.

Clark, Kenneth B. "Alternative Public School Systems." *Harvard Educational Review,* 1968, *38,* 100–13.

Clark, Kenneth B. *Youth in the Ghetto.* New York: Haryou, 1964.

Coleman, James S. "The Concept of Equality of Education Opportunity." *Harvard Educational Review,* 1968, *38,* 7–22.

The Commission on Urban Education. A Report to the General Assembly of Illinois. Chicago: State of Illinois, February 1971.

Cook, Desmond L. "Management Control Theory as the Context for Educational Evaluation." *Journal of Research and Development in Education.* 1970, *3*, 13–26.

Cook, James M., & Sadker, David. "Current trends in Teacher Education Curriculum." Paper Presented at the Annual AERA Meeting. New York, February 6, 1971.

Corwin, Ronald G. *A Sociology of Education.* New York: Appleton-Century-Crofts, 1965.

Daniels, Roger, & Kitano, Harry H. L. *American Racism.* Englewood Cliffs, New Jersey: Prentice-Hall, 1970.

Deutsch, Martin. "Organizational and Conceptual Barriers to Social Change." *Journal of Social Issues,* 1969, *25*, 5–18.

Division of School-Community Relations and the Office of School Decentralization. *Detroits' Schools Make History With Decentralization.* Detroit: Board of Education of the City of Detroit, October 1970.

Dodson, Dan W. "The Uncivilized Right to Revolt." Unpublished, 1968.

Doll, Russell C. "Alternative Models of Institutional Change in the Slum School." *Phi Delta Kappan,* 1971, *52*, 334–37.

Downs, Anthony. "Alternative Futures for the American Ghetto." *Daedalus.* 1968, *97*, 1331–78.

Draft of Plan for Hyde Park-Kenwood Board of Education. March 30, 1970. (Mimeographed)

Dunn, Joan. *Retreat from Learning.* New York: David McKay Co., 1955.

Ebel, Robert L. "Behavioral Objectives: A Close Look." *Phi Delta Kappan.* 1970, *52*, 171–73.

Educational Renewal: A Decentralization Proposal for the Los Angeles Unified School District. A Report by the Decentralization Task Force. Los Angeles: Los Angeles Unified School District, February 22, 1971.

Fantini, Mario D. "Discussion: Implementing Equal Educational Opportunity." *Harvard Educational Review,* 1968, *38*, 160–75.

Fantini, Mario D., & Magot, Richard. "Decentralizing Urban School Systems." In A. Toeffler (Ed.), *The Schoolhouse in the City.* New York: Praeger Publishers, 1968. Pp. 110–35.

Farmer, James A. "Indigenous Interactional Research." Paper Presented at the Annual AERA Meeting. New York, February 5, 1971.

Fein, Leonard J. "The Limits of Liberalism." *Saturday Review,* June 20, 1970, 83–85, ff.

Fisher, John H. "School Parks for Equal Educational Opportunities." *Journal of Negro Education,* 1968, *37*, 301–9.

Flynn, Michael. "Community Control and the Public Schools—Practical Approach for Achieving Equal Educational Opportunity: A Socio-Legal Perspective." *Suffolk University Law Review*, 1969, *4*, 308–42.

Forehand, G. A. "Curriculum Evaluation as Decision-Making Process." *Journal of Research and Development in Education*. 1970, *3*, 27–37.

Friedenberg, Edgar Z. *The Vanishing Adolescent*. New York: Dell Publishing Co., 1962. (Originally published by Beacon Press, 1959)

Friedenberg, Edgar Z. *The Dignity of Youth and Other Atavisms*. Boston: Beacon Press, 1966.

Frumier, Jack R. "Why Students Rebel." *Educational Leadership*, 1970, *27*, 346–50.

Gittell, Marilyn. *Participants and Participation*. New York: Praeger Publishers, 1967.

Gittell, Marilyn. "Urban School Politics: Professionalism vs. Reform." *Journal of Social Issues*, 1970, *26*, 69–84.

Glenn, Norval D. "The Role of White Resistance and Facilitation in the Negro Struggle for Equality." *Phylon*, 1965, *26*, 105–16.

Glenn, Norval D. "The Kerner Report, Social Scientists, and the American Public." In J. L. Frost & G. R. Hawkes (Eds.), *The Disadvantaged Child*. Boston: Houghton Mifflin, 1970. Pp. 442–47.

Glickstein, Howard A. "Federal Educational Programs and Minority Groups." *Journal of Negro Education*, 1969, *38*, 303–14.

Goodland, John I. "The Reconstruction of Teacher Education." *Teachers College Record*, 1970, *72*, 61–72.

Gordon, Edmund W., & Wilkerson, Doxey A. *Compensatory Education for the Disadvantaged*. New York: College Entrance Examination Board, 1966.

Gottlieb, David. "Goal Aspirations and Goal Fulfillments: Differences Between Deprived and Affluent American Adolescents." *American Journal of Orthopsychiatry*, 1964, *34*, 934–41.

Guidelines for Regional and Central Boards of Education of the School District of the City of Detroit. Detroit: Board of Education of the City of Detroit, October 26, 1970. (Pamphlet contains text of Public Act 48, State of Michigan, 75th Legislature, Regular Session of 1970.)

Havighurst, Robert J., Smith, Frank L., & Wilder, David E. *A Profile of the Large-City High School*. Washington, D.C.: National Association of Secondary School Principals, 1970.

Hentoff, Nat. *Our Children Are Dying*. New York: The Viking Press, 1966.

Herzog, Elizabeth. "Social Stereotypes of Social Research." *Journal of Social Issues*, 1970, *26*, 109–25.

Hicklin, Charles R. "Student Dissent." *Illinois Education*, 1971, *33*, 117–20.

Hicks, E. P. Changing the Role of the Cooperating Teacher." *Journal of Teacher Education*, 1969, *20*, 153–57.

Highland, John H. "Student Dress Codes: Fact or Fiction?" *Illinois Education*, 1971, *33*, 114–16.

"Hobson v. Hansen: Judicial Supervision of the Color-Blind School Board." *Harvard Law Review*, 1968, *81*, 1511–27.

Hodgkins, Benjamin J., & Stakenas, Robert G. "A Study of Self-Concepts of Negro and White Youth and Segregated Environments." *Journal of Negro Education*, 1969, *38*, 370–77.

Hoffer, Eric. *First Things, Last Things*. New York: Harper and Row Publishers, 1971.

Holt, John. *How Children Fail*. New York: Pitman Publishing Corp., 1964.

House, James E. *A Study of Innovative Activities in Selected Secondary Schools in Wayne County, Michigan*. Unpublished Doctoral Dissertation, Wayne State University, 1969.

Howe, Harold, Clark, Kenneth B., & Allen, James E., *et al. Racism and American Education*. New York: Harper and Row Publishers, 1970.

Hunter, Madeline. "Expanding Roles of Laboratory Schools." *Phi Delta Kappan*, 1970, *52*, 14–19.

Jablonsky, Adelaide. "Some Trends in Education of the Disadvantaged." *IRCD Bulletin*, 1968, *4*, 1–11.

Jackson, Phillip W. *Life in Classrooms*. New York: Holt, Rinehart & Winston, 1968.

Janowitz, Morris. *Institution Building in Urban Education*. New York: Russell Sage Foundation, 1969.

Jencks, Christopher. "Educational Vouchers." *New Republic,* July 4, 1970, 19–21.

Jensen, Arthur R. "How Much Can We Boost IQ and Scholastic Achievement." *Harvard Educational Review*, 1969, *39*, 1–123.

Jonas, Gilbert. "Who is Guilty?" *New York Times,* December 26, 1970, 17.

Katz, Daniel, & Kahn, Robert L. *The Social Psychology of Organizations*. New York: John Wiley & Sons, 1966.

Katz, Irwin. "Factors Influencing Negro Performance in the Desegregated School." In M. Deutsch, I. Katz, & A. R. Jensen (Eds.), *Social Class, Race, and Psychological Development*. New York: Holt, Rinehart & Winston. Pp. 254–89.

Katz, Irwin. "A Critique of Personality Approaches of Negro Performance, With Research Suggestions." *Journal of Social Issues*, 1969, *25*, 13–27.

Kelly, Earl C. *In Defense of Youth*. Englewood Cliffs, New Jersey: Prentice-Hall, 1962.

Keniston, Kenneth. "Youth, Change, and Violence." *American Scholar*, 1968, *37*, 227–45.

Keniston, Kenneth. "Youth: A 'New' Stage of Life." *American Scholar,* 1970, *39,* 631–54.

Knowles, Laurence W. "Student Rights Find a Friend in Court(s)." *Nation's Schools,* 1971, *87,* 46–48.

Levine, Daniel U., & Havighurst, Robert J. "Social Systems of a Metropolitan Area." In Robert J. Havighurst (Ed.), *Metropolitanism: Its Challenge to Education.* Part I. National Society for the Study of Education, Yearbook 1967. Chicago: University of Chicago Press, 1968. Pp. 37–70.

Lierheimer, Alvin P. "Charging the Palace Guard." *Phi Delta Kappan,* 1970, *52,* 20–25.

Lifton, Robert J. "Notes on a New History, Part I: The Young and the Old." *Atlantic,* 1969, *18,* 47–54.

Lopate, Carol, Flaxman, E., Bynum, Effie M., & Gordon, Edmund W. "Decentralization and Community Participation in Public Education." *Review of Educational Research,* 1970, *40,* 135–50.

Mahan, Thomas W. "The Busing of Students for Equal Opportunities." *Journal of Negro Education,* 1968, *37,* 291–300.

March, James G., & Simon, Herbert A. *Organizations.* New York: John Wiley and Sons, 1958.

Marland, Sidney P. "The Education Park Concept in Pittsburgh." *Phi Delta Kappan.* 1967, *48,* 328–32.

Marx, Gary T. "Racism and Race Relations." In M. Wertheimer (Ed.), *Confrontation.* Chicago: Scott, Foresman and Co., 1970. Pp. 100–102.

Mayor's Advisory Panel of Decentralization of the New York City Schools. *Reconnection for Learning—A Community School for New York City.* New York: Ford Foundation, 1967.

McCabe, John. (Ed.), *Dialogue on Youth.* Indianapolis: The Bobbs-Merrill Co., 1967.

McGowan, William N. "About Student Unrest," *Journal of Secondary Education,* 1968, *43,* 225–59.

Miller, S. M. "Theoretical Issues in Poverty Research." *Journal of Social Issues,* 1970, *26,* 169–74.

A Multiple Option Approach to School—Community Participation. Report on the Commission on Decentralization and Community Participation. Philadelphia: Philadelphia Board of Education, July 22, 1970.

Nash, Robert. "Commitment to Competency: The New Fetishism in Teacher Education." *Phi Delta Kappan,* 1970, *52,* 240–43.

New York Times, July 16, 1967, Section E, 1, 12.

New York Times. July 26, 1970. Section E, 7.

New York Times, April 21, 1971, 1, 28–30. (a)

New York Times, June 6, 1971, Section E, 2. (b)

Olivero, James L. "The Meaning and Application of Differential Staffing in Teaching." *Phi Delta Kappan,* 1970, *52,* 36–40.

Ornstein, Allan C. "Preparing and Recruiting Teachers for Slum Schools." *Journal of Secondary Education,* 1967, *42,* 368–72.

Ornstein, Allan C. "Teaching the Disadvantaged." *Educational Forum,* 1967, *31,* 215–23.

Ornstein, Allan C. "What it Is Really Like for Most Slum-School Teachers." *Integrated Education,* 1967, *5,* 48–52.

Ornstein, Allan C. "Improving Teachers for Slum Schools." *Improving College and University Teaching,* 1968, *16,* 120–24.

Ornstein, Allan C. "Theory as a Basic Guide for Teaching the Disadvantaged." *Clearing House.* 1968, *42,* 434–42.

Ornstein, Allen C. "What Type of Teacher for the Disadvantaged?" *Contemporary Education,* 1968, *40,* 85–94.

Ornstein, Allan C. "Discipline Practices for Teaching the Disadvantaged." In A. C. Ornstein & P. D. Vairo (Eds.), *How to Teach Disadvantaged Youth.* New York: David McKay Co., 1969. Pp. 163–93.

Ornstein, Allan C. "Toward the End of the Teaching Strike." *Journal of Secondary Education,* 1969, *44,* 260–64.

Ornstein, Allan C. "Decentralization: Problems and Prospects." *Journal of Secondary Education,* 1970, *45,* 219–23.

Ornstein, Allan C. "Recent Historical Perspectives for Educating the Disadvantaged." *Urban Education,* 1971, *5,* 378–99.

Ornstein, Allan C. *Understanding and Teaching the Disadvantaged.* New York: David McKay Co., 1972.

Ornstein, Allan C. "Urban Teachers and Schools: Fashionable Targets." *Educational Forum,* 1971, *35,* 359–66.

Ornstein, Allan C., & Milberg, Toby. "Problems Related to Teaching in Low Socio-Economic Areas." *Negro Educational Review,* 1967, *18,* 79–82.

Parker, Don H. *Schooling for What?* New York: McGraw-Hill Book Co., 1970.

Payne, David A. *The Specification and Measurement of Learning Outcomes.* Waltham, Massachusetts: Blaisdell, 1968.

Perel, William M., & Vairo, Philip D. *Urban Education,* New York: David McKay and Co., 1969.

Pillard, Matthew J. "Teachers for Urban Schools." In B. J. Chandler, L. J. Stiles, & J. I. Kitsuse (Eds.), *Education in Urban Society.* New York: Dodd Mead, 1962. Pp. 193–210.

Project Beacon Conference. *Improving Teacher Education for Disadvantaged*

Youth: What University Professors Can Learn from Classroom Teachers. Yeshiva University. New York, May 15–17, 1966.

Proshansky, Harold, & Newton, Peggy. "The Nature and Meaning of Negro Self-Identity." In M. Deutsch, I. Katz, & A. R. Jensen (Eds.), *Social Class, Race, and Psychological Development.* New York: Holt, Rinehart & Winston, 1968. Pp. 178–218.

Rabb, Earl, & Lipset, Seymour M. "The Prejudiced Society." In E. Rabb (Ed.), *American Race Relations Today.* Garden City, New York: Doubleday & Co., 1962. Pp. 29–55.

Riessman, Frank. *The Culturally Deprived Child.* New York: Harper & Row, Publishers, 1962.

Rivlin, Harry N. "A New Pattern for Urban Teacher Education." *Journal of Teacher Education,* 1966, *17,* 177–84.

Rosenthal, Jack. "Hunger: Half a Bowl, Say Critics, is not Good Enough." *New York Times,* March 7, 1971, Section E, 3.

Ruebhausen, Oscar M., & Brim, Jr., Orville G. "Privacy and Behavioral Research." *American Psychologist,* 1966, *21,* 423–37.

Shanker, Albert. "The Real Meaning of the New York City Teachers' Strike." *Phi Delta Kappan,* 1969, *50,* 434–41.

Shanker, Albert. "Violence in the Schools." *New York Times,* December 27, 1970, Section 3, 7.

Simmons, J. L., & Wineograd, Barry. *It's Happening: A Portrait of The Youth Scene Today.* Santa Barbara, California: Marc Laird Publications, 1966.

Smith, Calvert H., & Hazard, William R. "On Decentralized School Systems." *Illinois School Journal,* 1971, *51,* 17–27.

St. John, Nancy A. "Desegregation and Minority Group Performance." *Review of Education Research,* 1970, *40,* 111–33.

Stake, Robert E. "The Countenance of Educational Evaluation." *Teachers College Record,* 1967, *68,* 523–40.

Stanley, J. C. *Measurement in Today's Schools.* Englewood Cliffs, New Jersey: Prentice-Hall, 1964.

Stattler, Jerome M. "Racial 'Experimenter Effects' in Experimentation, Testing, Interviewing, and Psychotherapy." *Psychological Bulletin,* 1970, *73,* 137–60.

Stupak, Ronald J. "The Students as an Enemy of the Student." *Phi Delta Kappan,* 1970, *52,* 79–81.

"Suburbia: The New American Plurality." *Time* Magazine, March 15, 1971, 14–20.

"The Supreme Court Votes Against the Poor." *Time* Magazine, May 10, 1971, 16–17.

Tanner, James R. "Inservice Training for Teachers of the Disadvantaged." Paper Presented at the Proceedings of a Conference on the Disadvantaged at the University of Wisconsin. Milwaukee, June 8–9, 1967.

Thompson, Charles H. "Race and Equality of Educational Opportunity: Defining the Problem." *Journal of Negro Education,* 1968, *37,* 191–203.

Thompson, Ralph H. "Where Teacher Education Programs Fail." *Journal of Teacher Education,* 1970, *21,* 264–69.

U.S. Riot Commission. *Report of the National Advisory Commission on Civil Disorders.* New York: Bantam Books, 1968.

Usdan, Michael D. "Learning from New York City's Mistakes." *Urban Review,* 1969, *4,* 9–12.

Usdan, Michael D., & Bertolaet, Frederick (Eds.), *Development of School-University Programs for Pre-Service Education of Teachers for the Disadvantaged through Teacher Education Centers.* Washington, D.C.: U.S. Government Printing Office, 1965. (Research Grant No. F-068)

Vairo, Philip D., & Perel, William M. "Prerequisites for the Preparation of Teachers of Disadvantaged Youth." In A. C. Ornstein & P. D. Vairo (Eds.), *How to Teach Disadvantaged Youth.* New York: David McKay Co., 1969. Pp. 347–65.

Van Til, William. "In a Climate of Change." In R. R. Leeper (Ed.), *Role of Supervisor and Curriculum Director in a Climate of Change.* Washington, D.C.: ASCD, 1965. Pp. 7–29.

Warner, Lloyd. *American Life.* Chicago: University of Chicago Press, 1953.

Westin, Alan F., De Cecco, John P., & Richards, Arlene. *Civic Education for the Seventies.* Center for Research and Education in American Liberties. New York: Teachers College, Columbia University Press, 1970.

"What People Think About the High School." *Life,* May 16, 1969, 22–33.

Wilcox, Preston R. "The Community-Centered School." In A. Toeffler (Ed.), *The Schoolhouse in the City.* New York: Praeger Publishers, 1968. Pp. 97–109.

Wirth, Patty. "My Ideal School Wouldn't Be a School." *Teachers College Record,* 1970, *72,* 57–59.

Name Index

191

Subject Index